STUDIEN ZUR DEUTSCHEN LITERATUR

Band 90

Herausgegeben von Wilfried Barner, Richard Brinkmann
und C~~~~d Wiedemann

Stephen D. Dowden

Sympathy for the Abyss

A Study in the Novel of German Modernism:
Kafka, Broch, Musil, and Thomas Mann

Max Niemeyer Verlag Tübingen 1986

This book was published with the help of a grant from the Frederick W. Hilles Publication Fund of Yale University.

CIP-Kurztitelaufnahme der Deutschen Bibliothek

Dowden, Stephen D.: Sympathy for the abyss : a study in the novel of German modernism: Kafka, Broch, Musil, and Thomas Mann / Stephen D. Dowden. – Tübingen : Niemeyer, 1986.
(Studien zur deutschen Literatur ; Bd. 90)
NE: GT

ISBN 3-484-18090-0   ISSN 0081-7236

Satz: pagina GmbH, Tübingen
Druck: Allgäuer Zeitungsverlag, Kempten
Einband: Heinr. Koch, Tübingen

Table of Contents

For my parents

Steve H. Dowden & Dell E. Dowden

INTRODUCTION: Eurydice Lost

> Die So-geliebte, daß aus einer Leier
> mehr Klage kam als je aus Klagefrauen.
>
> Rilke, »Orpheus. Eurydike. Hermes«

It is revealing that, at least since Nietzsche, the modern writer has frequently envisioned himself as an avatar of his earliest mythic precursor. Before Proust it was Orpheus who went in search of time lost, and because he indulged himself in this presumptuous and hopeless quest – condensed into the image of a fateful backward glance – he was made to suffer not once but twice the loss of his beloved wife Eurydice. In his redoubled grief, Orpheus became a singer of lamentations for his lost wife. The poet's word is thus an act of rememoration, but it is more than simple expression of nostalgia. Humbled but undaunted, the poet sings now not to recover the past, but to understand it. His lamentation is the negative articulation of a powerful utopian longing. It is a cry of outrage, an eloquent refusal to accept the world as it is.

A related sense of loss draws the modernist writer to his legendary counterpart. An epoch that witnessed not only unprecedented upheavals in its systems of beliefs and values but also experienced undreamt-of political bestiality in the shape of two World Wars found itself bereft of the fundament that had traditionally made artwork the work of celebration. The motivations and assumptions that nourished the imagination of Schiller and Beethoven cannot not ring true in the era of Kafka and Berg. In the absence of joy and beauty, in the absence of Eurydice, celebration has been transformed into lamentation. Yet Adorno's dark pronouncement – that there can be no poetry after Auschwitz – stands not so much as a denial of the possibility of art itself; it is much more an index to the indecency of perpetuating a tradition predicated on ideals of beauty that history has swept away. After the death of Eurydice, lamentation is not only possible, it is necessary.

Perhaps this aesthetic of loss and lamentation is nowhere more conspicuous than in the novel of German modernism: as an oppressive absence of beauty in Kafka; as the relentless demystification of cher-

1

ished illusions in Musil and Broch; or as that ubiquitous »sympathy for the abyss« in the fiction of Thomas Mann, a paradoxical sympathy that reaches its profoundest and most chilling expression in Adrian Leverkühn's articulate cry of pain, *Dr. Fausti Weheklag* – a lamentation written on the loss of the composer's young nephew.

But even when the novel does not take up lamentation as an explicit theme, it enacts its sense of loss formally as the revolt against illusion and representation, as the dissatisfaction of the novel with its tradition and with itself.[1] It is by now a critical commonplace that the general current of modern fiction in the wake of Cervantes, Sterne, and the German Romantics has been against the idea that art is a verisimilar replica of the world. This trend is most fully developed in the fiction of modernism and in its post-modern aftermath. The modernist novel typically meditates on and unmasks by means of irony its artistic-artificial nature. The modernist generation of novelists were deeply suspicious of mimesis in the *received sense* of a fictional illusion that seeks to attain the fullest possible correspondence to perceived reality. Nevertheless, it seems likely that much postmodern talk about the »death of literature« and the »failure of representation« has been overstated and insufficiently differenciated. Undone on one hand by the autotelic play of signifiers, and on the other by political culpability, literature in the modern and post-modern era has been proclaimed opaque or dead or both. Yet the nihilistic anti-realism of modernist writing that has given rise to these positions is simultaneously an opening up of art to new possibilities of expression, a contribution toward what is spoken of in *Doktor Faustus* as the »Rekonstruktion des Ausdrucks.«

Given that the modernist novel insists emphatically on aesthetic autonomy, and granted that it gathers much of its energy from an irony that seeks to undercut the conventional wisdom that the novel can be a mirror held up along the road of life, it is reasonable to suggest that we as readers ought to address this fiction not primarily as a »representation of reality« but instead as the imaginative articulation of a *counter-reality*. Seen in this light, the putative failure of representation is not really one at all; sanctimonious obituaries on the death of literature are premature. Far from being undone by the destruction of time-honored assumptions, the novel thrives in the clearing that has opened up, and the seeming »failure« turns out to be the very condition of the possibility of well imagined fiction. Emancipated from the obligation to de-

---

[1] See esp. Theodor W. Adorno, *Ästhetische Theorie*, hrsg. von Gretel Adorno und Rolf Tiedemann (Frankfurt am Main: Suhrkamp Taschenbuch Verlag, 1981), 168–79.

scribe the world as it is, the literary mind is free to render as word and image our sensibilities of what ought to be. This hermeneutic challenge demands a renewal of our concept of mimesis toward what is, in Robert Musil's phrase, »ein auf ›Herstellung‹ gerichteter Vorgang, ein ›Vorbildzauber,‹ und keine Wiederholung des Lebens oder von Ansichten darüber, die man ohne sie besser ausdrückt. . .«.[2]

Ironically, it is the poetic word's utopian *separation* from mere reality that is fundamental to a mimetic project that reaches beyond the confines of a narrowly conceived verisimilar realism. As Paul Ricoeur has written with elegance and precision: »The more imagination deviates from that which is called reality in ordinary language and vision, the more it approaches the heart of reality which is no longer the world of manipulable objects, but the world into which we try to orient ourselves by projecting our innermost possibilities upon it, in order that we *dwell* there, in the strongest sense of that word.«[3] This view motivates the studies that follow. They are an attempt to elaborate the ways in which certain major novelists in the era of German modernism have worked to break down the traditional constraints of representational mimesis in order more fully to explore the other mimesis, the one that Ricoeur invokes.

From this perspective, literary expression is not the recuperative imitation of reality – a *Nachvollzug* of the world's apparent objectivity – but is instead a constitutive activity in itself, the *Vollzug* of a gesture that reconstrues the world according to the principles of narrative imagination. Fiction is thus one of the means whereby a culture discloses to itself the indistinct contours of its ever-emerging ethos. Art in general and narrative in particular function to preserve, but also to re-shape and replenish the values and attitudes that make up our *Lebenswelt*; and the act of interpretation marks the site at which dialogue occurs between literary monuments of the past and critical imagination of the present. It is here that the difficult question of hermeneutics and interpretive method arises.

Because fiction and criticism both are historically conditioned, and because any new voice in the conversation between them is necessarily preceded by the history of that dialogue, I have chosen to enter the hermeneutic circle at a historical point of embarkation. Chapter One

---

[2] Robert Musil, »Literat und Literatur,« in his *Gesammelte Werke in neun Bänden*, hrsg. v. Adolf Frisé, vol. 8 (Reinbek bei Hamburg: Rowohlt, 1978), 1224–25.

[3] Paul Ricoeur, »The Function of Fiction in Shaping Reality,« *Man and World,* 12 (1979), 139. Cf. also *After Babel. Aspects of Literature and Translation* (New York, London: Oxford University Press, 1975), 227–35.

offers an account of the background and development of the idea of literary modernism – what the Germanists sometimes refer to as »die klassische Moderne« – in its relation to the German novel. The essays that follow it are fueled especially by the notion that, for the modernist, there exists between narrative fiction and conventional reality a great rift. Probably the simplest generalization to be made about German modernism is that its novel tends to reflect ironically in theme and structure on its own fictional status. The uses of irony as metafiction and autocommentary will the be the object of special attention throughout this inquiry and, it may be added, what holds true for narrative fiction certainly also holds true for narrative criticism. It too must be aware of its mediated nature. Like the fiction it addresses, criticism is also the product of a historical time and place, a confluence of the manifold »Vorverständnisse« that converge on and inform the reasoning of critical imagination. Ironic fiction ought to evoke an ironic response, if »ironic« in this context may be understood as a healthy self-critical skepticism expressed as a willingness to make serious and binding assertions (response implies responsibility) without striking a posture of rigid finality.

Apart from the German modernist's characteristic irony and the various other aspects of these novels that the literary historian can neatly categorize, there exists a powerful yet indistinct pivotal center that pulls these works into concentric orbits. It is what might be described as a certain ethical sensibility that becomes articulate in modernist fiction as the expression of grief and lamentation. It is a sensibility that resists conceptual definition, that must be brought to language as metaphor and fiction. It will be the task of the chapters that follow to trace out the contours of this sensibility.

It is a central insight of German modernism that imaginative literature – and, by way of extrapolation, the criticism that proceeds from it – does not fix and define. Instead it is an evocation of, and invitation to creative thinking. I have attempted to approach Franz Kafka, Hermann Broch, Robert Musil, and Thomas Mann as a listener attentive to the overriding historical features that join them together as German modernists, but I have also attempted to draw out the unique particularities of their works that make them distinct and irreducible to a set of prefabricated literary categories. For this reason each of the following essays can also stand alone as a study whose line of inquiry conforms to the individuality and integrity of the text in question.

4

CHAPTER I

THE MODERNIST TURN

Storytelling in one form or another is a mode of behavior that is basic to mankind. Sacred narrative, tribal myth, fables, heroic epic, the sagas, chivalric romance, and the other ways of telling tales always belong to specific times and places, serving to mediate the world to a given community. The novel is European modernity's most characteristic narrative medium, and it has risen to its place of prominence for two main reasons. The first reason is the ascendancy of the bourgeoisie, a broad social class with the education, leisure time, and financial wherewithal necessary to make use of the books that the relatively new craft of printing had made available.[1] The second precondition of the novel's widespread popularity is its characteristically »realist« mode. The genre began by distinguishing its themes and forms from the fantasies and mannerisms of courtly romance.[2] In contradistinction to romance, the

---

[1] Ian Watt, »The Reading Public and the Novel,« in *The Rise of the Novel. Studies in Defoe, Richardson, and Fielding* (London: Chatto and Windus, 1957), pp. 35–59. Watt discusses only the English novel, but it is reasonable to assume that his thesis holds true for the European novel in general. Cf. also Harry Levin, *The Gates of Horn. A Study of Five French Realists* (New York: Oxford Univ. Press, 1963), pp. 31–39. On the specific German situation see Marianne Spiegel, *Der Roman und sein Publikum im 18. Jahrhundert 1700–1767*, Abhandlungen zur Kunst-, Musik, und Literaturwissenschaft, 41 (Bonn: Bouvier, 1967); Leo Balet and E. Gerhard, *Die Verbürgerlichung der deutschen Kunst, Literatur und Musik im 18. Jahrhundert*, hrsg. v. Gert Mattenklott, Ullstein Buch, 2995 (Frankfurt am Main: Ullstein, 1973), esp. pp. 464–68.

[2] Ian Watt, »Realism and the Novel Form,« in his *Rise of the Novel*, pp. 9–34. Cf. Levin, 39–48. It is not clear why the German novel did not develop a strong tradition of its own, especially after Grimmelshausen's contribution in the seventeenth century. Not until the English novel of the eighteenth century had provided a model did German novel-writing establish itself with Wieland, Goethe, and the Romantics. For the nineteenth century in general it was the realism of the eighteenth-century novel and not its irony that was exemplary (the German Romantics and Gogol are notable exceptions). Verisimilar realism gradually edged out elements of the marvelous and the fantastic even in German as the fabulous world of E. T. A. Hoffmann yielded to the sober portraiture of Theodor Fontane. See Hildegard Emmel, *Geschichte*

novel emphasizes the individuality of plausible characters and events, and abandons the standardized plots, settings, and figures of the chivalric world. It also rejects the decorous language of the courtly epic so that it can address its audience in the more down-to-earth idiom of prose.

Cervantes' *Don Quixote* stands at the beginning of the novel's tradition. In it we witness the resonant clash of two ancient foes locked in combat. One of them is the fabulous world of proud knights, winsome maidens, and noble ideals fading endlessly into the twilight of imaginary worlds. Its sworn enemy is the prosaic or even brutal factuality of the world outside books. The demystifying vision of *Don Quixote* reveals the heroes and monsters and fine ladies of romance to be phantasms of literary dream-reality. It sets in opposition to them a world of men and women engaged in the toil of everyday existence, a world in which the line separating books from life seems as clear as the difference between a common barber's basin and the legendary helmet of Mambrino. The realism of *Don Quixote* and of the genre of the novel as a whole is to be sought first of all in its fidelity to the facts of ordinary life and in its antagonism toward the unfulfilled wishes of romantic fancy.

Cervantes' work also stands at the beginning of an era with an unprecedented interest in establishing the facts. This demand for the verifiable truth of things unencumbered by myth and magic is the rise of empirical rationalism. Between 1600 and 1800 the scientific revolution conceived and exploited a method of discovering the facts that was more rigorous and more reliable than any previous technique in history. Observing nature with an impartial eye, the scientific mind set about the task of discovering and modelling nature's objective laws in the precise language of mathematics. The crowning achievement of this style of thinking was the formulation of Newtonian mechanics, statements about the physical world that unambiguously and impartially represent actual events. The verifiable certainty of a correspondence between a model and an objective event became the criterion for validity in scientific knowledge. Something is said to be true when there is isomorphy between a fact and its representation.

Such a notion of truth has a direct bearing on the claims of literary narrative. The demand that legends and tales must *in some way* be

---

des deutschen Romans, Sammlung Dalp, 103, I (Bern, München: Franke, 1972), pp. 58–146; Fritz Wahrenburg, *Funktionswandel des Romans und ästhetische Norm*, Studien zur allgemeinen und vergleichenden Literaturwissenschaft, 11 (Stuttgart: Metzler, 1976), pp. 119–131; Bruno Hillebrand, *Theorie des Romans*, I (München: Winkler, 1972).

truthful is no doubt as old as storytelling itself, but the idea that a story ought to legitimize its truth-claims in a verifiable correspondence to facts is probably an expectation as recent as the scientific revolution and the birth of the novel.[3] When Cervantes submitted the fictional world of romance to the test of correspondence with reality, poetic imagination became suspect. Throughout the Christian Middle Ages truth had expressed itself as divine revelation in Holy Scripture and in the Book of Nature. God presided over the unity of things and authenticated the forms of knowledge as an unscientific code of resemblances. Language – the stuff of literature – was also a part of the divine order, even after the unpleasantness at Babel had clouded its pristine clarity. After Babel, an *ars interpretandi* founded in the hermeneutical learning of tradition made it possible to unlock the signs and make them speak their truth. But when in the course of a few decades mankind's relationship to nature changed and divine authority began to slacken, both language and nature were cut loose from their theocentric moorings. Science and humanism began to regard them not in their relation to God but instead in their relation to man himself and the new practices of representation, experimentation, and verification.

The subsequent fortunes of narrative are closely linked to the success of science and technology. The old hermeneutical skills and knowledge, symbolic and allegorical habits of mind, and the traditional faith in the word took on an air of quixotry. The novel offered a new kind of fiction, one that purported to mirror the moral, social, and psychological facts of the world. Certainly there are also novels that reject »realism,« but on the whole the popular success of the genre has to do with its nearness to the facts of lived experience. The outrageous wit and fancy of the Romantic novel provoked the same snort of disgust in the nineteenth-century realists that the lofty tomfoolery of Renaissance epic had engendered in Cervantes. No Romantic novel is a serious challenge to the achievement of the great novels of nineteenth-century realism.

It is surely no coincidence that principles of verisimilar representation triumphed over Romantic fabulation in a century that committed itself fully to science and technology in an Industrial Revolution whose influence touched virtually every aspect of public and private life. A

---

[3] This proposition cannot be proven with certainty, but Michel Foucault has offered persuasive arguments that situate an important shift in literary expectations in the waning sixteenth century. Michel Foucault, *The Order of Things. An Archeology of the Human Sciences* (New York: Vintage Books, 1973), esp. chapter two. Foucault follows up his specifically literary thoughts in »La pensée du dehors,« *Critique*, 22 (1966), 523–46.

preference for the representation of real life dominated more than ever the reading public's tastes. In France, England, and even in mystical Russia the novel became, in Stendhal's phrase, a mirror held up along the road of life. However, the situation in the German-speaking countries was somewhat different. For reasons that are still not entirely clear, the realist novel did not rise to the position of predominance that it held in Europe's other major literary languages. In spite of its general popularity, the German novel remained inferior in prestige – and probably in actual achievement as well – to lyric and drama.[4] Nevertheless, the powerful current of European realism pulled along the German novel in spite of its relative laggardliness.

By the end of the century, the realist mode's latent scientism became overt in Naturalism's programmatic stance. The new generation of writers turned to the positivistic-materialistic theories of the natural and social sciences in order to find secure foundations upon which to erect the edifice of a new art. The model of Zola was decisive for much of the literary intelligentsia throughout Europe. His quasi-objective descriptions of individual problems and of social conditions were persuasive by virtue of the aura of factuality that surrounded them. But the crucial factor in their rhetorical effect was not so much any truly scientific approach; it was much more the foregone conclusion that truth in fiction was a matter of accurate representation of the facts. The literary term *mimesis* as it is customarily used refers to this prejudice.

The German novel emerged from its provincial isolation into the European mainstream in 1901 with the publication of Thomas Mann's *Buddenbrooks*. It was received as an objective depiction of modern decadence; and in fact the correspondence between fact and fancy in it was accurate enough to outrage the Lübeck burghers who took the novel to be a libelous *roman à clef*. This little controversy can be understood as a pivotal moment in the history of the German novel. Thomas Mann began his career as a writer at a time when realist/naturalist assumptions dominated the serious novel. The commercial and academic success of the *Buddenbrooks* at the time of its publication is a testament to the conventional expectations of the era.[5] Against this background, Mann responded to accusations that his novel was a

---

[4] Cf. Helmut Koopmann, »Vom Epos und vom Roman,« in *Handbuch des deutschen Romans*, hrsg. v. H.K. (Düsseldorf: Bagel, 1983), pp. 11–30.

[5] Not only was *Buddenbrooks* readily accepted into the academic canon of major literary works, but it was also Germany's number-one bestseller between 1915 and 1940. Donald Ray Richards, *The German Bestseller. A Complete Bibliography and Analysis 1915–1940*, German Studies in America, 2 (Bern: Peter Lang, 1968), pp. 55.

slanderous transcription of Lübeck reality by writing a newspaper article entitled »Bilse und Ich« (1906). In it Mann defends his novelistic practices by reminding his readers of the obvious: a rigorous distinction must be made between reality and the fictional shadow that it casts. A work of art, he claims, lives not by the virtue of its correspondence to the facts but in its own aesthetic right, autonomously.[6] Mann does not elaborate in any precise way exactly what he considers the aesthetic quiddity of a literary artwork to be. But it is highly significant that he has relegated to a position of lesser importance the criterion of accurately representing the supposed facts. Even in a novel as obviously »realistic« as *Buddenbrooks*, it is not the factuality of the fictional world that is ultimately interesting. It is much more its suggestive counterfactuality – the part of it that is sheerly and provocatively imaginary – that appeals to our natural sense of the aesthetic.

By the time Thomas Mann wrote *Buddenbrooks*, the realistic trend of the nineteenth-century novel had become a dogma. But as Thomas Mann realized, the essence of narrative fiction is not and cannot lie principally in the much-invoked concept of an imitation of nature. The fate of Biblical narrative in the modern period exemplifies the far-reaching consequences of a literature that restricts itself to copying appearances. The idea that art – including sacred texts – ought to represent verifiable facts led to a crisis from which theology has not yet recovered entirely. Its solution is a matter of concern to literary critics as well as theologians. If the Bible is not a record of facts, if it must be »demythologized,« how are we to understand it, if at all?

In answer to this question, Rudolf Bultmann's thesis is centrally important. He proposes that Scripture is not primarily a representation of reality but is instead an articulation of the conditions and possibilities

---

[6] I wish to make clear that by »aesthetic autonomy« there are two things I do *not* mean. First of all, I do not intend to join the tradition that subscribes to a notion of the artwork as an elevated object of disinterested contemplation in the manner of Kant and Schiller. Secondly, I do not intend to suggest that an artwork is a sheerly beautiful artifact that exists apart from ethical and truth claims (*l'art pour l'art*). A work of art is a kind of impassioned game in which the meaning of human being is always at stake to a greater or lesser degree. It is a field of play upon which real decisions are made in unreal situations. The rules of the game are contingent upon the exigencies of life lived in the present and on hopes projected into the future. The *ludic* dimension is the point of conjuncture for art and life. Each is the result of an ongoing process of shaping, submitted only to the authority of imagination within the parameters of creativity defined by history and tradition. It is a reenactment of nature's own movement through time, an evolutionary becoming that is outside of finality.

9

for a spiritually sound existence in the world.[7] His solution is in need of much clarification, but it is no doubt a step in the right direction, and it

[7] Insofar as literary criticism wishes to become more than a descriptive discipline it will be necessary for it to develop a hermeneutic program that is as binding for secular literature of the modern era as was the Biblical hermeneutics of former times. In the same way that Holy Scripture once reflected the mind of man and his place in a theocentric universe, so also does the secular literary canon reflect the essence of man in the modern world. *Literaturwissenschaft* must develop the critical tools it needs to discuss these essential matters in a direct, coherent, and non-dogmatic fashion. The sphere of ethics is an obvious example of one of the categories of essence that is omnipresent in literature but that contemporary literary criticism has little to say about. In the present study there is a strong interest in the presence of ethical considerations in the modernist novel. It stems not from a theological frame of reference but instead out of a cryptic comment that Ludwig Wittgenstein and Robert Musil made independently of each other, namely that ethics and aesthetics are identical.* However, this undercurrent remains largely submerged because literary criticism is not at present equipped methodologically to deal with these knotty issues.** Musil's work is a concrete example: it is clear that he was vitally interested in the nature of the relationship between literature and »the good.« But literary criticism – functioning under the aegis of the historical-critical method – can determine only what Musil said and wrote. Its tacit aim is to reconstruct Musil's intentions in textual exegesis. But it cannot offer a scientific judgment concerning the truth of the text's claims nor even concerning its *beauty* (the feeling of embarrassment that this last word generates is an index to a conspicuous problem in literary criticism, which after all is a branch of aesthetics). If *Literaturwissenschaft* is to become a *Wissenschaft* that is epistemologically, ethically, and aesthetically responsible, it must also be able to take a critically reflected stand on the truth-claims of literature. It is for this reason that I invoke the name of Rudolf Bultmann. He and his successors – e.g. Ernst Fuchs, Gerhard Ebeling, or Eberhard Jüngel – are theologians who have made significant contributions to a Biblical hermeneutics that stresses the priority of Scripture as a *narrative* phenomenon. Secular literary hermeneutics can learn much from the advances they have made toward a science of the Word as an articulation of the »essence« of man and his place in the order of things. Rudolf Bultmann, *Glauben und Verstehen*, 4 Bde. (Tübingen: Mohr, 1933ff); Ernst Fuchs, *Marburger Hermeneutik* (Tübingen: Mohr, 1968); Gerhard Ebeling, *Wort und Glaube*, 3 Bde. (Tübingen: Mohr, 1960ff.); Eberhard Jüngel, »Metaphorische Wahrheit. Erwägungen zur theologischen Relevanz der Metapher als Beitrag zur Hermeneutik einer narrativen Theologie,« *Evangelische Theologie*, Sonderheft (1974), pp. 71–122. By way of introduction to the relationship between literary criticism and contemporary theology see Richard Brinkmann, Max Seckler, Paul Ricoeur, and Jakob J. Petuchowski, »Literarische und religiöse Sprache,« *Christlicher Glaube in moderner Gesellschaft*, Enzyklopädische Bibliothek in 30 Teilbänden, hrsg. v. Franz Böckle, et al., Bd. 2 (Freiburg, Basel, Wien: Herder, 1981), pp. 71–130. * Ludwig Wittgenstein, *Tractatus Logico-Philosophicus*, edition suhrkamp, 12 (Frankfurt am Main: Suhrkamp, 1968), p. 113: »Ethik und Ästhetik sind Eins.« Robert Musil, *Tagebücher*, hrsg. v. Adolf Frisé (Reinbek bei Ham-

is an insight of great relevance to literary criticism. The novel of modernism presents the literary critic with a problem that is similar to Bultmann's. I will attempt in the following chapters to show that the modernist trend away from so-called »mimetic realism« amounts to a demythologization of the idea that narrative is first and foremost a representation of reality. Because the modernists were acutely aware of the limits of representation, they attempted to find ways of superseding these limits in order to address the more elusive aspects of life, especially the ethical.

For the moment, it is important to offer a working definition of what constitutes the »modernism« of a novel. Principally, it is a reaction against the quixotry of dogmatic realism, against the positivistic optimism that narrative fiction can really be the impartial reflection of objective reality. Within this general framework at least three characteristic traits are discernible. The first of these is a critique of the traditional concept of a stable, objective reality. The second is a critique of the idea of representation in language and literature. The third is the valorization of subjectivity as the new locus of reality. These tropisms – the turn away from external reality, the linguistic turn, and the inward turn – are familiar topoi in the literary criticism that the novel of modernism has generated.[8] But the literature on this topic is so diffuse, especially in Germanistics, that a short summary of these categories is not superfluous.

---

burg: Rowohlt, 1976), p. 777: »Ich habe von Jugend an das Ästhetische als Ethik betrachtet.«

** Dietmar Mieth's idea of a »narrative ethics« is an interesting exception to the rule. D.M., *Epik und Ethik: Eine theologisch-ethische Interpretation der Joseph-Romane Thomas Manns*, Studien zur deutschen Literatur, 47 (Tübingen: Niemeyer, 1976).

[8] The term »modernism« is not current in German literary criticism, but its characteristic features are well known and much discussed. The following list of studies includes both those which use the term and those which do not. It should be noted that literary modernism is related to but not identical with the movement in Catholic theology that bears the same name and also began around 1900. For relevant discussions of literary modernism see: T.S. Eliot, »The Modern Mind,« in *The Use of Poetry and the Use of Criticism: Studies in the Relation of Poetry to Criticism in England* (London: Faber and Faber, 1933), pp. 113–35; Wolfgang Kayser, »Die Anfänge des Romans im 18. Jahrhundert und seine heutige Krise,« *DVjs*, 28 (1954), 417–46; Paul Kluckhohn, »Die Wende vom 19. zum 20. Jahrhundert in der deutschen Dichtung,« *DVjs*, 29 (1955), 1–19; Erich Heller, *The Disinherited Mind* (Cambridge: Bowes & Bowes, 1952); Nathalie Sarraute, *The Age of Suspicion. Essays on the Novel*, trans. Maria Jolas (New York: George Braziller, 1963), orig. pub. in French as *L'ère du Soupçon*, (Paris, 1956); Renato Poggioli, *The Theory of the Avant-*

1. Wirklichkeitsverlust

> Wirklichkeit – Europas
> dämonischer Begriff: glücklich
> nur jene Zeitalter und
> Generationen, in denen es
> eine unbezweifelbare gab . . . .
>
> Gottfried Benn[9]

»It goes without saying that you will not be able to write a good novel unless you possess the sense of reality.«[10] Such was Henry James' opin-

---

[9] *Garde*, trans. Gerald Fitzgerald (Cambridge, Mass. and London: The Belknap Press of Harvard, 1968), orig. pub. in Italian as *Teoria dell' arte d' avanguardia* (Società editrice il Mulino, 1962); Stephen Spender, *The Struggle of the Modern*, (London: Hamish Hamilton, 1963); Erich Kahler, »The Transformation of Modern Fiction,« *Comparative Literature*, 7 (1955), 121-28, »Untergang und Übergang der epischen Kunstform,« *Neue Rundschau*, 64 (1953), 1-44, »Die Verinnerung des Erzählens,« *Neue Rundschau*, 68 (1957), 501-46 and, 70 (1959), 1-54, 177-220; Georg Lukács, *Wider den mißverstandenen Realismus* (Hamburg: Claasen, 1958), esp. 13-48; Irving Howe, »The Culture of Modernism,« in his *Decline of the New* (New York: Harcourt, Brace & World, 1963), 1-33; Harry Levin, »What Was Modernism?« in his *Refractions. Essays in Comparative Literature* (New York: Oxford Univ. Press, 1966), 271-95; John Barth, »The Literature of Exhaustion,« *The Atlantic*, Aug. 1967, pp. 29-34, »The Literature of Replenishment,« *The Atlantic*, Jan. 1980, pp. 65-71; Gerhard Bauer, »Die ›Auflösung des anthropozentrischen Verhaltens‹ im modernen Roman,« *DVjs*, 42 (1968), 677-701; Theodore Ziolkowski, *Dimensions of the Modern Novel* (Princeton: Princeton Univ. Press, 1969); Maurice Beebe, »What Modernism Was,« *Journal of Modern Literature*, 3 (1974), 1065-84; Matei Calinescu, *Faces of Modernity: Avant-Garde, Decadence, Kitsch* (Bloomington: Univ. of Indiana Press, 1977); Hans Ulrich Gumbrecht, »Modern, Modernität, Moderne,« in *Geschichtliche Grundbegriffe. Historisches Lexikon zur politisch-sozialen Sprache in Deutschland*, hrsg. v. Otto Brunner, Werner Conze, Reinhard Koselleck, Bd. 4 (Stuttgart: Klett-Cotta, 1978), 93-131; *Modernism 1890-1930*, eds. Malcolm Bradbury and James McFarlane (Sussex: Harvester/New Jersey: Humanities, 1978); Peter Faulkner, *Modernism*, The Critical Idiom, 35 (London, New York: Methuen, 1980); Peter Bürger, *Theorie der Avantgarde*, Mit einem Nachwort zur 2. Aufl., edition suhrkamp, 727 (Frankfurt am Main: Suhrkamp, 1981); Beatrice Sandberg, »Der Roman zwischen 1910 und 1930,« and Joseph Strelka, »Der Roman zwischen 1930 und 1945,« both in *Handbuch des deutschen Romans*, hrsg. v. Helmut Koopmann (Düsseldorf: Bagel, 1983), 489-529.
[9] Gottfried Benn, »Lyrik des expressionistischen Jahrzehnts,« in his *Gesammelte Werke in zwei Bänden*, hrsg. v. Dieter Wellershoff, Bd. 2 (Wiesbaden: Limes, 1968), p. 1841.
[10] Henry James, »The Art of Fiction,« in *The Art of Fiction and Other Essays*, with an Intro. by Morris Roberts (New York: Oxford Univ. Press, 1948), p. 10.

ion in the 1880's. But only a generation later another author, the fictitious novelist of Hermann Broch's *Schlafwandler* trilogy, doubts that such a thing as the ›sense of reality‹ even exists:»Hat dieses verzerrte Leben noch Wirklichkeit? Hat diese hypertrophische Wirklichkeit noch Leben?«[11] His attitude is typical for writers of the modernist generation, the novelists who came of age between 1900 and the First World War. For them, objective reality had lost its accustomed fixity in an era of unprecedented change and shocking brutality. The authority of social and political institutions, the inviolability of religious beliefs, the indivisibility of the human psyche, and even the finality of time and space all proved to be static fictions that history and chance had imposed upon the flux of things in the world.

Looking back into recent history, this generation could see that the optimism of the *Gründerzeit* in Wilhelminian Germany and Habsburg Austria had been ill founded. The catastrophe of 1914–1918 and the subsequent rise of fascism meant not only the final dissolution of the old order but it also cast into doubt the entire ideology of progress and prosperity that animated enlightened bourgeois culture. At the same time, anthropologists began to spread knowledge of non-Western cultures, knowledge that served to undermine the authority of traditional European customs and assumptions. In particular, bourgeois manners and morality were revealed to be conventions grounded in cultural tradition instead of in a metaphysical absolute. Nietzsche abbreviated this decline and fall of the absolute as the »death of God.« War in Europe, revolution in Russia, international economic depression, political instability, cultural relativity and a general atmosphere of nervous exhaustion threw the era into a state of concentrated turmoil. It is not surprising that for many people »reality« began to seem a remote and phantomlike ideal.

Something like a large-scale schizophrenia settled in on the European mind at certain crucial junctures. One of these junctures, though not the only one, was literary imagination. The experience of isolation, madness and despair is commonplace in the literature of modernism, but in order to situate this literature historically it ought to be helpful to point out briefly some of the other flashpoints at which the crisis appears in sharp relief. In the interest of simplicity, I will invoke the names of Nietzsche, Marx, Freud, and Einstein as symbols for the lost sense of reality.

---

[11] Hermann Broch, *Die Schlafwandler*, in the Kommentierte Werkausgabe, hrsg. v. Paul Michael Lützeler, Bd. 1 (Frankfurt am Main: Suhrkamp, 1975), p. 418.

The Marxian critique of ideology codified for future generations the concepts of alienation and false consciousness. The idea that the economic, political, and social conditions of industrial Europe had brought about the estrangement of modern man from his old familiar place in the natural order of things was not new with Marx and Engels, but they gave it its popular and lasting formulation. The perception of superordinated powers as conspiratorial forces that sustain themselves by generating a web of illusions that only seem to be a necessary reality anticipates the modernist skepticism concerning the permanence of any political or social order. The Marxian strategy of unmasking appearances is a technique that is fundamental to the modernists' reading of the world.

The same gesture is basic to Freudian psychoanalysis. It rests upon a theory of the psychic apparatus in which false appearances play the central role. Like Marx, Freud intended to demystify the fictions that constitute the surface of an illusory reality. A slip of the tongue, a joke, or a dream are not simply what they seem, but are actually mechanisms of repression, distorted masks that we use to conceal the terrible truth about ourselves from our conscious minds. Beneath an ostensibly harmless surface, down in the inky blackness of the unconscious lurk the fears, taboos, and monstrous desires that made Freud so unpopular with the general public and philistine academy of his day. Marx and Freud, each in his own sphere, showed that apparent reality had a false bottom, that the cherished institutions and beliefs of enlightened culture were historical constructs.

Both Marx and Freud thought and wrote within the framework of nineteenth-century positivism. Each believed that his scientific method of analysis could uncover the hidden bedrock of authentic reality. In contradistinction to them, Nietzsche mounted a critique of culture and knowledge that abandoned this presupposition. The final truth cannot be discovered because it does not exist. When old myths must be discarded, new myths and not final truths must replace them. There is no inert background against which to judge reality. The foundations of knowledge float freely in the abyss and can validate themselves only by being more or less useful in a given time and place. It is for this reason that Nietzsche proclaimed in *Die Geburt der Tragödie* that life can be justified only as an aesthetic phenomenon. Apparent truth is always only a biologically and historically conditioned understanding of a surface that is continually subject to being shaped and re-shaped. Absolute knowledge is impossible because any knowledge is a function of the medium in which it occurs, especially language.[12]

---

[12] For a helpful examination of the Nietzschean critique of reality see J.P. Stern,

14

Tough-minded skeptics might object that poets and philosophers are well known for inventing problems where there are none. Marx, Freud, and Nietzsche were, after all, *Geisteswissenschaftler* whose disciplines did not require of them the same exacting respect for the facts to which the propositions of natural scientists must conform. But in point of historical fact, it was the hardest of the hard sciences – physics – that dealt the most damaging blow to conventional beliefs about the stability of external reality.

Two important developments brought traditional physics to a turning point. One of these was Einstein's relativity theory of 1905; the other was the emergence of atomic physics. Together they challenged the received understanding of the world's physical properties. Newtonian mechanics was a model based on the experience of average reality in Euclidean space and linear time. The discovery of electromagnetic phenomena presented later physicists with a problem that Newton's laws failed to explain. Newton had assumed that linear time and three-dimensional space were invariants of material reality. Einstein's theory of relativity toppled this assumption by showing the limits of its applicability. Only the speed of light is absolute; time and space are always relative to the observer's position and state of motion.[13] His theory and its subsequent vindication in experiment disabused the scientific and popular mind of its illusions about the universality of reality's most fundamental categories: space and time.

While Einstein was shaking the foundations of traditional presuppositions about time and space, other scientists were exploring the submicroscopic realm atomic phenomena. It was known that material reality comprised atoms, but the materials that constituted the atoms

---

»'Only as an aesthetic phenomenon',« in his *A Study of Nietzsche* (Cambridge: Cambridge Univ. Press, 1979), pp. 171–202. During the modernist era a student of Nietzsche's philosophy developed an »as-if« theory of reality that was well known and influential: Hans Vaihinger, *Die Philosophie des Als-Ob: System der theoretischen, praktischen und religiösen Funktionen auf Grund eines idealistischen Positivismus* (Berlin: Reuther & Reichard, 1911). In his study of modernism, Frank Kermode develops the idea of reality as a system of heuristic fictions at some length: F.K., *The Sense of an Ending. Studies in the Theory of Fiction* (New York: Oxford, 1967). Cf. also Roy Pascal, »Narrative Fictions and Reality. A Discussion of Frank Kermode's *The Sense of an Ending*,« *Novel*, 11 (1977–78), 40–50.

[13] In the next chapter I will take up the influence of Einstein's theory on Hermann Broch. Newtonian physics assumed that the scientific observer was a detached witness to objective events. Einstein's theory reintroduced the observer into the world of events and showed how the meaning of space and time was a function of that observer's position and state of motion. Broch developed an analogous theory of the narrator in fiction.

15

themselves remained to be discovered. Classical physics operated under the assumption that the ultimate building block of the material universe would be solid matter. But theories and experiments in subatomic physics since the beginning of this century have shown that the material world is an illusion of sorts. Subatomic particles and light quanta do not have a »material« existence in the ordinary sense of the word. Prior to mass and matter is energy, and »energy,« writes Werner Heisenberg, »is in fact the substance from which all elementary particles, all atoms and therefore all things are made . . .«[14]. Subatomic particles are not tiny building blocks of matter but are instead shimmering nothings that are constantly engaged in a high-energy game of vanishing and appearing. The end effect of this game is the phenomenon of solid-seeming material reality.[15]

Certainly the world is still real enough for all practical purposes, but after Nietzsche, Marx, Freud, and Einstein many of our tacitly understood metaphysical assumptions about the order of things in the world can no longer be taken for granted. The concept of ultimate authority has been undermined, and like the man in Kafka's »Türhüterlegende,« the modern mind is confronted with an interminable succession of guarded doorways. The absolute, the position held by God in the medieval imagination, has receded from the grasp of knowledge. In terms of modernist literary production, the recognition that reality is a fluid and metaphysically insecure postulate of daily life has had two results. Firstly, it caused writers to think more about the relationship of their medium to the world it attempts to recreate. The bond of language and literary convention with reality could no longer be taken for granted. The idea of »representation« would have to be rethought. Secondly, when external reality began to drift out of reach for novelists, they automatically turned inward for a more secure sense of the real. The life of the mind – and also the life of language – began to enjoy a new prominence in the literature of modernism.

---

[14] Werner Heisenberg, *Physics and Philosophy. The Revolution in Modern Sciences,* Harper Torchbook, 549 (New York: Harper and Row, 1962), p. 63.
[15] For a more detailed discussion and further references see Gary Zukav, *The Dancing Wu Li Masters. An Overview of the New Physics* (Toronto, New York: Bantam, 1979).

16

2. Verinnerung

Wir haben nichts als das Außen zum
Innen zu machen, daß wir nicht mehr
Fremdlinge sind . . . .

Hermann Bahr[16]

In an essay of 1931 on Proust, Samuel Beckett draws attention to »the only world that has reality and significance, the world of our own latent consciousness.«[17] The turn away from objective realism through impressionism rests on the quasi-scientific insight that external reality in its absolute truth is inaccessible to the perceiving mind. Individual subjectivity knows reality only as it appears to consciousness, only in the categories that consciousness has at its disposal.[18] The stream-of-consciousness techniques associated with Joyce, Schnitzler, and Faulkner mark the literary breakthrough into this way of thinking about the world. Programmatic movements, especially Expressionism and Surrealism, often radicalized this insight under the hyperbolic signs of madness and solipsism.

---

[16] Hermann Bahr, »Die Moderne,« in *Hermann Bahr. Zur Überwindung des Naturalismus. Theoretische Schriften 1887–1904*, hrsg. v. Gotthart Wunberg, Sprache und Literatur, 46 (Stuttgart: Kohlhammer, 1968), p. 37.

[17] Samuel Beckett, »Proust,« in S.B. and Georges Duthuit, *Proust/Three Dialogues* (London: John Calder, 1965), p. 13.

[18] I say semi-scientific because the writers in question were often working under the influence of scientist-philosophers. Ernst Mach, for instance, influenced many German and Austrian modernists. Judith Ryan, »The Vanishing Subject: Empirical Psychology and the Modern Novel,« *PMLA*, 95 (1980), 857–69. Cf. also Heiner Willenberg, »Die Darstellung des Bewußtseins in der Literatur. Vergleichende Studien zu Philosophie, Psychologie und deutscher Literatur von Schnitzler bis Broch,« Diss. Frankfurt, pub. by Studienreihe Humanitas, Akademische Verlagsgesellschaft, 1974. Also: Jürgen Peper, *Bewußtseinslagen des Erzählens und erzählten Wirklichkeiten. Dargestellt an amerikanischen Romanen des 19. und 20. Jahrhunderts insbesondere am Werk William Faulkners*, Studien zur amerikanischen Literatur und Geschichte, 3 (Leiden: E. J. Brill, 1966). It should not go unremarked that the objectivity of nineteenth-century realism was largely undergirded by a latent subjectivity: Richard Brinkmann, *Wirklichkeit und Illusion. Studien über Gehalt und Grenzen des Begriffs Realismus für die erzählende Dichtung des neunzehnten Jahrhunderts*, 3. Aufl. (Tübingen: Niemeyer, 1977). When in the course of this study I make reference to the »objectivity« of nineteenth-century prose I do so principally from the point of view of the modernists, who received it as a prescriptive dogma. I am not speaking of the realists' perception of themselves nor am I making any claims about the actual status of realist prose; rather, I am working from the modernists' perception of the realist tradition.

17

Obviously the writers of fiction were not working in a vacuum. Empirical psychology, phenomenology, psychoanalysis, neo-Kantianism, the concept of the aesthetic »Erlebnis« and the entire, ultimately Cartesian tradition of introspection flowed together to establish subjectivity as a major theme and structural principle of modernist prose and poetry. This turn in literary history is nothing other than the belated appearance of Kant's »Copernican Turn« in the arts.

Ever since Descartes, the world has been divided into two halves: subjective mind and objective nature. By the end of the nineteenth century, it had become clear to even the most »objective« of the natural sciences that the observing subject is trapped within his conceptual categories and that these categories impose form upon nature, at least to a certain extent. The lesson of this epistemological doctrine was that, when the fixity of the external world fell into doubt, the reasonable solution to the dilemma was to turn inward to the conscious mind as a stable locus for reality. Descartes' *cogito ergo sum* had established the immutable fixity of consciousness with apparently indubitable certainty.[19] In this historical situation the poet no longer conceived of his task as representing reality. Instead, he was to use the means at his disposal to represent reality as it appears to the mind's eyes: memory, dream, passive perception, active imagination, tradition, desire.

For the purposes of synthesis, it is convenient to refer now to a central document of literary criticism, namely Erich Auerbach's *Mimesis*. The book's final chapter – »Der braune Strumpf« – takes Virginia Woolf as a representative case for the modernist era. It illustrates the era's characteristic response of literary criticism to the idea that mind is prior to external reality. Auerbach takes *To the Lighthouse* (1927) as an exemplary instance of the mimetic situation in the prose of Woolf's generation. She had schooled herself on James Joyce, and her essay »Modern Fiction« of 1919, which is often taken to be a manifesto of modernism, sings his praises for shifting the focus of prose onto the inner life.[20] Her own prose – like that of Rilke, Proust, Broch, Schnitzler, Faulkner, Belyi, Musil and many others – reflects a similar concern for the life of the mind.

---

[19] The certainty of consciousness's self-presence has recently fallen into considerable doubt because of the critiques offered by C. S. Peirce, Jacques Lacan, and Jacques Derrida. Cf. Walter Benn Michaels, »The Interpreter's Self: Peirce on the Cartesian 'Subject',« *Georgia Review*, 31 (1977), 383–402.

[20] Virginia Woolf, »Modern Fiction,« in her *Collected Essays*, vol. 2 (London: Hogarth, 1966), pp. 103–110. The same essay appeared in German translation as »Der moderne englische Roman,« in *Die Neue Rundschau*, 41/II (1930), 112–20.

The theme of Auerbach's book is mimesis, or in the formulation of his subtitle: »Dargestellte Wirklichkeit in der abendländischen Literatur.« Using Woolf as his example, he understands represented reality in the modernist era to be »natürliche und sogar wenn man will, natüralistische Wiedergabe der Bewußtseinsvorgänge in ihrer durch keine Absicht beschränkten und durch keinen bestimmten Gegenstand des Denkens dirigierten Freiheit.«[21] For Auerbach, imitation of reality is the representation of the contents of consciousness.

The problem with Auerbach's view is that he assumes language is a neutral, endlessly pliable medium. »Die innere Welt,« wrote Kafka, »läßt sich nur leben, nicht beschreiben.«[22] The mind's interiority is in its essence as elusive as nature's exteriority. This is so because language and literature lead a historical existence of their own beyond the spatial metaphor of a static inner/outer reality. The individual writer must make use of a medium that precedes him. As language, the poetic word's grasp of reality – inner and outer – is restricted by its grammatical and rhetorical categories; as literature, its tradition and conventions define the limits of its ability to represent persuasively. Whatever

---

[21] Erich Auerbach, *Mimesis. Dargestellte Wirklichkeit in der abendländischen Literatur*, 2. verb. und erw. Aufl. (Bern: Francke, 1959), p. 500. In the meantime the centrality of consciousness has become a touchstone for literary criticism, especially in connection with modernism but also for other literary periods. See: Theodor W. Adorno, »Form und Gehalt des zeitgenössischen Romans,« *Akzente*, 1 (1954), 410-16. Wilhelm Emrich's essays collected under the title *Protest und Verheißung. Studien zur klassischen und modernen Dichtung* (Frankfurt am Main: Athenäum, 1960) contain many observations that are relevant to modernism, including the importance of subjectivity. Erich von Kahler attempts a concise history of the development of subjectivity in literature in an essay originally published as »Die Verinnerung des Erzählens,« in *Die Neue Rundschau*, 68 (1957), 501-46 and 70 (1959), 1-54, 177-220. Its final, revised form is available only in English: *The Inward Turn of Narrative*, trans. Richard and Clara Winston, The Bollingen Series, 83 (Princeton, New Jersey: Princeton Univ. Press, 1973). Hans-Georg Gadamer's proposition that Kantian critique subjectified aesthetics is of central importance. It is a more precise tool than Kahler's blurry notion of »Verinnerung:« *Wahrheit und Methode. Grundzüge einer philosophischen Hermeneutik*, 2. Aufl. (Tübingen: Mohr, 1965), pp. 39ff. Cited as Gadamer. Richard Brinkmann has showed how the category of subjectivity is also intrinsic to the supposedly objective German Realists: *Wirklichkeit und Illusion. Studien über Gehalt und Grenzen des Begriffs Realismus für die erzählende Dichtung des neunzehnten Jahrhunderts*, 3. Aufl. (Tübingen: Niemeyer, 1977); on pp. 326-24 Brinkmann discusses the transition from realism to modernism in terms of the emergence of subjectivity from its latent realist form into its overt modernist form.

[22] Franz Kafka, *Hochzeitsvorbereitungen auf dem Lande und andere Prosa aus dem Nachlaß*, hrsg. v. Max Brod (Frankfurt am Main: S. Fischer, 1953), p. 72.

19

exists outside of linguistic and literary convention – i.e. all that is unique – slips through its coarse-woven grid and escapes representation. The modernists' self-understanding on this point is often blurry. Some of them pursued a way of representing the inner life. Broch and Musil took this path. Others, such as Kafka and Mann, were rather more aware of the literary word as a more or less autonomous category somewhere between mind and nature. I hope to shed some light on this confusing point during the course of this study. In any case, the contemporary critic is not obliged to adopt a given writer's theories or self-interpretations. Certainly the priority-of-consciousness theme is a major aspect of the modernists' general self-understanding, but their intentions are not necessarily the end-station of critical observation. The ›phenomenological bias‹ of modernism and much of the literary criticism it has generated usually feels compelled to render an account of the »Sprachkrise,« or the problematic relationship between the speaking, writing subject and the medium of representation. Too often the historical autonomy and momentum of language has been left out of consideration. In other words, the modernists and their critics have not sufficiently explicated the interaction of mind and language. In order to clarify the nature of this tension, we must turn now to the idea of literary representation in the modernist era.

3. Sprachkrise

> Joyce's writing is not *about* something: *it is that something* itself.
>
> Samuel Beckett[23]

»Daß man erzählte, wirklich erzählte, das muß vor meiner Zeit gewesen sein.«[24] This complaint, spoken here by Rilke's Malte, is frequent in the narrative of modernism. The objective world eludes the grasp of language, and it no longer seems possible to tell stories about what happens outside of the Self. Some modernist narrative attempts to narrate the inner world. Kafka, for instance, is often thought to be a novelist principally aiming to describe »die ungeheure Welt« of his own

---

[23] Samuel Beckett, »Dante... Bruno.. Vico.. Joyce,« in *Our Exagmination Round his Factification for Incamination of Work in Progress* (London: Faber and Faber, 1972), p. 14; orig. pub. 1929.
[24] Rainer Maria Rilke, *Sämtliche Werke*, hrsg. v. Rilke Archiv, Bd. 6 (Frankfurt am Main: Insel, 1966), p. 844.

mind.[25] Yet if the crisis of representation is thought through to its logical conclusion, any connection between language and the Self becomes at least as tenuous as the link between language and external reality. It is necessary to ask whether language is the instrument of the subject or whether the subject is a function of language.

The trend of recent theory has shifted in the favor of ascribing epistemic privilege to language. Following Heidegger, Hans-Georg Gadamer has developed the idea that linguisticality – the word-character of the literary act – is a fundamental hermeneutic category.[26] In a similar vein, the Russian formalists, the structuralists, and poststructuralists have elaborated theories of culture and literature that »decenter« the so-called »speaking subject.«[27] The individual inhabits a variety of semiotic systems, of which language is perhaps the most basic, that constitute man in his present form. Man the speaker is always already spoken; this idea is an axiom of post-structuralist thought. The limits of spirituality are tacitly present in the various systems that precede and govern the intellectual interplay of an individual with his historical environment. Consciousness is therefore not the primary site of reality. It is secondary insofar as it is the nexus at which the multiplicity of already existing semiotic systems intersect and become articulate. Individual creativity is the act of articulation within the latent paradigm of all that can possibly be known and spoken in a given era.

Within the limited context of literary history, this paradigm consists mainly of poetic and narrative tradition. The modernist generation found itself heir to a tradition that no longer spoke to the present with a voice of authority. The exhausted forms of the past were perceived as being unable to grasp the life of the present. Narrative seemed to be an

---

[25] Franz Kafka, *Tagebücher 1910–1923*, hrsg. v. Max Brod (Frankfurt am Main: Fischer Taschenbuch Verlag, 1980), p. 192. In chapter IV I try to show the limits of this orthodox reading of Kafka.

[26] Gadamer, pp. 361–82 (cf. note 21).

[27] Victor Erlich, *Russian Formalism. History – Doctrine*, Slavistic Printings and Reprintings, 4 (S'-Gravenhage: Mouton, 1955); Emile Benveniste, »Subjectivity in Language,« in his *Problems in General Linguistics*, trans. Mary Elizabeth Meek, Miami Linguistics Series, 8 (Coral Gables, Florida: Univ. of Florida Press, 1971); Claude Levi-Strauss, *The Savage Mind* (Chicago: Univ. of Chicago Press, 1966); Roland Barthes, *S/Z*, trans. Richard Miller (New York: Hill and Wang, 1974); Jacques Lacan, *The Language of the Self*, with an essay by Anthony Wilden (Baltimore: Johns Hopkins, 1968); Michel Foucault, *The Archeology of Knowledge*, Harper Torchbooks, 1901 (New York: Harper and Row, 1976); Jacques Derrida, *Speech and Phenomena and Other Essays on Husserl's Theory of Signs* (Evanston: Northwestern Univ. Press, 1973); Julia Kristeva, »The System and the Speaking Subject,« *Times Literary Supplement*, 12 Oct. 1973, pp. 1249–50.

epistemologically dubious undertaking, no matter whether it purported to represent the outer world of objective reality or the inner world of subjective experience. The link between the word and the Self was as insecure as the link between language and the independent being of external things.

This troubled relationship between word and world gave rise to radical experiments in poetic language and narrative form. One aspect of this experimentation was the attempt to represent the contents of consciousness, as in the work of Woolf or Schnitzler. It is the most conservative side of modernism inasmuch as it holds fast to the principle of representation. Another relatively conservative side of modernism is its tendency toward parody and critique. The fiction of Musil and Broch always contains an essayistic metalevel of critique that is supposed to serve as a point of interpretive orientation for the reader. Thomas Mann was aware of himself as a critical parodist of the great novelistic tradition of the nineteenth century. His *Bildungsromane* mock the genre of the *Bildungsroman*. Unable to forge ahead into the authentic storytelling that Malte longs for, the modernist parodies and critiques the limitations of the shopworn forms that the tradition has bequeathed him.

A third side of modernism is its often disturbing tendency toward opacity. Trakl's lyric poetry and prose narrative belongs in this category, and so does much other Expressionist and Surrealist production. But the outstanding example of virtual narrative, inscrutable in its austerity, is Franz Kafka's *Schloß*. No other modern novel, with the possible exception of *Finnegan's Wake*, thwarts exegesis so fully as Kafka's masterpiece.

It is the opaque literature of modernism that vivifies the life of the poetic word carried on apart from represented reality. Its aloof severity forces the linguisticality and narrativity of its being into the foreground. Its sheer »aestheticness« serves as a reminder that the seeming clarity of more conventional works is apt to be deceptive. Even a realistic narrated world exists in aesthetic autonomy that is only masked by the referential purport of its mode. It is extraordinary that a novel as uninterpretable as *Das Schloß* should be so compelling. The critics have not been able to determine what the story is *about* – indeed, it is perhaps not »about« anything in the sense that realist novels are about this or that problem or event – but it is clear that something is at work in the narrative that functions apart from the way we conceive of a realistic connection between the world and a story about it. It is this obscure but provocative aesthetic *specificum* that keeps serious readers returning to *Das Schloß*.

Even the less »difficult« fiction of modernism partakes of the crisis in representation that reaches its peak in Kafka. The general confusion about how an imaginative narrative ought to hook onto reality gave rise to a fourth characteristic feature of modernism that has seldom received systematic treatment. This aspect is that of self-reflection or self-consciousness. When it is no longer obvious how fiction and reality are connected, one way of addressing the problem is to build into the novel a narrative layer that reflects on the possibility or impossibility of such a connection.

4. Self-Consciousness and Mimesis

> Je commence à entrevoir ce que j'appellerais le »sujet profond« de mon livre. C'est, ce sera sans doute la rivalité du mond réel et de la représentation que nous nous ens faisons.
>
> André Gide[28]

As Thomas Mann was making a leisurely Atlantic crossing in 1934, he passed his time on shipboard reading *Don Quixote*. Like many other major literary works that passed within range of his voracious imagination, *Don Quixote* was devoured, digested, and finally transformed into a literary essay, the »Meerfahrt mit *Don Quixote*.« Mann records that he took special delight from the passage in Part II, Chapter 30 in which the old knight and his squire meet a beautiful huntress in the forest. As it turns out she is a duchess, and when Sancho has executed the requisite formalities of courtly introduction for his master, she asks this question:

> »Tell me brother squire,« she said, »is not your master the one concerning whom they have printed a story called *The Ingenious Gentleman Don Quixote de la Mancha*, and who has a lady of his heart, a certain Dulcinea del Toboso?«
> »He is the same my lady,« replied Sancho, »and I am that squire of his that figures, or is supposed to figure, in the story, the one named Sancho Panza – that is to say, unless they changed me in the cradle – I mean, in the press.«[29]

---

[28] André Gide, *Les Faux-Monnayeurs* (Paris: Gallimard, 1925), p. 261.
[29] Thomas Mann, »Meerfahrt mit *Don Quixote*,« in his Gesammelte Werke, Frankfurter Ausgabe, hrsg. v. Peter de Mendelssohn, Bd. 8 (Frankfurt am Main: S. Fischer, 1982), pp. 1035f. I have cited Cervantes according to Samuel Putnam's translation, vol. 2 (London: Cassel and Cassell, 1953), pp. 705f.

Thomas Mann, himself an avowed ironist, is attracted to the witty game that Cervantes is playing with the fictional status of his figures. He forces the illusion of reality to its limit, to the ironic point at which the believability of fiction collides with the knowledge that these people are after all not real, the knowledge that Sancho and his Ingenious master were conceived in the mind and born in the printing press.

This element of self-consciousness in narration is a trait that has been with the novel since its beginnings. It is true that the genre is by and large »realistic,« but it is also true that realism has its limits. There is no unbroken continuity between fiction and life, and Cervantes is a pains to point this out to his readers. Even realist fiction is, above all, fiction.

This playful ironization of the narrated world has a distinguished place in the history of the novel. Robert Alter has written a partial history of the novel as a self-conscious genre and returned this theme to its rightful prominence. His study begins with Cervantes, traces the phenomenon up through the landmark works of Fielding, Sterne, and Diderot, and then on into the present day.[30] Predictably, the nineteenth century with its belief in a fixed reality and its scientistic ideals of objective representation was not a period in which self-conscious fiction was greatly esteemed. Aside from Gogol and the German Romantics, the rest of novel-writing and novel-reading Europe did not like for the stories it told about itself suddenly to melt into thin air. Shakespeare may have believed that we are such things as dreams are made

---

[30] Robert Alter, *Partial Magic. The Novel as a Self-Conscious Genre* (Berkeley, Los Angeles, London: Univ. of California Press, 1975). Unfortunately, Alter does not explore the variations and development of the self-conscious novel in German fiction. As is well known, Cervantes and Sterne exercised a great deal of influence on the German novel at the end of the eighteenth century, and especially on the German Romantics. Romantic Irony and novelistic self-consciousness are closely related, but it does not lie within the scope of this study to pursue this important topic. However, the relation of the modernists to the Romantics must briefly be mentioned. It is tempting to suggest that the modernists' use of irony is a reprise of the Romantics' use of it, but I do not believe that this is the case. The Romantics took over ironic self-consciousness from Sterne and Cervantes, but they also added to it a complex interpretation derived from their reading of Kantian and Fichtean Idealism (see Ingrid Strohschneider-Kohrs, *Die romantische Ironie in Theorie und Gestaltung*, 2. durchges. u. erw. Aufl., Hermaea, N.F., 6 (Tübingen: Niemeyer, 1977). With the possible exception of Broch, the modernists' literary technique remained free of a programmatic interaction between irony and philosophical doctrine. I am suggesting that modernist techniques of self-consciousness are first of all literary phenomena based in literary tradition and not derivative from Idealist philosophy in any overt way.

of, but the nineteenth century knew better. Reality was serious business – social, political, economic, and moral – and it was the serious novelist's obligation to recreate faithfully its appearances. The literary projects of Stendhal, Balzac and Tolstoy, or of Fontane and Zola were not intended to be received as dream-realities but as the veracious image of our waking life reflected in the impartial mirror of scrupulously wrought fiction.

However, by the end of the nineteenth century and with the rise of modernist thinking, the vogue of self-conscious fiction entered a period of renewal that is still in progress.[31] It should become clearer in the following chapters that the German novel has participated in this trend to a degree not yet accounted for by its critics. Owing to the influence that the novel of realism exerted upon critical expectations, ironic self-consciousness in the modern German novel has not received its proper share of systematic attention. When for instance Kommissär Bärlach of *Der Richter und sein Henker* needs some information to further a homicide investigation, the novelist sends him – ironically, of course – to a supreme authority in the universe of detective fiction: Bärlach seeks out a figure known as the »Schriftsteller.« In the film version, Bärlach finds him at home playing a game of chess with himself, and the role is acted, naturally, by Dürrenmatt himself. There can be no doubt that this is a selfconscious writer who is calling attention to the limits of his illusion-world and to the ludic nature of his own and his reader's undertaking.

But the game is not an idle diversion. In it, the truth-claims of narrative are at stake. The theme and practice of self-consciousness in narrative is one way of coping with the problematical relationship between life in the real world and the representations that storytellers make of it. The fictional novelist in André Gide's *Counterfeiters* expresses precisely these sentiments, and the real author of the novel intends his reader to ponder this matter with him. Such considerations are typical for the novel in the era of modernism, a time when external reality has become transient and amorphous, when internal reality also lacks fixity, and when the medium – linguistic and literary convention – is discovered to have intrinsic limitations. Because they were skeptical about the traditional assumptions concerning literary representation, the novelists of modernism inserted into their novels a metafictional

---

[31] Alter, pp. 138–79. Cf. also Maurice Beebe, »Reflective and Reflexive Trends in Modern Fiction,« in *Twentieth Century Poetry, Fiction, Theory*, eds. Harry R. Garvin and John D. Kirkland (Lewisburg: Bucknell Univ. Press, 1977), pp. 13–26; Beebe includes a bibliography on p. 13.

layer that reflects on the possibilities of how fiction can be related to reality. In the following chapters this phenomenon will be a helpful critical tool.

CHAPTER II

VIENNESE BAROQUE:
Temporality and Allegory in *Die Schlafwandler* of
Hermann Broch

> »Wie gern wollte ich dir das Wort
> ›Symbol‹ zugestehen, wäre es nicht
> schal geworden, daß michs ekelt.«
>
> Hofmannsthal[1]

It is sensible to begin this study with Hermann Broch and *Die Schlafwandler* (1928–31) not for chronological reasons – Kafka wrote his *Prozeß* in 1914, more than a decade before Broch went to work on his
trilogy – but instead because of Broch's strong awareness of himself as a
modernist. Writing after the novelists he admired, namely Gide, Joyce,
and Dos Passos, Broch purposefully set about the business of develop-
ing for the German novel a form that suited the era's perception of
itself. Viewing the world from inside Vienna after the collapse of imperial Austria-Hungary and taking his cues from eminent novelists of
his time, Broch attempted to establish new formal possibilities for the
novel, in hopes of making it a therapeutic force in an unhealthy epoch.

It will be the task of this chapter not only to describe the modernist
traits of Broch's trilogy but also to do justice to its individuality. This
individuality, however, is entrenched in the Austrian tradition of which
Broch was a part, and it leads directly back to the mainstream of modernist tendencies. This tradition is the Baroque with its typical mode of
representation: allegory. In the modernist period, allegory reappears in
various forms that will become clear in the pages that follow.

Broch's intentions in his novels were cosmopolitan and had little to
do with any narrowly Austrian sense of identity or tradition. Indeed, at
first glance Broch seems to be opposed to Austria's nostalgic self-esteem
as the heartland of Baroque culture. In his study »Hofmannsthal und
seine Zeit,« Broch critisizes modern Austria's nostalgic affinity for the

---

[1] Hugo von Hofmannsthal,»Gespräch über Gedichte,« in *Gesammelte Werke
in 10 Einzelbänden*, hrsg. v. Bernd Schoeller in Beratung mit Rudolf Hirsch,
Erzählungen, Erfundene Gespräche und Briefe, Reisen (Frankfurt am Main:
Fischer Taschenbuch Verlag, 1979), p. 501.

splendor of a bygone era. According to Broch, the decadent present was clutching vainly at memories of its vigorous past in an attempt to stave off the chaos that was growing all around it. Yet at the same time Broch himself was actually renewing the Baroque, though not out of any self-absorbed sentimentality.

The link between modernists such as Broch and the Baroque era is in part a formal one. Arnold Hauser, for instance, has noted that the stylistic claims of art and literature from Baudelaire to Proust and Kafka shares with the Baroque the characteristic tendencies of mannerism.[2] On the thematic level there are also interesting parallels that unify modernism with the Baroque, especially Viennese modernism. Mutability and death are central topoi of both eras.[3] The ephemerality of earthly things is reflected in the dualism of the typically Baroque distinction between material appearances and the truer realm of divine spirit. Similarly, modernism experiences the world as illusion and deception, but instead of religious conviction, modernism offers Kantian epistemology and the findings of advanced physics as the grounds for its views.[4]

There are other possible thematic links between modernism and the Baroque – the sacrificial hero, the apocalypse, the world as a stage[5] – each of which is a prominent theme in Broch's work. But the strongest links, the ones that will help to clarify the purport of Broch's *Schlafwandler*-trilogy in its generality as a programmatic modernist experiment and in its particularity as an individual work of art, are the

---

[2] Arnold Hauser, *Der Manierismus. Die Krise der Renaissance und der Ursprung der modernen Kunst* (München: Beck, 1964), pp. 355–94.

[3] On the theme of death in modernism see Theodore Ziolkowski, »The Metaphysics of Death,« in his *Dimensions of the Modern Novel. German Texts and European Contexts* (Princeton, New Jersey: Princeton University Press, 1969), pp. 215–57. Cited as Ziolkowski, *Dimensions of the Modern Novel.* On the peculiarly Austrian obsession with death see William Johnston, *Austrian Mind. An Intellectual and Social History 1848-1938* (Berkeley, Los Angeles, London: University of California Press, 1972), pp. 165–80. Cited as Johnston, *Austrian Mind.*

[4] See Chapter I.

[5] See Frank J. Warnke, *Versions of the Baroque. European Literature of the Seventeenth Century* (New Haven, London: Yale University Press, 1972). Cited as Warnke. Modernism is populated with »absurd« sacrificial heroes: August Esch, Josef K. and Adrian Leverkühn are obvious examples. Intimations of the Apocalypse are frequent in modernist prose, esp. in Expressionism but also in Broch and many others. In this regard see Frank Kermode, *The Sense of an Ending* (New York: Oxford, 1967). The world as a stage is important in Nietzsche, Hofmannsthal, Sartre and, as the next chapter will show, it plays an important role in Musil's concept of reality.

themes of death and false appearances.[6] The seventeenth century's preoccupation with human mortality finds a close analogue throughout the writings of Hermann Broch, and its doctrine of the world as illusion is a close parallel to his Platonic philosophy.[7] Broch believed the physical world to be the broken reflection of the greater supersensible realm of Platonic ideas that exist beyond time and death.

The link between death and material existence is the problem of temporality. My thesis in this chapter is that *time* is Hermann Broch's fundamental concern and that this concern conditions his turn to allegory. The theme of temporality and its expression in allegory are the decisive points of connection between modernism and the Baroque. The concept of self-reflection that I attempted to elaborate in the previous chapter is actually a kind of allegory – self-allegory – and functions like seventeenth-century allegory except for one major difference: the seventeenth-century mind was able to take for granted a divine order of things. It functioned for the era as an unquestioned and indisputable *tertium comparationis* that sustained the meaning of literary allegories. The modernist writer has lost confidence in the divine, invariant order of things. This loss of a collective faith in a secure metaphysical order means that allegory must fold back on its origin; and this origin is the autonomous imagination of individual artists. In the case of Hermann Broch, a certain philosophy of history and values fills the place once occupied by a securely grounded *tertium comparationis*: Broch allegorizes his philosophical theories in the action of his novels.[8] Before clarifying the connection between temporality and allegory, it will be necessary first to turn to Broch's specific conception of allegory and self-representation in the novel: *Die Schlafwandler* allegorizes a

---

[6] On death and false appearances as Baroque themes cf. Warnke, pp. 21–65.

[7] On Broch's Platonism see esp. Hermann Krapoth, *Dichtung und Philosophie. Eine Studie zum Werk Hermann Brochs*, Literatur und Wirklichkeit, 8 (Bonn: Bouvier, 1971).

[8] On one level this insight is nothing new. Ever since Richard Brinkmann's key article of 1957, Broch students have been explicating the relationship of his historicist *Wertphilosophie* to the action of the novel. At present, little remains to be added on this count. What I am trying to do here is to go behind the reflexive pair theory/action in order to get at their common origin and the significance of the allegorical form of presentation. The origin is the problem of temporality, and I hope to show that it expresses itself in the narrative rhetoric of allegory. On the relation between Broch's theories and his stories see Richard Brinkmann, »Romanform und Werttheorie bei Hermann Broch,« *DVjs*, 31 (1957), 169–97; rpt. in *Deutsche Romantheorien*, hrsg. v. Reinhold Grimm (Frankfurt am Main: Athenäum, 1968), pp. 347–73, and in *Hermann Broch. Perspektiven der Forschung*, hrsg. v. Manfred Durzak (München: Fink, 1972), pp. 35–68.

29

specific theory of history and values as well as the origin of this theory in individual subjectivity.

I

When Broch submitted an early version of *Die Schlafwandler* to the Rhein-Verlag in 1930 to be considered for publication, its editor-in-chief – Daniel Brody – handed over the manuscript to Yvan Goll for evaluation. Goll raised the objection that Broch should not allow the authorial voice to intrude into the fictional world. He justified his objection on the grounds that the model of Flaubert's narrative technique had long since discredited the old-fashioned intruding narrator. His comment is an index to the standards of realism that prevailed at the time Broch was writing. These standards demanded that the believability of the novel's illusion-world not be compromised by the intrusion of exterior reality. The modernist Broch refused to accept the Flaubertian imperative and insisted upon such archaic-modern devices as the use of an authorial *wir*, an occasional apostrophe to the reader, and, especially, the introduction of an author-narrator called Bertrand Müller into the story. In defense of his position, Broch wrote to Brody:

> Zu der Bemerkung Golls: das Heraustreten des Autors ist ein ebenso legitimes Kunstmittel wie seine Verborgenheit; es muß bloß wie alles Technische dem Architektonischen untergeordnet werden. Hier gibt es keine Regeln, auch wenn sie von Flaubert aufgestellt sind. Überall, wo die Darstellungstechnik mit zum Inhalt des Dargestellten wird, muß natürlich die werkende Hand mit zum Vorschein kommen, vide ganze Kapitel im Ulysses, Gide, etc. (eine Erscheinung, die sicherlich und, wie ich glaube, auch nachweisbar zur Denkstruktur unserer Zeit gehört). Bei den Schlafwandlern wird das Technische mit der zunehmenden Versachlichung des Inhaltes immer mehr bloßgelegt, und es versteht sich daher, daß man im III. Teil die Stimme des Autors am deutlichsten hört; im I. Teil geschieht dies bloß im allerletzten Satz, der damit zur Vorbereitung und als Überleitung zum Kommenden dient. (13/1: 91)[9]

This passage adumbrates part of the theory that Broch developed around his reading of Joyce's *Ulysses*, a theory that expands and clarifies his notion of the intruding author-narrator.

---

[9] Broch's works are cited throughout according to the *Kommentierte Werkausgabe*, hrsg. v. Paul Michael Lützeler, 13 vols. (Frankfurt am Main: Suhrkamp, 1978ff). Cf. Flaubert's famous dictum:»An author in his book must be like ›God‹ in the universe, present everywhere and visible nowhere. Art being a second Nature, the creator of that Nature must behave similarly. In all its atoms, in all its aspects, let there be sensed a hidden, infinite impassivity.«

In his essay »James Joyce und die Gegenwart« (1936) Broch discusses the problem of mimesis in a world whose reality has become so fragmented as to be »unabbildbar.« He writes that traditional narrative practices can no longer produce mirror-images of reality because neither the objective certainty of reality nor the power of words to capture it can be taken for granted. His tentative solution to this crisis of representation is to step back from the situation by writing at a metafictional level. In his novels, Broch wants not only to tell a story but also to tell the story of the telling. In explanation of this concept Broch calls on Einstein's theory of relativity for an analogy, suggesting that relativity is related to classical mechanics as the modernist novel is to the novel of realism (9/1: 77–79).

Newtonian mechanics operated under the assumption that events in the material world occur in absolute time and space, independent of the impartially observing scientist. Contradicting classical physics, Einstein theorized that only the speed of light was absolutely invariant and that time and space were in fact relative to the position of the observing subject, viz. to his state of motion. These findings meant that in order to represent any given event truthfully, the observer of that event as well as the act of observation must also be taken into consideration. By way of Einstein's theory, Broch proposed that the writing of a novel functions according to analogous principles. Like the impartial observer of classical physics, the objective »Flaubertian« narrator of the classical novel – i.e. the novel of nineteenth-century realism – turns out to be a participant in the observed event. The action of the novel is always relative to his point of view.[10] In both science and poetry no »object« of investigation is ever separable from the methods of observation, procedures of isolation and the analytic tools that transmute it into knowledge.

Because the observer is always already present, and because the act of observation is actually a part of the observed event, Broch felt compelled to acknowledge the epistemological situation by introducing an

---

[10] The first critic to pay close attention to this »introduction of the observer into the field of observation« was Theodore Ziolkowski, »Hermann Broch and Relativity in Fiction,« *Wisconsin Studies in Contemporary Literature*, 8 (1967), 365–76. It was he who originally noted the special role of Bertrand Müller (pp. 373f), but he rather overestimates the uniqueness of Broch's dramatized narrator (p. 375). Certainly Broch's *justification* for this device is unique, but the device itself is as old as *Don Quixote, Tristram Shandy*, and the German Romantics. In Broch as in the pre-realist novel, the intruding narrator serves to ironize that which is narrated. The following chapters will attempt to show how this sort of irony occurs not only in Broch but also in Musil, Kafka, and – most conspicuously – in Thomas Mann.

31

observing subject – a narrator – into the field of observation. In this way the various points of reference that work together to determine meaning emerge more fully into view so that their limitations and their plenitude can be assessed.

For a proper understanding of how Broch attempts to show the writing hand is at work in his novels, it is important to note the three-part structure of his model. In ostensible reference to Joyce, Broch suggests, »daß man das Objekt nicht einfach in den Beobachtungskegel stellen und einfach beschreiben dürfe, sondern daß das Darstellungssubjekt...und nicht minder die Sprache, mit der er das Darstellungsobjekt beschreibt, als Darstellungsmedien hineingehören. . . . Das Werk soll selber aus der Beobachtung entstehen, der Beobachter ist immer mitten drin, er stellt dar und stellt sich und seine Arbeit gleichzeitig mit ihr dar« (9/1: 78). The three decisive features of fiction's narrative epistemics are for Broch: 1) the represented object 2) the representing subject, and 3) the medium of representation. These distinctions are important because in *Die Schlafwandler* – the first of Broch's two major novels – it is the representing subject that dominates the fictional world. Bertrand Müller's presence in the narrative foreground functions as a perspectivistic reality-principle. In Broch's vexed magnum opus, *Der Tod des Vergil*, it is the medium of representation – language itself – that dominates the narrative foreground. The novel's ponderous linguisticality consumes both subjective and objective realms and amalgamates them in a third modality that is neither one nor the other.[11] In *Die Schlafwandler* the presence of the novelist/narrator Bertrand Müller provides a point of self-reflection; in *Der Tod des Vergil* it is the almost palpable density of the language itself that awakens the reader to its own mediating presence. Before continuing with an analysis of the *Schlafwandler*'s baroque rhetoric, it will be useful to pause over the problem of self-reflection in both novels, inasmuch as it contitutes a feature of modernist fiction in general and is ultimately akin to the concept of allegory that links modernism to the Baroque.

In the case of *Die Schlafwandler*, Broch's notion of introducing the observing subject into the sphere of observation helps to clarify his defense against Yvan Goll's critique. The intrusion of the authorial voice into *Pasenow* and *Esch*, and the literal presence of the author

---

[11] Broch studies have not yet examined adequately the linguisticality of Vergil's consciousness and of the world he perceives. The basic question that will have to be asked is how the »public« idiom of narrative language is related to the hypothetically »private« vision of Vergil's mind. Broch criticism has thus far failed to make this distinction, which Broch himself made, between the representing subject and the medium of representation.

figure in *Huguenau* establish the locus of reality in the trilogy as his fictionalized consciousness: all that *is* proceeds from the mind of Müller. This writer and his individual subjectivity are the principle of unity that organizes and sustains the manifold diversity of the imaginary world. By re-introducing the narrator into the imaginary world of the novel, Broch marks his fiction with a technique that various other modernists were concurrently helping to revive.[12]

In his letter to Brody, Broch pointed out his kinship to Gide and Joyce, two other modernists who were at the forefront of the era's renewed interest in the self-conscious novel.[13] As Ziolkowski has suggested, it is likely that Gide's *Counterfeiters* (1925) influenced Broch with regard to the idea of writing a novel that self-reflexively includes within itself a figure who is supposed to be the author of the novel.[14] Gide's protagonist, Edouard – the similarity to Müller's own aesthete alter ego, Eduard von Bertrand, is probably no accident – is a man writing a journal that he plans to turn into a novel to be entitled *The Counterfeiters*. Gide has set into his tale a mirror that reflects the telling of the tale, a narratological device that he referred to as *mise en abyme*. By duplicating itself within itself, the novel asserts its autonomous integrity and independence from external reality. This type of novel is not so much an outward-turned reflection of things along the road of life as it is an inward-turned reflection of the life of the imagination. The self-reflecting novel asserts itself as verbal imagination existing a world apart from life outside the mirror.

Broch's version of this device shows the ironic way in which an autonomous narrative construct takes hold of reality. Its tenuous link with the outside world is the subjectivity of Bertrand Müller, author of the novels and author of the value-theory essays set *en abyme*. It is important to be aware that the much-discussed relationship between the *Werttheorie* and the action of the novel does not constitute the novel's primary claim on reality. Its reality-principle is first of all Bertrand Müller's individual consciousness. His imagination is the common origin of the novelistic and essayistic portions of the trilogy. He is the *Darstellungssubjekt* spoken of in the Joyce essay, and his personal

---

[12] Robert Alter, »The Modernist Revival of Self-Conscious Fiction,« in his *Partial Magic. The Novel as a Self-Conscious Genre* (Berkeley, Los Angeles, London: University of California Press, 1975), 138–78. Cited as Alter. Cf. also John R. Frey, »Author-Intrusion in Narrative: German Theory and some Modern Examples,« *Germanic Review*, 23 (1948), 274–89.

[13] Alter, pp. 140–44, 161–78.

[14] Theodore Ziolkowski, »Zur Entstehung und Struktur von Hermann Brochs *Schlafwandlern*,« *DVjs*, 38 (1964), pp. 58f, 64. Cited as Ziolkowski, »Ent.«

vision of things serves to bias whatever might look as if it were supposed to be an impartial reflection of objective reality.

Twenty years after completing *Die Schlafwandler*, Broch wrote that »Philosophie, welche die metaphysische Grenze zu überschreiten trachtet – sie tut das bereits überall dort, wo sie sich mit ethischen und ästhetischen Problemen beschäftigt – , nur dann haltbar ist, wenn sie auf einem theologischen Dogmengebäude fußt; eine säkularisierte Philosophie gibt es nicht, d.h., sie bleibt in Rahmen der subjektiven Meinung befangen, und so wollte ich eben diese Erkenntnis radikal zu Ende führen, indem ich das Subjektive, also das Dichterische zur Instanz gemacht habe und ihm die philosophische Überlegung unterzuordnen trachtete« (13/3: 532).[15] Broch himself points out here that even the philosophical parts of his novel are subordinate to subjective vision, the perspective that Müller represents. However, he also equates subjectivity with »the poetic,« an equivocation that implicitly raises the question of how the medium of poetic expression functions with regard to subject and object.

In the Joyce essay, Broch was careful to draw a line of distinction between the *Darstellungssubjekt* and the medium of representation. In *Die Schlafwandler* it is the representing subject that dominates the picture of reality. Turning now to *Der Tod des Vergil*, we see that the situation is somewhat altered. By the same token that Gide's Edouard was a precursor to Broch's Müller, Joyce's language in *Ulysses* and *Finnegan's Wake* showed the way to the idiom of *The Death of Vergil*.

In Broch's second major novel, the figure of the narrator-author disappears into the vastness of the novel's sea of words. A basic element of narrative technique in the *Schlafwandler*-novels had been the ironic distance between the limited minds of the three protagonists and the observations that Müller wanted to make about their vision of the world.[16] For instance, when August Esch looks at a travel poster that depicts a ship putting out to sea, he begins to consider emigrating to America. Starting from Esch's point of view, the narrator gradually

---

[15] Cf. Ziolkowski, »Ent.« pp. 62f., 69. It is customary to think of poets as subjective observers, but Müller (and Broch) the philosopher must also be thought of as subjective or »poetic.« Certain contemporary philosophers, although they have abandoned the concept of transcendental subjectivity to which Broch subscribed, have asserted the »poetic« status of the philosophical text: see Richard Rorty, »Philosophy as a Kind of Writing: An Essay on Derrida,« *New Literary History*, 10 (1978), 141–60.

[16] In this regard see Dorrit Cohn's comments on »psycho-narration« in her *Transparent Minds. Narrative Modes for Presenting Consciousness in Fiction* (Princeton, New Jersey: Princeton University Press, 1978), pp. 52–7.

34

shifts away from his protagonist's slow-witted meditations and develops them into a rhapsodic soliloquy of his own. At its conclusion, he jerks the reader back down to his hero's banal reality with a tongue-in-cheek reminder: »So dachte Esch sicherlich nicht« (1: 254). In *Der Tod des Vergil* the protagonist and the narrator converge in the figure of the dying poet, whose mind and language are adequate to voice the thoughts that Broch would like to express.

Yet if we read Broch against the grain of his phenomenological premises and take seriously the extraordinary or even oppressive weight of his novel's word-character, i.e. the linguisticality of Vergil's imagination, then it becomes clear that not only external reality but also Vergil's personal subjectivity are subordinate to the language that precedes them and in which they occur. Linguisticality – or, at the level of the literary text, what might be called »narrativity« – is the primary locus of reality. It mediates both the subjective and objective realities of the novel, impresses upon them its temporal forms and grammatical categories, and gives a seemingly objective form to the wispy nothingness of mind. The near-opaque density of the novel's profusion of words calls attention to itself by the sheer weight of its verbal substance. In so doing it reveals that it too is a thing in the material world, that it too has its own history, limitations, and autonomy. Vergil knows that his mind is caught in a net of words just as his soul is trapped in a living husk that is fated to decay and die. The novel's final word addresses that moment at which mind and soul lift away from earthly containment and become »jenseits der Sprache« (4: 454).

The knowledge and moment of death interested Broch uncommonly. It is in fact the crux of the impulse that underlies much of his philosophical and literary writing. In turning now to look more closely at *Die Schlafwandler*, we shall see the importance of the theme of death, and another mode of self-allegory will come into view.

II

The last three decades of Broch criticism have made it plain enough that his *Schlafwandler* trilogy is an allegory of his historicist theory of values. However, it is less clear and at least as interesting to note that the mode of allegory is somehow a function of Broch's fascination with *time*, a preoccupation that was common in the modernist generation. The emergence of time as a major theme in Broch and other modernists as well as the nature of its connection with allegory are in need of some explanation.

Two letters of May, 1925 – one to his father and another to his son – vouch for Broch's personal commitment to grappling with the problem of temporality, a commitment that surfaces more complexly in his literary production (13/1: 62–7). In these two letters he describes his understanding of the modern era and man's place in it, especially from the perspective of the final confrontation with death that every individual must make. In Broch's vision of the world, the collapse of traditional religious beliefs and values had left modernity with no spiritual foundation capable of assuring finite man of his continuity with infinite divinity: the prospect of a modern death leaves the temporal Self intolerably exposed to a monstrous nullity. His perception of this absurdity led him to conceive of the artist's task as diagnostic and therapeutic. The artist must help to impose order on the chaos, thus restoring at least in some small way a partial sense of meaning to a spiritually destitute culture. He did not believe that literature or philosophy could ever fully replenish the void left in the absence of traditional religion and authentic myth, yet he persisted in his literary and philosophical efforts. This gesture of defiance marks his refusal to accept temporality on empirical modernity's secular terms.[17]

This fascination with man's fate in a time-bound reality was not an idiosyncratic interest on Broch's part. It is much more a dominant feature of the modernist era.[18] In 1863, one of modernism's most important precursors, Charles Baudelaire, wrote: »La modernité, c'est le transitoire, le fugitif, le contingent, la moitié de l'art, dont l'autre moitié est l'éternel et l'immuable.«[19] The political, social, and scientific upheavals of the late nineteenth and early twentieth centuries shook the foundations of the »eternal and immutable« beliefs that previous generations had been able to take for granted. The result was a heightened awareness of the temporal flux of things, of their fragility and

---

[17] Doris Stephan, »Vom Ungenügen des Dichters: Anmerkungen zur Todeserkenntnis Hermann Brochs,« Forum, 8 (1961), 181–83; Beate Loos, Mythos, Zeit und Tod. Zum Verhältnis von Kunsttheorie und dichterischer Praxis in Hermann Brochs Bergroman, Gegenwart der Dichtung, 1 (Frankfurt am Main: Athenäum, 1971).

[18] See esp. Margaret Church, Time and Reality. Studies in Contemporary Fiction (Chapel Hill, N.C.: University of North Carolina Press, 1963); Theodore Ziolkowski, »The Discordant Clocks,« in his Dimensions of the Modern Novel, pp. 183–214.

[19] Charles Baudelaire, »Le Peintre de la Vie Moderne,« in his Oeuvres Completes, ed. Y.-G. Le Dantec, rev. Claude Pichois (Paris: Gallimard, 1961), p. 1163. For an excellent discussion on Baudelaire, temporality and modernism, see Matei Calinescu, Faces of Modernity (Bloomington: University of Indiana Press, 1977), pp. 46–57.

incertitude. Time pulls all things, including man, toward dissolution and destruction. The prospect of a death that empties life into mere nothingness unsettled the western imagination on a large scale. In the era of modernism, time develops into a major philosophical and literary theme from Bergson and Proust to Thomas Mann and Martin Heidegger.

Perhaps nowhere was this theme more dominant than in the Viennese milieu. It appears there, and in Broch's *Schlafwandler* trilogy, in its dual aspect: the motif of *death* is the sign of time's absolute power over finite beings; and the motif of *eroticism* serves as an ambiguous sign for the hope of somehow transcending temporal finitude. The intellectual atmosphere of fin-de-siècle Vienna was saturated with intimations of eros and thanatos. The morbid eroticism of Sezession painters and sculptors, the sexually funded theories of men such as Freud, Kraus, and Weininger, the recurring thematics of death and erotic desire in the work of Hofmannsthal, Schnitzler, Schaukal, Beer-Hofmann, Sacher-Masoch, Roth and many others are only the most obvious examples of a trend that bordered on the proportions of an obsession.[20] Hermann Broch came of age in a generation that knew itself to be witnessing the death-throes of a once virile *Kaiserreich* and, ultimately, its violent end in the First World War.

This generation's desire for personal and historical regeneration expressed itself in an ambivalent preoccupation with eroticism. It is ambivalent because its positive and negative aspects are often difficult to distinguish from each other. In fin-de-siècle aestheticism, the erotic generally appears as nihilistic self-gratification. The erotic sensibilities of Schnitzler's Anatol or of the various figures in his *Reigen* are typical. Anatol's erotic encounters are ecstatic but transitory escapes from his own mortality. He tries to suspend the knowledge of his death in the timeless space of erotic experience. Because this moment of erotic flight is itself temporal, Anatol attempts to hold it fast by aesthetisizing the experience. A lock of hair, a photograph, or any other memento be-

---

[20] For a concise discussion of the development of this situation, see Horst Fritz, »Die Dämonisierung des Erotischen in der Literatur des Fin de Siècle,« *Fin de Siècle. Zur Literatur und Kunst der Jahrhundertwende*, hrsg. v. Roger Bauer et al, Studien zur Philosophie und Literatur des 19. Jahrhunderts, 35 (Frankfurt am Main: Vittorio Klostermann, 1977), pp. 442–64. Johnston, *Austrian Mind*, pp. 115–80 passim. For a fascinating speculative treatment of the interplay between the erotic, death, and the sacred, see Georges Bataille, *L'Erotisme* (Paris: Les Editions de Minuit, 1957). On the theme of death in modernist fiction, see Theodore Ziolkowski, »The Metaphysics of Death,« in his *Dimensions of the Modern Novel*, pp. 215–57.

comes the source of his tepid pleasure as he indifferently lets the live
women go their own ways.[21] Anatol lives only in his memory, among
the dead emblems of past adventures, while true life passes him by. His
keepsakes are unchanging and eternal. They signify for him his con-
quest not only of various women but also of time and death. Actually,
Anatol is already dead because he denies himself a truer life in the
temporal flux of human love. Like Hofmannsthal's Claudio, Anatol
isolates himself in an artificial paradise. In his futile struggle against
change and the passage of time, in his attempt to make time stand still
in symbols, Anatol succumbs even more to the *Todesverfallenheit* of
loveless, mechanical sexuality.

The post-aestheticist generation of writers in Vienna – in particular
Broch and Musil – also takes eroticism as a major theme, but in a
different way. They reject the sterile, time-denying erotics of dandyism,
preferring instead to present erotic experience as an affirmation of temporality. It shows their desire for a rapprochement with the ›dionysian‹
sources of myth and the sacred. Ulrich's attachment to his sister, Agathe, in *Der Mann ohne Eigenschaften* is charged with the erotics of a
creativity that brushes aside even the most forbidding taboos of society.
Chapter III of this study will discuss their relationship in greater detail.
The erotic violence that concludes *Die Schlafwandler*--Huguenau's
rape of Esch's wife – has nothing to do with love, but it is nonteles
meant to be a propitious sign. Within the framework of Broch's historicist metaphysics, the murder of Esch and the rape of his wife signify
the death of the old epoch and the procreation of that which is to come.
In Broch and Musil, the erotic is not an escape from time but is instead
an act that is in harmony with time's forward motion. Its commitment
is not to escape but to creativity.

Temporality underlies the motifs of death and eros for the aesthetes
and post-aesthetes alike. It is also noteworthy that there is an interesting
parallel between modernism – especially in Austria – and the Baroque
with regard to the importance of temporality. The modernists renewed
the old *memento mori* theme as a spontaneous aesthetic response to the
perceived loss of timeless and eternal values – what Nietzsche tele-
graphically labeled the »death of God.«

Like the early seventeenth century, the early twentieth century was a
time of devastating historical upheaval. World War One and the Thirty
Years War left entire nations in the deepest misery of ideological, material, and spiritual pandemonium. Such a historical experience condi-

---

[21] Arthur Schnitzler, *Anatol*, in his Gesammelte Werke in zwei Bänden, I
(Frankfurt am Main: S. Fischer, 1962).

tions the sort of metaphysical pessimism expressed in a literature that dwells on the fragility, mutability, and meaninglessness of earthly things. The Baroque mind dismisses mere reality as deception and illusion, a distortion of the truer reality beyond this world. Life, in Calderón's central formulation, is a dream: *la vida es sueño*; and it is in this selfsame dreamlife that Broch's sleepwalkers drift about. It is so because their path »nur mehr Symbol und Andeutung eines höheren Weges ist, den man in Wirklichkeit zu gehen hat und für den jener bloß das irdische Spiegelbild ist, schwankend und unsicher wie das Bild im dunklen Teich« (1:379f). Broch's Platonism has much in common with Baroque habits of mind. The pious seventeenth century rejected the priority of the objective reality around them on religious grounds, in celebration of God's timeless heavenly order. The twentieth century has lost confidence in objective reality for reasons of secular epistemology and because of a disappointment in the failure of enlightened humanism to fulfill the utopian expectations that it had generated. The Baroque flight into religion is no longer possible: Broch reduces the Church to a shabby and impotent Salvation Army Band. This pathetic group of proselytizing tambourine-bangers is all that remains of traditional Western religiosity in the world of Broch's sleepwalkers. It is the merest vestige of what was once a mighty bulwark against the immensity of death and time.

One of Broch's contemporaries, also writing in the 1920's worked out a provocative hypothesis concerning the relationship between temporality and literary form. In his *Ursprung des deutschen Trauerspiels* (Berlin, 1928), Walter Benjamin writes: »Unter der entscheidenden Kategorie der Zeit ... läßt sich das Verhältnis von Symbol und Allegorie sich festlegen.«[22] He suggests that symbol, which is the master

---

[22] Walter Benjamin, *Ursprung des deutschen Trauerspiels*, hrsg. v. Rolf Tiedemann, Suhrkamp Wissenschaft Taschenbuch, 225 (Frankfurt am Main: Suhrkamp, 1982), pp. 144f. Cited as Benjamin. For a conveniently brief survey of the aesthetic rivalry between symbol and allegory see Gunter Reiß, *»Allegorisierung« und moderne Erzählkunst. Eine Studie zum Werk Thomas Manns* (München: Fink, 1970), pp. 11–40. Reiß operates with a notion of allegory similar to the one I am trying to develop here, but he does not appreciate the relevance of temporality to the rise of allegory in the modernist era. He explicitly rejects it (p. 33). Paul de Man is more sympathetic to Benjamin's thesis, which he modifies and develops: P.d.M., »Allegorie und Symbol in der europäischen Frühromantik,« in *Typologia Litterarum*, Festschrift für Max Wehrli, hrsg. v. Stefan Sonderegger, Alois M. Maas, and Harald Burger (Zürich: Atlantis, 1969), pp. 403–25; »The Rhetoric of Temporality,« in *Interpretation. Theory and Practice*, ed. Charles Singleton (Baltimore: Johns Hopkins University Press, 1969), pp. 173–209.

trope of the Renaissance and the *Goethezeit*, is the figural mode proper to a world firmly rooted in a sound metaphysics: »Als symbolisches Gebilde soll das Schöne bruchlos ins Göttliche übergehen.«[23] Its temporality is that of the mystical instant of timeless continuity between earthly beauty and ideal divinity; it is the immanence of God in the world. But the disruptive intrusion of time as history – as a war, for instance, that no pious mind can understand as a reflection of the continuity between man and divine perfection – into this unity ruptures the continuum, signaling the presence of death in paradise and the retreat of God into a distant transcendence. The trope that enacts this separation from the divine, and that admits of temporality and death, is allegory. Its function is to reconcile differences between appearances in the phenomenal world and the ideality of spiritual reality.

Allegorical thinking in the seventeenth century typically devalued empirical reality to the status of a sign. The world represents but is not identical with the Platonic (Christian) realm beyond appearances. The twentieth century, similarly immersed in the turmoil of political, religious, social and intellectual crisis, has shown a like affinity for allegory, especially in the large-scale trend toward reflective and reflexive practices in fiction.[24] The felt need for a self-reflective level in narrative no doubt has to do with a metaphysical insecurity so thoroughgoing that even linguistic signification is set into question. Separation from traditional absolutes conditions the predominance of allegory as postulated meaning not governed by the *tertium comparationis* of an indubitable authority.

The important difference between modernism and the Baroque is the finality of the separation of lived reality from the transcendent order. In spite of its profound distress, the seventeenth century ultimately retained its confidence in the divine authority of God as manifestation of Church and State. This order, invariant because of collective faith in its divine sanction, provides the Baroque allegorist with a stable *tertium comparationis*. The twentieth century – after Kant, after Nietzsche, and after the failure of its cherished institutions to prevent a war of shocking inhumanity – has not been able to retain its confidence in absolute authority, divine or earthly. Modern allegorists lack the frame-

---

[23] Benjamin, p. 139.
[24] Maurice Beebe, »Reflective and Reflexive Trends in Modern Fiction,« in *Twentieth Century Poetry, Fiction, Theory*, Bucknell Review, ed. Harry Garvin (London: Associated University Presses, 1977), pp. 13–26. However, Beebe makes no connection between reflexivity and the tradition of allegory. On the modern rise of allegory see Edwin Honig, *Dark Conceit. The Making of Allegory* (London: Faber and Faber, 1959).

work of an invariant plane of reference. In its absence they must fall back on the resources of individual imagination: because he cannot refer to a divine order, Bertrand Müller must allegorize a theory of history (i.e. of temporality).

Broch was aware of the allegorical tendencies of modern fiction, but he did not consciously associate them with the problem of temporality. He cites Hofmannsthal and Joyce as examples of modern allegorists. The crisis of modern literature as Broch understood it is summed up in the autonomy of the subject, who must posit new values for himself. The modern Self is cut off from the transcendence guaranteed in the symbolism of myth and sacred narrative. Broch takes Hofmannsthal's Chandos-Letter to be the breaking point between the metaphysics of symbolism and the disrupted signification of the allegorical figure: »die mystische Intuitiv-Einheit von Ich, Ausdruck und Ding ist ihm [Hofmannsthal] mit einem Schlag verlorengegangen, so daß sein Ich jählings zu hermetischer Isolierung gebracht ist . . .« (9/1:305). According to Broch, Hofmannsthal tentatively finds his way out of this dilemma in a ploy of self-reflection: »Dichtung ist Traum, aber einer, der sich seines Träumens immer wieder bewußt wird« (9/1:307). Writing about Hofmannsthal's *Frau ohne Schatten*, Broch contends,

> der Symbolstrom hat zwar wieder zu fließen begonnen, aber die natürliche unmittelbare Verbindung zwischen Assoziation, sprachlichem Ausdruck, Symbol und Ding hat sich nicht wieder eingestellt; eine gewisse Symboler-starrung ist eingetreten, und um die Mitteilung verständlich und flexibel zu erhalten, müssen immer mehr Symbole ins Spiel gebracht werden, freilich in ihrer Überfülle nun erst recht den Erstarrungsprozeß fördernd, da sie - und das ist der Übergang vom Symbol zur Allegorie - überhaupt nicht mehr verständlich wären, wenn sie nicht in einen fixen, eben allegorischen Kanon gebracht werden würden, das Gegenextrem zur unmittelbaren Mittelbarkeit. Und weil es ein Erstarrungsprozeß ist, haftet der Allegorie etwas homunku-loid Lebloses an, von dem sie ebensowohl in Versteinerungs- wie in Verflüch-tigungsgefahr gebracht wird. (9/1:322)

The modern writer's symbols become allegories because the writer himself must also posit their *tertium comparationis*--what Broch here calls a »fixed or allegorical canon« of meanings. Such is precisely Broch's own solution for himself when he builds in an essayistic me-talevel that reflects and interprets the action of the three *Schlafwand-ler*-novels.[25] It should also be noted - especially in view of the fact that

---

[25] In a letter of 4 April 1935 to Herbert Burgmüller Broch explains himself: »In den Exkursen des Huguenau habe ich einen Ausweg gefunden: wenn schon der Autor eine Sinngebung mit Objektivitätsanspruch für unerlässlich hält, so möge er es offen und ehrlich tun, d.h. also wirkliche Objektivitätssphären einbauen« (13/1:340).

many Broch critics try to find a symbolic-mythic level in his works – that Broch is explicitly aware of the limitations which allegorizing imposes: any allegorical structure is the postulate of an »isolated ego« and therefore cannot attain to the effectively objective character of genuine myth.[26] He nevertheless attributes to Hofmannsthal a special insight that affirms the creative, perhaps mythopoeic potential of the autonomous Self. Broch reads the Kaiser's dream in the *Frau ohne Schatten* as the tale's allegory of itself. A dream in a story is a dream in a dream:

> Hofmannsthal symbolisiert also – ein geradezu Joycescher Trick – nochmals den Allegorisierungsprozeß, symbolisiert im Inhalt sein eigenes Darstellungsmittel, und auf diese Weise durchbricht er mit nochmaligem Raffinement das lediglich Allegorische, das lediglich Raffinierte, das lediglich Mittelbare und gewinnt ihm die zweite Unmittelbarkeit, die schöne Einfalt, ohne die das Märchen kein Märchen wäre. (9/1: 323)

In this passage Broch is straining to regain some sense of symbol and myth, but his proposition that metafiction achieves a »zweite Unmittelbarkeit« is unconvincing. His philosophical premise of an autonomous subject forestalls the claims he would like to make on a literature of unmediated vision.

Nevertheless, his observation that allegory and self-allegory are important features in Hofmannsthal and Joyce is compelling. Broch does not explain what he means by saying that Hofmannsthal's ironic self-reflection in the *Frau ohne Schatten* is a »joycean trick,« but the allusion is reasonably clear. Joyce's allegorical impulse manifests itself as parody. His *Ulysses* is a parody – i.e. allegory – of Homer's *Odyssey*. The classical epic provides him with a continuous plane of reference according to which he organizes his conspicuously unheroic world.[27]

---

[26] Along with many other writers of his generation, Broch was interested in fulfilling the Romantics' call for a new mythology, but he realized the unlikelihood of him or anyone else actually managing the job of composing sacred texts: See his »Geist und Zeitgeist. Ein Vortrag,« 9/2: 177–201, esp. p. 197. Cf. also 13/1: 398.

[27] Maurice Beebe has suggested that a defining characteristic of modernist fiction is the use of myth not »as a discipline for belief or a subject for interpretation, but as an arbitrary means of ordering art,« M. B., »Ulysses and the Age of Modernism,« in *Fifty Years »Ulysses*,« ed. with an Intro. by Thomas F. Staley (Bloomington, London: Indiana University Press, 1974), p. 175. Beebe's observation is in principle true, but it is too narrow. Allegory or allegorization describes more exactly what is decisive because it includes but goes beyond the mythologizing that Beebe has singled out. Many authors do allegorize myths, but other authors – who operate under the influence of the same need to posit a verifying *tertium comparationis*–allegorize other preformed systems. Freudian and Jungian psychoanalytic theories are obvious examples of such systems that some authors refer to; Broch's theory of values

Homer could construct an imaginary world according to the real world's divine plan; his modern counterpart, Joyce, must construct his imaginary world in the absence of divinity. Under these circumstances he ironically bases it not upon reality – spiritual or historical – but instead upon the *stories* that have traditionally been told about it. The vision of the world that Joyce offers is mediated through the optic of narrative tradition.

One of the staggering implications of his achievement is that there is something profoundly narrative and interpretive about the way we set about determining what is real and what is not. The ›stories‹ told about the world – scientific, historical, and poetic – are projections not only of facts but also of values and beliefs that we impose upon the coordinate system of nature and history. Values and beliefs are the special province of the poetic word, which has in its subliminal keeping the inchoate future. This future is not present in the form of some particular idea or other that some particular poet or other writes down for posterity to translate into fact. Instead, the future is manifest in the capacity of literature's most evocative images to stir a receptive imagination into renewed creativity. These evocations reinforce but also subtly redefine the beliefs and values that will determine the bounds within which the future will take shape.

III

Broch's narrative technique in *Die Schlafwandler* incorporates aspects of the self-allegory he mentions in connection with Hofmannsthal and of the parodical allegory to be associated with Joyce. As self-allegory, the trilogy duplicates itself within itself in the form of Bertram Müller's philosophical disquisition. His essay on the disintegration of values reflects and interprets the narrative in which it occurs. It functions as a *tertium comparationis* for the events in the fictional world.[28] In the

---

is another. It is the need to allegorize and not any particular allegorical content that is modernism's defining characteristic. Cf. Angus Fletcher, *Allegory. The Theory of a Symbolic Mode* (Ithaca: Cornell University Press, 1964), 304–59, esp. 317–21.

[28] The relationship between the essays and the novel is of course the most often interpreted aspect of *Die Schlafwandler*. My intention here is not to offer another interpretive paraphrase of how he translates his theories into fiction; previous critics have already made this aspect sufficiently clear. Rather, I want to demonstrate the allegorical character of his technique and trace it to its source in the experience of temporality. For studies of the relationship between Müller's (Broch's) theory and the course of the trilogy's fictional action see esp. Richard Brinkmann, (cf. note 4) but also Karl Robert Mandel-

absence of any superordinated, universally valid frame of reference Broch has found it necessary to fabricate one that will make his tale systematically intelligible. Yet Broch also knows his philosophical theory to be a fabulation in its own right. It is only a tentative substitute that cannot attain to the binding universality of myth and religion. Broch acknowledges the fictionality and fallibility of the »Zerfall der Werte« by setting them, along with their author, *en abyme*. Müller's presence is the sign that the essays arise from a specific individual in a particular historical setting. They are bound to the limitations of his personal perspective. There is no Archimedean point, no *tertium comparationis* outside of fictionality.

Part of Müller's essay can serve as a key to the parodical form of allegory that is also at work in the trilogy. The present age, asserts Müller, lacks an authentic artistic style of its own. »Style« in his special sense is the objectivation of an epoch's spirituality, and the purely ornamental flourish – especially in architecture – is the point at which this inner logic of values becomes visible. But the aesthetic object is only one of the ways in which the transpersonal system of values reaches expression. This structure is the matrix from which emerge all the thoughts, deeds, and judgments that precede and inform the character of a historical people. Müller's interest focuses on the aesthetic object because it is the purest expression of an era's inner logic.

It is here that Müller makes his most direct statement about the connection between temporality and aesthetics. He understands the threat of time and the fear of death to be the underlying source of the aesthetic impulse:

Vielleicht wäre es müßig über Stil nachzudenken, wenn nicht das Problem dahinter stünde, das allein alles Philosophieren legitimiert: die Angst vor dem Nichts, die Angst vor der Zeit, die zum Tode führt. . . . Denn was immer der Mensch tut, er tut es, um die Zeit zu vernichten, um sie aufzuheben, und

kow, *Hermann Brochs Romantrilogie »Die Schlafwandler.«* *Gestaltung und Reflexion im modernen deutschen Roman*, Probleme der Dichtung, 6 (Heidelberg: Carl Winter, 1962); Rolf Geißler, »Hermann Brochs *Die Schlafwandler*,« in *Möglichkeiten des modernen deutschen Romans*, hrsg. v. Rolf Geißler, 3. Aufl. (Frankfurt am Main: Diesterweg, 1962); Leo Kreutzer, *Erkenntnistheorie und Prophetie. Hermann Brochs Romantrilogie »Die Schlafwandler*,« Studien zur deutschen Literatur, 3 (Tübingen: Niemeyer, 1966); Hartmut Steinecke, »*Die Schlafwandler*. Beispiel eines polyhistorischen Romans,« in H.S., *Hermann Broch und der polyhistorische Roman* Bonner Arbeiten zur deutschen Literatur, 17 (Bonn: Bouvier, 1968), 101-55; Hartmut Reinhardt, *Erweiterter Naturalismus. Untersuchungen zum Konstruktionsverfahren in Hermann Brochs Romantrilogie »Die Schlafwandler*,« Kölner germanistische Studien, 7 (Köln: Böhlau, 1972).

diese Aufhebung heißt Raum. Selbst die Musik, die bloß in der Zeit ist und die Zeit erfüllt, wandelt die Zeit zum Raume, und daß alles Denken im Räumlichen vor sich geht, daß der Denkprozeß eine Verquickung unsagbar verwickelter vieldimensionaler logischer Räume darstellt, diese Theorie besitzt allergrößte Wahrscheinlichkeit. (1: 445)

Aesthetically wrought space annihilates time insofar as it reifies and reaffirms the symbolic continuity of man with values that are beyond time and death. The poverty of the modern era, says Müller, is that it lacks a distinctive sense of ornament and is therefore defenseless against the annihilating movement of time. This alleged lack of style is the manifestation of man's discontinuity with any transcendent order.

As a novelist in an era with no intrinsic style of its own, Müller has posed an interesting problem for himself. What is to be the style of his own artistic work? His solution – like the actual solutions of James Joyce and Thomas Mann – is to write novels in self-critical parody of past styles. He casts *Pasenow* in the manner of Fontane's realism and gives to *Esch* the characteristic patina of naturalism. He composes the *Huguenau* in a systematically fragmented anti-style that is meant to reflect the chaotic disorder of the lives of those living in the styleless era of World War I. The tentative unity of the three novels arises from yet another level of reference. This level is that of mythology, but once again this level is a dream that knows itself to be dreaming: the mythologizing can only be ironic. Broch harnesses eclectically borrowed (i.e. parodied) mythological motifs in order allegorically to represent his theory of history and values. We turn now to take a close look at the machinations of allegory in the three novels.

Students and critics of Broch's trilogy have taken careful note of the »parodistic« relationship between *1888 Pasenow oder die Romantik* and the conventions of realism familiar in the works of Theodor Fontane.[29] However, in this case the term »parody« is not to be understood as an attempt to satirize or ridicule Fontane for comic effect. Instead, Broch is making use of typically Fontanesque elements in order to awaken certain expectations in his readers. The setting in Berlin among the landed gentry of the Prussian countryside, as well as the theme of a young officer's choice between two attractive young women evokes in the reader a sense of pleasant familiarity. The reader knows the style and therefore has a general idea of how the plot ought to move forward. The expectation is that serious and touching conflicts will develop, that

---

[29] See esp. Andreas Bertschinger, *Hermann Brochs »Pasenow« – ein künstlicher Fontane-Roman? Zur Epochenstruktur Wilhelminismus und Zwischenkriegszeit*, Zürcher Beiträge zur deutschen Literatur und Geistesgeschichte, 55 (Zürich: Artemis, 1982).

painful choices will be made, but finally that the order of things will be reaffirmed. Broch undermines these expectations by unmasking the terrible confusion that lies only slightly beneath the genteel surface of his protagonist's stiff uniform and polished manners.

The young officer is Joachim von Pasenow, and his problem is that he must find and take his rightful place in Wilhelminian society. Unlike a true Fontane hero, this protagonist finds himself snarled in an anarchical jumble of elemental experiences that he is unable to untangle or even identify. He undergoes two decisive experiences. One of these is the senseless death of his brother, Helmuth, who is killed in a duel for the sake of an outdated notion of honor. This personal confrontation with death is profoundly unsettling for Joachim. It forces him toward a reckoning with his own inner strength against the inevitability of death. As his friend Bertrand once pointed out to him, Joachim's only spiritual stability lies in superficial convention, which his military uniform represents. Such outward signs, suggests Bertrand, have supplanted the inner fortification that the Church had once provided (1: 24–28; 58–61). Superficial convention in the form of a nonsensical code of honor sent Helmuth to his grave, and now Joachim also has been made to feel the threat of meaninglessness and an absurd death.

The other major event in Joachim's development occurs, significantly, at the same time as his brother's death. This event is his erotic encounter with the passionate Ruzena. His night of lovemaking with her immediately precedes the news of Helmuth's killing, thereby bringing the experience of eros and thanatos into a conspicuous juxtaposition for him and for the reader. Like death, sex belongs to the elemental part of life that largely escapes convention and is therefore a threat to Joachim, who seeks refuge in the familiarity and clarity of convention. Ruzena is an outsider, an exotic casino-hostess who, in her elemental simplicity, does not even have a full command of the cultivated German language. She exists beyond the precincts of Wilhelminian society. She is a temptress who draws Joachim out of his accustomed reality into a dangerously unfamiliar world.

Her opponent for his affections, such as they are, is the blond-haired blue-eyed Elisabeth Baddensen. Like Joachim, she belongs to the upper classes and leads her life entirely within the protected boundaries that convention has established for young people of their station. Broch uses this well-heeled maiden and her family to exemplify how convention strives to contain the temporal threat of eros and death within artificial boundaries. With the Baddensens as his example, the narrator introduces the theme of temporality into the novel. Because the burden of time oppresses them, he explains, they have become enthusiastic collectors of things. In order to assemble for themselves a familiar unchanging world they surround themselves with inanimate things, especially art objects. It means for them an »Aufhebung des Todes« (1 : 80f). They immure themselves within a fortress of cultural detritus for much the same reason that Schnitzler's Anatol prefers keepsakes to live women. It is an aesthetisization of the real world that attempts to staunch the flow of time by stopping it at symbolic points and holding it fast.

In contradistinction to the stillness associated with the Baddensens' collection of objects, Broch connects Ruzena with the dynamic fluidity of water imagery (e.g. 1:44f). He distinguishes her as the carrier of mutability and time. Her erotic vitality, although it seems sinister to Pasenow, is a principle of life that affirms itself tragically, in full acceptance of its temporality. Ruzena suffers for it, but there is more of life in her than in any other figure in the trilogy. She is embedded in the ebb and flow of things. Elisabeth, by way of contrast, swoons into the arms of an unrecognized death. Her favorite place is her father's well-manicured garden at the family's country estate. Because change frightens her, she seeks refuge in the accustomed surroundings of his collection and his garden:

zwar wußte Elisabeth nicht, daß jeder Sammler . . . , aufgehend in seiner Sammlung, auch die Erreichung seiner eigenen Absolutheit erhofft und die Aufhebung seines Todes, Elisabeth wußte es nicht, aber umgeben von all den vielen schönen toten Dingen, die um sie angesammelt und aufgehäuft waren, umgeben von den vielen schönen Bildern, ahnte sie dennoch, daß die Bilder an die Wände gehängt waren, als sollten sie die Mauern verstärken, und als sollten all die toten Dinge etwas sehr Lebendiges bergen . . . . Sie ahnte die Angst, die dahinter stand und die den Alltag, der das Altern ist, im Festlichen zu übertönen suchte, Angst, die sich immer wieder vergewisserte – stets neu erlebte Überraschung – , daß sie lebendig und geboren und definitiv beisammen waren und ihr Kreis ewiglich geschlossen. Und so wie der Baron immer neue Strecken seines Bodens in den Park einbezog, dessen dichter dunkler Bestand nun schon fast von allen Seiten mit weiten Flächen freundlichen lichten Jungholzes umgeben war, so schien es Elisabeth, als wünschte er mit fast weiblicher Fürsorge ihrer aller zu einem immer größeren eingefriedeten Park voll anmutiger Raststationen zu machen, . . . auf daß Elisabeth sich für immer in ihm ergehen möge. (1 : 80f; cf. 1 : 37, 110)

Elisabeth resists all that is outside of her little garden, secure in the knowledge that no outsider will penetrate its bounds. She fears the loss of her virginity and is afraid of coming into the temporal flow of a world where things change and people die. Yet even her father cannot bring time to a standstill. Joachim rejects Ruzena and takes Elisabeth as his wife. The pathological prudery of their wedding night is the final demonstration of their will to resist the temporal truth of eros and thanatos.

47

In the same way that Fontanesque elements serve as a bonding device for the external structure of *Pasenow*, familiar topoi of the naturalist novel give to *Esch* its outward appearance. The aura of gentility that characterizes the *Pasenow*-novel gives way to the harsh tones and unsavory details of life among the Rhineland's working class. The novel's ostensible theme is the confrontation of its dimwitted protagonist, August Esch, with the hard facts of proletarian life. His job-problems, woman-troubles, and his personal campaign against social injustice make up the external events depicted in the tale. Its actual theme goes behind the naturalistic backdrop to get at the deeper sources of Esch's impotence and despair. These sources are metaphysical, and are not finally different from those uncovered in *Pasenow*.

Esch's epiphany of death and eros comes to him when he visits a music hall in the company of Erna and Balthasar Korn, the brother and sister from whom he rents a room. The evening's amusements include watching a juggler whose routine climaxes with a knife-throwing act. His target is a beautiful girl, who stands »crucified« against a black background. She placidly awaits the remotely phallic knives of her partner while Esch, tense with fear and excitement, expects her at any moment to be plunged into the blackness of death. It is unpleasantly comical that this burlesque tableau moves Esch deeply, awakening his stunted religious sensibilities. His driving ambition from then on is to save the beautiful girl, to *redeem* her – »Erlösung« is a key word in this novel – and to sacrifice himself in her place:

Fast hätte Esch die Arme selber gegen den Himmel erhoben, selber gekreuzigt, hätte er gewünscht, vor der Zarten zu stehen, mit eigenem Körper die drohenden Messer aufzufangen, und hätte der Jongleur, wie dies zu geschehen pflegt, gefragt, ob ein Herr aus dem Publikum den Wunsch hege, auf die Bühne zu kommen, um sich vor das schwarze Brett zu stellen, wahrlich, Esch hätte sich gemeldet. Ja, es war ihm ein fast wollüstiger Gedanke, daß er allein und verlassen dort stünde, und daß die langen Messer ihn an das Brett anheften könnten wie ein Käfer, doch müßte er dann, korrigierte er, mit dem Gesicht gegen das Brett gewendet sein, da kein Käfer vom Bauche her aufgespießt wird: und der Gedanke, daß er gegen die Finsternis des Brettes gekehrt wäre, nicht wissend, wann das tödliche Messer von hinten heranfliegt, das Herz ihm zu durchbohren und es an das Brett anzuheften, war von so außerordentlichem und geheimnisvollem Reiz, war Wunsch von so neuer Stärke und Reife, daß er wie aus Traum und Seligkeit auffuhr, als mit Trommelwirbel und Paukenschlag und Fanfaren das Orchester den Jongleur begrüßte, der ... dem erlösten Publikum sich verneigten. Es waren die Fanfaren des Gerichtes. Der Schuldige wird wie ein Wurm zertreten; warum soll er nicht wie ein Käfer aufgespießt werden? warum soll der Tod nicht statt der Sense eine lange Stecknadel tragen, oder zumindest eine Lanze? (1: 203f)

Esch's desire for a sacrificial death and the image of being pierced from behind prefigure the mode of his death in the next novel. Huguenau will bayonet him in the back. The scene's immediate significance, though, is the spiritual awakening of August Esch. His initial response is the desire to consummate the experience in Erna Korn's bed.

Sex and women are not foreign to August Esch, who has the reputation of being something of a rake. When he is feeling low and has time to kill, it lifts his spirits to make a list of all the women he has ever slept with (1: 233). But the association of lust with these vaguely religious stirrings is something new for him. It signals a distinction between carnal self-indulgence and the possibility of lasting fulfillment in an erotic union that will shelter him from the omnipresent threat of death (1: 220). Unfortunately for him, Erna Korn's response is negative, and so Esch finds himself compelled to still his primal urges at a nearby brothel.

Nevertheless, he has undergone an experience that will continue to drive him forward. The desire to redeem Ilona – the girl from the knife act – becomes an obsession with him; and so does his desire to set right the injustice done to his friend, Martin Geyring. Geyring is a political organizer whom the authorities have jailed on trumped-up charges. August Esch, a bookkeeper by profession, believes that he has uncovered glaring errors in the credit and debit columns of the cosmos. This accountant-saviour takes upon himself the mission of seeing to it that the Geyrings will be set free and that the Ilonas will be preserved from the imminence of death at the hands of knife-throwing men.

When Teltscher – the juggler – and Gernerth – the manager of the music hall – decide to get into a new line of the entertainment business, they offer Esch the opportunity to participate. Esch seizes on this chance as a way of redeeming Ilona and, as long as it is for a good cause, earning a few marks. In a mood of ascetic self-sacrifice he quits his job, renounces his romantic aspirations toward both Erna and Ilona, and joins in the new business venture. The idea of throwing in with Teltscher and Gernerth overtakes Esch as a sudden illumination one evening as he readies himself for bed:

> Und ohne Ordnung in den Büchern gab es auch keine Ordnung in der Welt, und solange keine Ordnung war, würde Ilona weiter den Messern ausgeliefert sein, würde... Martin... ewig im Kerker schmachten. Er dachte scharf nach, und wie er jetzt die Unterhose fallen ließ, ergab es sich zwanglos: die andern hatten ihr Geld dem Ringkampfunternehmen zur Verfügung gestellt, also mußte er, der kein Geld besaß, nun eben doch mit seiner eigenen Person zahlen .... (1: 243)

Naturally Esch's profound insight is about as momentous as the falling of his undershorts. The impecunious hero will offer his services to Teltscher and Gererth by rounding up women who are so down and out that they are willing to scuffle about in a public rink for the prurient entertainment of idle men. Esch has conveniently forgotten that his »renunciation« of Erna and Ilona was not of his own choosing. Erna has designs on Lohberg, the marriageable owner of a prosperous tobacco shop, and Ilona is having a shabby affair with Balthasar Korn. Because Esch is not one to let mere facts dampen his messianic enthusiasms, and because business is business, he invests his energies in the new undertaking with great fervor. »Besser Ringkämpfe als Messerwerfen,« says Esch philosophically (1: 264).

Parallel to the vulgar sexuality of his wrestling show, there develops for Esch a new romance. He spends an increasing amount of time with the widowed proprietress of a small cafe in Cologne. She is known to the regulars there as »Mutter Hentjen.« Esch hopes that an erotic union with Mutter Hentjen will be his redemption, an abrogation of time (1: 286f). It is significant that in Esch's fogged mind an overlap occurs between the image of Mutter Hentjen's dead husband – she keeps his photograph in the café – and that of Eduard von Bertrand, the shipping magnate whom Esch holds responsible for Martin Geyring's imprisonment. It is also important that Esch alternately loves and hates this Bertrand: hates him for his passive role in the world's injustices and because he is a homosexual (i.e. not procreative), but also loves him because he is »etwas Besseres,« a grand patriarch of the sterile capitalist society in which Esch lives. Appropriately, Bertrand is the president of the company for which Esch worked. The overlap between Bertrand and Father Hentjen sets into motion the oedipal scenario that Esch plays out in his dreamlike confrontation with Bertrand. Esch wants to overcome »the father« – Hentjen/Bertrand – and take »Mutter« Hentjen as his wife:

> Denn nun war kein Zweifel mehr, daß er, der Lebende, von dem die Frauen das Kind empfangen durften, daß er sich hingebend an Mutter Hentjen und an ihren Tod, daß er durch diese außergewöhnliche Maßnahme nicht nur die Erlösung Ilonas vollendet, nicht nur auf ewig sie den Messern entrückt, nicht nur ihre Schönheit ihr wiedergewinnt und alles Sterben rückgängig macht, rückgängig bis zu neuer Jungfrauschaft, sondern daß er notwendig damit auch Mutter Hentjen vom Tode errettet, lebend wieder ihr Schoß, jenen zu gebären, der die Zeit aufrichten wird. (1: 354)

Esch wishes to accede to the role of the Father in order to become the progenitor of the coming saviour. But before he can take the old queen – Mutter Hentjen's »crown« is the stiff, blond hair-do that she constantly fumbles with (1: 357) – her husband the king must first be toppled. After his dream-talk with Bertrand, Esch returns to Mutter Hentjen, where he casts a challenging glance at the dead Hentjen's photograph (1: 357) and proceeds to write out a statement to the police charging Bertrand with illegal homosexual activities. This accusation brings about the »second death of Herr Hentjen« (1: 337) when it produces Bertrand's suicide. The news of his death coincides with the removal of old Hentjen's photograph from the wall of the café as Mutter Hentjen becomes Esch's fiancée. (1: 362f).

That the new king will be »August« Esch – his name means *emperor* in Latin and *clown* in German – is not so much mythopoeic profundity as it is mytho-parodic allegorizing. Its irony is similar to that of *Der Zauberberg*, which revives the German Bildungsroman in the intentionally dubious setting of a tuberculosis clinic for the moribund well-to-do; it is an irony that is also similar to Joyce's when he reduces the magnificent Odysseus to the stature of the ludicrous Leopold Bloom. In all three cases the use of previous literary models is first and foremost a framing device that provides formal organization on the level of structure and ironic commentary on the level of content. This literary allegorizing points up these artists' sense of themselves adrift in a cultural »Spätzeit« with no mythic orientation of its own.

Broch had originally intended to frame the trilogy's final instalment, *1918 Huguenau oder die Sachlichkeit*, as an Odysseus parody.[30] But the appearance of Joyce's *Ulysses* during the writing of the *Huguenau* made this idea seem unwise (13/1: 99). Nevertheless, mythological schemata underlie and organize the third novel's avant-garde surface style. Writing perhaps under the influence of John Dos Passos, Broch structured *Huguenau* as a fragmented series of loosely connected narratives about lonely people – including the narrator himself – caught up in the final dissolution of their society. Even the war is not a cause but an effect of this process of disintegration that has made a shambles of their lives and left them unprotected against the terror of death-bringing time.

---

[30] Cf. Paul Michael Lützeler, »Lukács *Theorie des Romans* und Brochs *Schlafwandler*,« in *Hermann Broch und seine Zeit*, Akten des Internationalen Broch-Symposiums Nice, 1979, hrsg. v. Richard Thieberger, Jahrbuch für Internationale Germanistik, Reihe A, Bd. 6 (Bern, Frankfurt am Main, Las Vegas: Peter Lang, 1980), pp. 54f. In this article, Lützeler suggests that Broch's Sleepwalker-trilogy allegorizes Georg Lukács' theory of the novel. He also shows that Joachim Pasenow is a parody of Faust, that Esch is a Quixote-figure, and that Wilhelm Huguenau is parody of Wilhelm Meister.

Broch's Odysseus is the devious Wilhelm Huguenau, an absolutely amoral representative of goal-oriented *Sachlichkeit*. After he has abandoned his post on the battlefront, Huguenau comes slouching toward a village near Trier, where the aged Joachim von Pasenow has been reactivated by the military as the town's commandant. The childless August Esch runs the local newspaper with his wife, Gertrud, formerly known as Mutter Hentjen. The *Esch*-novel ended on a note of foreboding. The new king discovered that his frigid mate was barren: »Es schauderte ihn, und unentrinnbar wußte er, daß ihr Schoß getötet war, oder schlimmer noch, eine Mißgeburt zu gewärtigen hatte« (1: 378). Yet because Esch did at last manage to seduce Erna Korn, it may be that he is not childless after all. She became pregnant and it seems unlikely to Esch that her fiancé, whom he usually refers to as a »keuscher Josef,« can be the father.

The names of these characters reveal Broch's technique of eclectic mythologizing. »Korn« is the traditional emblem of fertility associated with Ceres or Demeter, the goddess of bounty and marriage. »Erna« suggests *die Ernte*, the harvest of planted seed. That this child-bearer is married to a »keuscher Josef« makes Broch's intention obvious. Esch fears that her child is his because he knows it was conceived in an illicit and lascivious moment, »in dem drohend der Mord rasselte« (1: 376) and therefore does not promise the redemption for which he had hoped. The portent of an unholy son and the intimation of murder find fulfillment in the coming of Huguenau.

Wilhelm Huguenau is not the son of Erna Lohberg, but he assumes a role that nevertheless makes him the answer to Esch's dark forebodings. When he arrives in the town on the Mosel, Huguenau's business-like mind sizes up the local power structure to determine the most efficient course of action. Posing as the representative of a »patriotic« but unnamed business interest, he weasels his way into the good graces of local dignitaries. From them he raises funds necessary to buy out Esch's newspaper. He and Esch strike a bargain whereby Huguenau, in addition to instalment payments, actually moves into the Esch household. As time passes he behaves increasingly as a son in his family's midst. The orphan child Marguerite is a reflection of Huguenau in this respect. She too has been adopted by the Esches, is also a French-speaker, and, most importantly, is also an ethical *tabula rasa*. Like Huguenau, she is interested only in money; both of them are cold, unemotional, attracted instinctively only to Esch's printing press. Marguerite and Huguenau sense their kinship with the machine's insensate functioning, for they live in precisely the same mechanical way (1: 489–93).

Huguenau rises rapidly to a place of respect in the life of the community. It is he, for instance, who is the master of ceremonies at a victory celebration for the battle of Tannenberg. The novel's entire cast of characters assembles for this exercise in quasi-religious nihilism, and Huguenau, the arch-nihilist, presides over festivities that the clear-minded physician Dr. Kuhlenbeck refers to as an »etwas hysterische Kirchweih« (1: 572). Broch has cast the public dance as a parody of religious observance. Its high priest of nihilism, Huguenau, conducts services in honor of his deity for the townspeople and for the walking wounded from the military hospital. Public drunkenness, facetious but meaningful cries of »es lebe der Krieg,« and ostensibly tame social dancing are the thinly veiled correlatives for primitive rites of destruction and regeneration. If Broch were to develop his protagonist Huguenau according to the models of Pasenow and Esch, this scene of reverie would no doubt provide him with a suitable frame for Huguenau's experience of eros and death. But Huguenau will have no such epiphany because his pragmatic mind is closed to the possibility of spiritual illumination. Experience that does not involve calculable, material gain is categorically beyond Huguenau's grasp. Nevertheless, from his point of vantage outside of the dance, the narrator interrupts with a digression that reintroduces his temporality-theme as Huguenau and a woman whirl around the dance floor together:

Es ist der Tänzer dieser Welt entrückt. Eingeschmiegt in die Musik, hat er sein freies Handeln aufgegeben und handelt dennoch in höherer und luziderer Freiheit. In der Strenge des Rhythmus, der ihn führt, ist er geborgen und eine große Gelöstheit kommt über ihn aus der Geborgenheit. So bringt die Musik Einheit und Ordnung in das Verworrene und in die Wirrsäligkeit des Lebens. Die Zeit aufhebend, hebt sie den Tod auf und läßt ihn trotzdem in jedem Takte neu erstehen . . . . (1: 567f)

Huguenau sieht nicht seine Partnerin, die den Kopf empfangend zurückgeworfen, sich seiner starken, dennoch kaum sichtbaren Leitung hingegeben hat, er merkt nicht, daß die Musik eine zartere und straffere Kunst des Geschlechts in seiner Dame auslöst, eine bacchantische Weibheit, wie sie dem Gatten der Dame, wie sie ihrem Liebhaber, wie sie ihr selber ewig unbekannt bleiben wird, er sieht auch nicht das ekstatische Lächeln, mit dem die andere Dame zahnfleischentblößend an ihrem Herrn hängt, er sieht bloß diesen, sieht bloß diesen feindlichen Tänzer, der, ein hagerer Weinagent in Frack mit schwarzer Krawatte und Eisernem Kreuz, ihn selber, der bloß den blauen Anzug zur Verfügung hat, an Eleganz und heldischer Auszeichnung überstrahlt. So könnte auch der hagere Esch hier tanzen, und darum, die Frau ihm zu rauben, heftet Huguenau nun den Blick in die Augen der vorübergleitenden Tänzerin, und er tut es so lange, bis sie den Blick erwidert, sich ihm mit den Blicken schenkt, so das er, Wilhelm Huguenau, nun beide Frauen besitzt, sie besitzt, ohne sie zu begehren, denn es geht ihm nicht um die Gunst der Frauen, mag er jetzt auch um sie werben, – es geht ihm nicht um Liebeslust, vielmehr verdichtet sich ihm dieses Fest und dieser geräumige Saal immer enger um die weißgedeckte Tafel dort, und seine Gedanken richten sich immer unbedingter auf den Major, der weißbärtig und schön hinter den Blumen sitzt und ihm zusieht, ihm, Wilhelm Huguenau in der Mitte des Saales: er ist der Krieger, der vor seinem Häuptling tanzt. (1:569)

This portrayal of the dance scene is reminiscent of Edvard Munch's erotically charged dances of death.[31] Munch's nightmarish allegories share with this victory celebration the feel of a subdued yet ghastly carnival of decay and powerlessness. It is the music of erotic desire and not individual will that drives us; the cycle of procreation and death is master over the helpless individual. Like Broch's characters, Munch's figures seem to be sleepwalking in a dream-life, unaware of the macabre drama that they are compelled to enact.

The grinning, dancing Huguenau is supremely unaware of the omnipresence of death and decay. Its fullest expression is the war itself, which Huguenau's Baroque death dance is celebrating. But life in a dream is not less exacting than life in a reality, for the apocalypse will soon engulf and annihilate what seems to the dreaming sleepwalkers to be a secure little world. Implicit in the death-dance of Tannenberg is a barely restrained frenzy that will momentarily irrupt from below, flooding the little town's daily life with an ungovernable tide of dionysian pandemonium. Broch's scaled-down representation for World War One as the outburst of an entire culture's bacchanalian drive to self-negation is the trouble that begins in the town's nearby prison. In it are interned the repressed passions and violence that threaten to overwhelm the village.

As they walk in the countryside, Esch and Pasenow suddenly become aware of a chanting cry from within the prison complex: »Hunger, Hunger, Hunger.« The child Marguerite laughs jubilantly and begins to chant along with the rebelling prisoners. This »Hunger« that they are experiencing presages the outbreak of demonic forces from within a weakened containment. Pasenow quells the potential uprising, but meanwhile Huguenau is complaining to his »Mutter« Esch about his own »Hunger,« encouraging her to make a dinner for him. Huguenau originally began to take the role of son to the Esches when he took a son's place at their dinner table (1: 499–502). By the time of the prison revolt he has come to perceive them as his »Mutter« and »Vater« (1: 610–12). Half-jokingly, half-seriously he even suggests that they adopt him:

---

[31] Cf. the so-called »Dance of Life,« (1899–1900) and the »Death and the Maiden« (1893).

54

»Mir schmeckt es bei Ihnen, Mutter Esch. . . . möchten Sie mich vielleicht adoptieren?« Er hätte gerne hinzugefügt, daß Esch dann den Sohn hätte, von dem er immer faselte und der das Haus bauen soll, – aber aus irgendeinem, ihm selbst unverständlichen Grunde war er tief indigniert und die ganze Sache kam ihm nicht mehr scherzhaft vor. (1: 628f)

Broch has once again set the stage for an oedipal drama. Huguenau is the ironic fulfillment of Esch's wish for a redeemer-son. But this redeemer is not a Christ; he is instead a Judas whose kiss will set in motion the impersonal wheels of history.

On November 3rd of 1918, Major von Pasenow dispatches soldiers to break up a demonstration of workers; the red glow on the horizon tells the townspeople that Trier is burning; the sound of rifleshots is heard near the prison. These are the signs that the fury of the apocalypse is about to break loose. As Huguenau the vigilante stands guard over the village with his rifle and bayonet poised emblematically between his legs, a series of thundering detonations from a munitions dump sounds the beginning of violence and general chaos. A crowd of people from the barracks rush down to the prison and break it open, thus releasing the pent up forces of madness and destruction that had always been latent in the sleepy hamlet. Broch epitomizes the event in the image of a prison guard being held down by two women while a man in hobnail boots uses a crowbar to break his bones. The apocalypse, also a favorite Baroque topos, is in Broch's chiliastic vision the historical catastrophe of World War One.

Meanwhile, Mutter Esch is worried about her husband. Huguenau, who by this time is by her side, takes advantage of the mass hysteria to make sexual advances to his proxy mother. She submits to his perfunctory rape and begs him to save Esch. Huguenau leaves her to go in search of Esch, but when he finds his »father« he attacks him from behind, running him through with the bayonet on his rifle. The combination of this rape and murder is the allegorical representation of that moment in history – or, more precisely, in Broch's *theory* of history's cyclical progress – in which the old order is razed. It is an act of nihilistic violence that simultaneously implants the seeds of the new. Huguenau, the new »father« is not a mover of history. He is only the tool of historical process.

The chaos and despair of the novel's conclusion is, at least to Broch's way of thinking, not final. It was his conviction that the present age of nihilism will eventually pass and that the course of history will at last take an upswing of its own accord. The Pauline quotation that closes the novel – »Tu dir kein Leid! denn wir sind alle noch hier« (1: 716; Acts 16: 28) – is intended to be a ray of sunlight in his otherwise gloomy depiction of the historical situation. The Huguenaus will not inherit the earth; their generation will in turn give way to ethical renewal. In a letter of 17 July 1933, Broch gives to Stefan Zweig a concise picture of the conviction that informs his literary and philosophical writings:

> Alles in allem muß man sich dabei klar sein, daß wahrscheinlich nichts fruchten wird: ich sage dies nicht aus prinzipiellem Pessimismus, sondern aus der Überzeugung – einer Überzeugung, die ich ja schon oft zu begründen versucht habe – , daß die ganze Bewegung, die wir so schmerzlich mitmachen, eine notwendige Entwicklungsphase des gesamten abendländischen Geistes darstellt, in ihrer autonomen Logik begründet und daher unaufhaltsam ist, genau so unaufhaltsam wie seine schließliche Rückkehr zum Platonischen, was aber an die 100 Jahre oder darüber währen wird. So lange sollte man leben können. (13/1: 241)

Viewing history from Austria between the wars, writing in the tradition of »Geschichtspessimismus« – also represented by Nietzsche, Spengler, Theodor Lessing and many of Broch's contemporaries[32] – and motivated by a chiliastic optimism for the regeneration of an ethically sound world, Broch experienced his era as a low point in the process of historical transformation.

This loss of faith in the world as it is, perceived as a loss of continuity between man and metaphysical absolutes, has exposed the individual to the laming fear of time because time brings change and death. This preoccupation emerges in modernist literature as allegory. Time is the theme of Broch's *Schlafwandler*, and allegory is the form of its presentation. *History* as the movement of time through culture becomes the foundation of an allegory that attempts to reconcile the ephemerality of human life with the ancient desire to overcome death.

---

[32] Christoph Eykman, *Geschichtspessimismus in der deutschen Literatur des 20. Jahrhunderts* (Bern: Francke, 1970). Although Eykman does not include him in this study, Broch and his work fit well into the pattern that he discerns.

CHAPTER III

THE CLOUD OF POLONIUS:
Rewriting Reality in Robert Musil's *Mann ohne Eigenschaften*

> Hamlet: Do you see yonder cloud that's almost in the shape of a camel?
> Polonius: By th' mass and 'tis, like a camel indeed.
> Hamlet: Methinks it is like a weasel.
> Polonius: It is back'd like a weasel.
> Hamlet: Or like a whale.
> Polonius: Very like a whale.
>
> *Hamlet* III.ii

In a note to himself concerning his leviathan novel fragment, *Der Mann ohne Eigenschaften*, Robert Musil wrote, »*Ein Hauptthema* fürs Ganze ist also: Auseinandersetzung des Möglichkeitsmenschen mit der Wirklichkeit« (5: 1881).[1] The »possibilitarian« is Ulrich, the novel's protagonist; and the »reality« he confronts is Musil's ironic portrait of Austro-Hungarian culture as it stood in complacent self-absorption on the brink of World War I. Musil's commentators have recognized the thematic importance of »Wirklichkeit« as a problem in *Der Mann ohne Eigenschaften*, and the world of illusion that characterizes the era portrayed in the novel has been much remarked.[2] Musil presents »Kakania«

---

[1] Citations from Musil's writings are taken from Robert Musil, *Gesammelte Werke in neun Bänden*, hrsg. von Adolf Frisé (Reinbek bei Hamburg: Rowohlt, 1978). Each citation is followed by the volume: page number. Where a »T« precedes the volume number, the reference is to Musil's *Tagebücher*, hrsg. von Adolf Frisé (Reinbek bei Hamburg: Rowohlt, 1976); where a »B« precedes the volume number the citation refers to Musil's *Briefe, 1901–1942*, hrsg. von Adolf Frisé (Reinbek: Rowohlt, 1981). In two instances, on page 72 and page 82, *Der Mann ohne Eigenschaften* is cited according to Frisé's earlier edition of the *Gesammelte Werke in Einzelausgaben*, vol. I (Hamburg: Rowohlt, 1952). This edition is marked by an asterisk following the page number.

[2] The premier expression of illusion and Austria's »merry apocalypse« is Hermann Broch's essay »Hofmannsthal und seine Zeit« (in H.B., *Kommentierte Werkausgabe*, hrsg. von Paul Michael Lützeler, IX/1 (Frankfurt a.M.: Suhrkamp, 1976), 111–284, but it does not deal specifically with Musil. Practically all of the critical literature on the *MoE* renders some account of this theme of confrontation between illusion and reality, and many develop it at length.

- his scatological pun on the official Austro-Hungarian abbreviation *k.k.*--as a culture so entrapped in the fictions and images of itself that it has inherited and invented, so enmeshed in a web of illusion, that it has lost touch with authentic human values. The feeble coherencies that pass for reality there are fictions that are powerless against the chaos that threatens to engulf Kakania as it blunders on toward massive destruction.

Musil's inquiry into the nature of reality does not exhaust itself in a critique of the specific Austro-Hungarian situation. He is more concerned with the underlying mechanisms that produce it and with the possibility of accounting for them in narrative prose. The novel is the medium of Robert Musil's confrontation with his world. This chapter elucidates the nature of this confrontation by pursuing the protagonist

---

Especially noteworthy is Peter Berger, »The Problem of Multiple Realities: Alfred Schutz and Robert Musil,« in *Phenomenology and Social Reality. Essays in Memory of Alfred Schutz*, ed. Maurice Natanson (The Hague: Martinus Nijhoff, 1970), 213-233. Berger develops a reading of the *MoE* with one foot in Schutzian phenomenological sociology and the other in his own theories of reality's social construction. His study is brief but clear and incisive. Philip Payne focuses on the role of the narrative's shifting perspective in the representation of reality: P.P., »Robert Musil's Reality - A Study of Some Aspects of Reality in *Der Mann ohne Eigenschaften*,« *Forum for Modern Language Studies*, 12 (1976), 314-28. In two articles David Heald discusses the problem of illusion at the instance of Musil's use of theater imagery: D.H., »All the World's a Stage - A Central Motif in Musil's *Der Mann ohne Eigenschaften*,« *German Life and Letters*, 27 (1973-74), 51-59; D.H., »Musil's Conception of ›Schauspielerei‹ as Novelist and Critic,« *Maske und Kothurn*, 23 (1977), 244-55. Ulf Schramm, *Fiktion und Reflexion. Überlegungen zu Musil and Beckett* (Frankfurt am Main: Suhrkamp, 1967) offers one of the more intelligent discussions of this problem in its relation to language as medium, pp. 20-60. Dietrich Hochstätter offers a detailed, intelligent commentary on the stylistic relation between the narrator's reality and the illusions of his figures in *Sprache des Möglichen. Stilistischer Perspektivismus in Robert Musil's »MoE«*, Gegenwart der Dichtung, 6 (Frankfurt a.M.: Athenäum, 1972), esp. pp. 9-113. Joseph Peter Stern offers a few useful remarks that situate the *MoE* between Vienna's historical milieu and Musil's abundant imagination: J.P.S., »Die Wiener Wirklichkeit im Roman *DMoE*,« *Literatur und Kritik*, 15 (1980), 525-31. Cf. also Helmut Arntzen, *Satirischer Stil. Zur Satire in Robert Musils MoE*, 2. erg. Aufl., Abhandlungen zur Kunst-, Musik-, und Literaturwissenschaft, 9 (Bonn: Bouvier, 1970); Frank Trommler, *Roman und Wirklichkeit. Eine Ortsbestimmung am Beispiel von Musil, Broch, Roth, Doderer, und Gütersloh*, Sprache und Literatur, 30 (Stuttgart, Berlin: Kohlhammer, 1966), esp. pp. 50-100; Frank Kermode, »Musil,« in his *Modern Essays* (Collins: Fontana Books, 1971), 182-204; Jochen Schmidt, *Ohne Eigenschaften. Eine Erläuterung zu Musils Grundbegriff*, Untersuchungen zur deutschen Literatur, 13 (Tübingen: Niemeyer, 1975), esp. 70f.

of his *Mann ohne Eigenschaften* throughout his own fictional »Auseinandersetzung mit der Wirklichkeit.«

In a letter of January 26, 1931, Musil posits a certain identity of purpose between himself and Ulrich that can serve as a hermeneutical point of entry into this interaction of fiction and reality. He writes, »Das Problem: wie komme ich zum Erzählen, ist sowohl mein stilistisches wie das Lebensproblem der Hauptfigur, und die Lösung ist natürlich nicht einfach« (B,I: 498). The work of a French critic, Marthe Robert, on Cervantes' *Don Quixote* and Kafka's *Schloß* helps to refine Musil's proposition into a form profitable for interpretive purposes. She suggests that »when imitation imposes a way of writing on the novelist and a way of living on the hero, it creates a functional identity between these two similar and disparate figures that tells us more than any external circumstance about the true extent of their relations.«[3] Though she did not have *Der Mann ohne Eigenschaften* in mind, her »functional identity« strikes close to Musil's own formulation of his relation to Ulrich. The special insight of Robert's comment is the idea that this identity is the problem of *imitation*. She has struck close to the heart of Musil's novel, for both Musil and his protagonist are plagued by the problem of imitation.

For Ulrich this problem is the Kakanian habit of living in imitation of models preordained by law, culture, peer pressure and tradition. In the same letter Musil briefly elucidates the situation:

> In unserer gegenwärtigen Welt geschieht größtenteils nur Schematisches (Seinesgleichen). d. i. Typisches, Begriffliches, und noch dazu ausgesogenes. U. sucht darum den Ausweg, eine wirkliche Determination seines Handelns .... (B,I: 498)

Parallel to Ulrich's problem of schematic patterns of life and experience is Musil's own »stilistisches« problem of writing a novel. It is the problem of mimesis, which is traditionally conceived of as the »imitation of nature,« but which Musil conceives of as the imitation of narrative models that convention has established in the minds of readers and writers. Both Musil and Ulrich would like to free themselves of the conventions that have been imposed on them and break through into originality and creativity.

The centrality of imitation in Ulrich's world and of mimesis in Musil's is a key to *Der Mann ohne Eigenschaften*. It is the point at which Musil's interests most significantly coincide with those of Ulrich, and it

---

[3] Marthe Robert, *The Old and the New. From Don Quixote to Franz Kafka*, trans. Carol Cosman (Berkeley, Los Angeles, London: University of California Press, 1977), p. 13.

is the point at which the narrative frees itself of the simple topicality of Austro-Hungarian thematics to engage the problematic relation between narrative fiction and objective reality.

I

Before turning to Ulrich's confrontation with this world's unacceptable reality, it will be necessary to establish Musil's attitude toward writing. The nineteenth century's ›realistic‹ novel had been concerned with creating and maintaining the uninterrupted semblance of a familiar reality, one that its reader could accept as an accurate and believable model of the real world. Its ideal of mimesis was one of holding a mirror up to nature, enabling us to see things as they »really« are. This undertaking is predicated on the assumption that some kind of objectivity is possible, that exterior reality and human nature are fixed and stable enough to be rendered in the fixed and stable framework of linguistic and literary conventions of representation.

Musil rejects this vision of literature and reality and its postulate that fiction is to be the isomorphic duplication of a possible reality. The two novellas joined under the title *Vereinigungen* are Musil's most radical departure from the traditional imitation-of-nature imperative in prose. One novella is the tale of a strange and improbable adultery, and the other revolves around a bizarre sodomy. Both are couched in difficult and highly artificial figurative language. Their themes break long-standing taboos, offending both bourgeois moral sensibilities and firmly entrenched habits of reading. The dense figurality of the novellas' style renders what little »realistic« content there is opaque and foreign.

In a response to his detractors, who deplored the lack of »realism« in the *Vereinigungen*, Musil wrote: »Es ist . . . die Realität, die man schildert, stets nur ein Vorwand,« by which he means that the apparent object of representation in the real world is only a pretext that grants access to the non-empirical world of »Gefühlserkenntnisse und Denkerschütterungen, . . . die allgemein und in Begriffen nicht, sondern nur im Flimmern des Einzelfalls . . . zu erfassen sind« (8: 997). Musil's writing is directed not toward transcribing this or that historical, social, or any other average reality, but instead toward inventing a more original world, a self-consciously ideational world, in which objects and events are not designed to duplicate those of the external world but which are instead intended to evoke a connotative »Flimmern« of cognition from the inner, human reality of emotion and consciousness.

Musil called this turn in his fiction an »Absage an den Realismus zugunsten einer idealistischen Kunst« (T,I: 929). However, by the time he wrote *Der Mann ohne Eigenschaften* he had relaxed his stand against conventional realism. The action of the narrative takes place in a world much more accessible than that of the *Vereinigungen*, a world of recognizable time and place, peopled by recognizable types from historically verifiable social milieux, who behave in a more or less psychologically plausible way. Still, the retreat from abstraction is more apparent than actual. The style of *Der Mann ohne Eigenschaften* reflects what Musil once referred to as a »realer Idealismus« (8: 1183), an expression suggesting that behind the façade of the apparently *real* world in a novel is an *idealistic* (or better: ideational) realm that principally addresses the inner reality of the human mind and feelings.

Musil's division between the real and the ideational is explicit in the famous fourth chapter of Book I in which the narrator presents the idea of a »Möglichkeitsmensch.« The ›possibilitarian‹ is someone who contests the privileged authority of the ›real‹ on the grounds that what we ordinarily accept as solid and substantial reality – bridges and buildings, political and cultural institutions, language and literature – consists of only isolated, and more or less random concretions of ideas: »Jede Ordnung ist irgendwie absurd und wachsfigurenhaft, wenn man sie zu ernst nimmt, jedes Ding ist ein erstarrter Einzelfall seiner Möglichkeiten. Aber das sind nicht Zweifel, sondern es ist eine bewegte, elastische Unbestimmtheit, die sich zu allem fähig fühlt« (5: 1509). ›Ideational reality,‹ a phrase that means as much as ›fiction,‹ is a vast quarry that precedes everyday reality, from which its realized forms are cut and chiseled.

Given that reality is a patchwork composition of various inventions of the mind, its relation to narrative fiction becomes evident. The ultimate source of each is imagination. From this common point of origin fiction finds its way into print, and reality makes its way onto the stage of human doings. Since the source of both is the same, Musil is not inclined to prize ›reality‹ above art: »Welche Verkehrtheit zu behaupten, das Leben sei wichtiger als die Kunst! Das Leben ist gut, soweit es der Kunst standhält: was nicht kunstfähig am Leben ist, ist Kitsch!« (7: 502). This confluence of art and life, of fiction and reality, establishes the point of »functional identity« between Ulrich and his creator.

Ulrich inhabits a world that has become Kitsch. Its reality proceeds according to paradigms transmitted under the authority of a tradition that no longer belongs to the present. The reiteration of these time-worn schemata in the lives of people, like the reiteration of standardized plots in fiction, reduces what ought to have been creative and original to something trite and lifeless. Ulrich complains to his friend Clarisse about this state of affairs, as his narrator reports:

> Das jetzt geltende System sei das der Wirklichkeit und gleiche einem schlechten Theaterstück. Man sage nicht umsonst Welttheater, denn es erstehen immer die gleichen Rollen, Verwicklungen und Fabeln im Leben. Man liebt, weil und wie es die Liebe gibt; man ist stolz wie die Indianer, die Spanier, die Jungfrauen oder der Löwe ... Vollends die erfolgreichen politischen Gestalter der Wirklichkeit haben, von den ganz großen Ausnahmen abgesehen, viel mit den Schreibern von Kassenstücken gemein; die lebhaften Vorgänge, die sie erzeugen, langweilen durch ihren Mangel an Geist und Neuheit, bringen uns aber gerade dadurch in jenen widerstandslosen schläfrigen Zustand, worin wir uns jede Veränderung gefallen lassen. So betrachtet, entsteht die Geschichte aus der ideellen Routine und aus dem ideell Gleichgültigen, und die Wirklichkeit entsteht vornehmlich daraus, daß nichts für die Ideen geschieht. (2: 364)

Reality becomes a parody of the past generated by the subliminal expectations that are always already present in the minds of life's actors. These expectations amount to stage directions, texts composed of convention and presupposition, in accordance with which people live, act, and even feel. Ulrich's »Auseinandersetzung mit der Wirklichkeit« focuses on this problem of imitation, the problem of a life that does not happen spontaneously and authentically but proceeds instead according to a principle of mimicking pre-established models. Musil dubs this principle »Seinesgleichen geschieht« and makes it the title of Book I, Part II.

The challenge that paradigms of lived experience present for Ulrich corresponds neatly with the challenge of writing an original novel for Musil. The novelist of modernism in general is likewise faced with a network of presuppositions and conventions in the minds of readers (and in his own mind) about what a novel is and how it ought to be written. D. H. Lawrence states the problem concisely: »All the rules of construction hold good only for novels which are copies of other novels.«[4] In the working-notes for his *Der Mann ohne Eigenschaften*, Musil poses the problem for himself as follows:

> Die Leser sind gewöhnt zu verlangen, daß man ihnen vom Leben erzähle und nicht vom Widerschein des Lebens in den Köpfen der Literatur u. der Menschen. Das ist aber mit Sicherheit nur soweit berechtigt, als dieser Widerschein bloß ein ver- armter, konventionell gewordener Abzug des Lebens ist. Ich suche Ihnen Original zu bieten, Sie müssen also auch ihr Vorurteil suspendieren. (5: 1937)

---

[4] Cited in Harry Levin, *The Gates of Horn. A Study of Five French Realists* (New York: Oxford University Press, 1963), p. 25.

The idea that fiction should be a vision of life itself, and not a vision of is mediation, is a prejudice to be overcome. Mediated vision in Musil's view is the source of originality as long as it holds itself apart from reductive and conventional patterns of representation. Musil's aim is not capture so-called objective reality. He wishes instead to articulate life as it appears to individual imagination. Mimesis in this sense implies a redefinition of the then, and possibly still, prevailing notion of literary imitation-of-nature. Even if the exterior world does remain fixed, our individual and collective imagination does not. It is this orientation of imagination that is the object of literary mimesis. Musil tirelessly reiterates his view that this non-objective realm is by nature a »Welt ohne feste Form,« a ceaselessly shifting fluid inaccessible to conceptual representation. »Die Wahrheit,« as Ulrich's narrator points out, »ist eben kein Kristall, den man in die Tasche stecken kann, sondern eine unendliche Flüssigkeit, in die man hineinfällt« (2: 533–34). In order to render this realm with accuracy, the writer must aspire to forms of expression that are both unique and undogmatic. Any fixed, conceptual or conventional formulation misrepresents »die Welt ohne feste Form« by falsifying its amorphous character.

The contrast Musil posits between »Leben« and the »Widerschein des Lebens« corresponds to the tension between the ›real‹ and the ›ideal‹ in his formulation of a »realer Idealismus.« He has asserted that any narrated world is actually a »Widerschein«: an ideational construct in the author's mind. Yet there is also something realistic about Musil's depiction of the world. It is Vienna in 1913, a real place full of real people on the threshold of a real war. It is also evident that Musil is at pains to minimize the authority of this apparent realism by exposing the artifice of literary construction that has gone into the making of this verbal citadel. The novel's *artificiality* is the twin of its »Idealismus.«

The narrator frankly avows his lack of commitment to verisimilar representation. In an apstrophe to the reader he asserts that »weder an dieser Stelle noch in der Folge der glaubwürdige Versuch unternommen werden wird, ein Historienbild zu malen und mit der Wirklichkeit in Wettbewerb zu treten« (1: 170). He is openly committed to the realm of imagination. The novel's first chapter offers a characteristic example of how Musil undermines the conventions of realism. He carefully sets the scene of action by building the detailed illusion of a Viennese street on a sunny August day in 1913. Next, he posits a hypothetical observer in this setting who recognizes it as Vienna. This observer is the reader's fictional proxy. The reader, like the observer, is a passive audience to the narrator's fictional world; and the reader, like the observer, is naturally inclined to accept as true what is apparent to the ordinary way of

63

looking at things. It is apparent to this hypothetical observer that he is in Vienna in the same way that reading habits make it apparent to the reader that the setting of the story *is* Vienna. But just as soon as the narrator has settled his observer/reader into the seemingly familiar milieu of a summer's day in 1913 Vienna, he gently slaps us in the face with a facetious comment that withdraws the relevance of the setting he has just described so carefully: »Die Überschätzung der Frage, wo man sich befinde, stammt aus der Hordenzeit, wo man sich die Futterplätze merken mußte« (1:9). The narrator also finds it odd that when it comes to being in a city, modern man »immer durchaus genau wissen möchte, welche besondere Stadt das sei,« and finally dismisses the whole matter as trivial: »Es lenkt von Wichtigerem ab« (1: 9–10).

Musil is ironically distinguishing between levels of reality. In the average reality of modern life it is just as important to be specific about cities as it was for the »Hordenzeit« to pay attention to the locations of its feeding grounds. When the narrator dismisses these matters as irrelevant he is actually pointing out that the reality of *this* Vienna in which the reader/observer finds himself is of a special order. It does not matter whether this city is corresonds to an actual Vienna because it is primarily present as an imaginary, narrative world. Musil is exposing the literary convention of setting as an arbitrary artifice and warning his reader not to accept the illusion uncritically. »Es lenkt von Wichtigerem ab.«

A striking instance in which the narrator subverts the illusion of reality occurs in the chapter that introduces Moosbrugger, the pathological killer whom all of Vienna is following in the newspapers. The narrator presents Ulrich's first »encounter« with the murderer:

> Ulrich war, als sein Blick auf dieses Gesicht mit den Zeichen der Gotteskindschaft über Handschellen traf, rasch umgekehrt, hatte einem Wachsoldaten des nahegelegenen Landesgerichts einige Zigaretten geschenkt und nach dem Konvoi gefragt, der erst vor kurzem das Tor verlassen haben mußte; so erfuhr er –: doch so muß derartiges sich wohl früher abgespielt haben, da man es oft in dieser Weise berichtet findet, und Ulrich glaubte beinahe selbst daran, aber die zeitgenössische Wahrheit war, daß er alles bloß in der Zeitung gelesen hatte. (1: 69)

This passage is first of all a good-humored parody. It makes Ulrich seem to be the hero of a bestseller, a man of stealth and resource engaged in some exciting and no doubt important undercover operation. But then the narrator takes it all back and conjectures with tongue in cheek that things probably used to happen that way since one reads so many such accounts. His Ulrich is no such dashing adventurer. He reads about Moosbrugger in the papers just as everyone else does.

Not only is Musil teasing the reader's expectation regarding the typical stylization of a hero, he is also flaunting the device of narration itself. By interrupting the passage and changing his story in mid-sentence the narrator reveals the whole of his narrative as artifice and Ulrich as his pawn. He is reminding his reader that there is a rift between the written world and the lived one, and admonishing him to read critically.

The narrator's treatment of the other figures in his tale reflects again his playful attitude toward the conventions of narrative representation. The novel's opening scene depicts a comfortable Viennese couple – also »realistically« portrayed – strolling on the streets in the summer day. Where we would ordinarily expect to find them identified and introduced by our omniscient narrator, we find instead that he is toying with our expectations.

> Angenommen, sie würden Arnheim und Ermelinda Tuzzi heißen, was aber nicht stimmt, denn Frau Tuzzi befand sich in August in Begleitung ihres Gatten in Bad Aussee und Dr. Arnheim noch in Konstantinopel, so steht man vor dem Rätsel, wer sie seien. (1: 10)

This passage is an interesting mixture of Musil's »real« and »ideal«. The strolling couple is not Ermelinda Tuzzi and Arnheim, but, as the phrasing implies, they may as well be. The narrator offers specific, realistic details of Arnheim's and Tuzzi's whereabouts, but once again he undercuts the illusion of realism by means of irony. If the narrator can place Tuzzi in Bad Aussee and Arnheim in Constantinople, he could also have placed them strolling on the streets of Vienna. This narrator wants us to understand the power he wields over the figures in his story. He can give them names or take them away; he can make his figures do things, make them present or absent, and deploy them as he wishes. Or, as is also the case in the opening chapter, he can have trucks run over them.

The novel's figures are not ›taken from life‹ in the sense of the nineteenth century's novel of character. Musil criticizes the view that the invented personae of a fictional world should fully simulate their three-dimensional counterparts: »Jene Dichter, die auf die komplette Lebendigkeit ihrer Gestalten so großen Wert legen, gleichen jenem etwas unverständlichen lieben Gott der Theologen, der den Menschen einen freien Willen verleiht, damit sie ihm den seinen tun« (8: 998). The creative achievement of good narrative is, then, not to be judged in its fidelity to reality, but in its strategic difference from that reality, in its service to undogmatic ideas.

The figures of fiction are not doubles for the figures of life. They are the bearers of abstracted feelings, thoughts, and human values that are

65

suspended between real-seeming illusion and self-conscious fictionality. Musil's reminders that his figures are only fictional constructs imprisoned in an artificial world might at first seem to belabor the obvious. His point is that fictional characters take shape under the governance of narrative convention and authorial imagination. In the course of *Der Mann ohne Eigenschaften* it becomes clear that the figures of life are subordinated to similarly exterior forces that shape character. As the artist's hand delineates a figure in fiction, so also does external circumstance – »der liebe Gott,« as it were – mold and shape human experience and personality in real life. Only the creative mind can, by an act of individual imagination, break free of the repressive order in which it finds itself confined. Ulrich is the personification of this idea. He points the way toward a freer way of thinking when he begins to realize that he is living in an elaborate fiction. Indeed, he is aware that he, like a character in a novel, inhabits a specifically narrative order (2: 650).

Musil's subversion of the reader's sense of realistic illusion is an attempt to establish his narrative not as a transcription of the real world but instead as a »durchstrichene Welt« (5: 1965, 1966), a fictional construct in which the illusion of reality is simultaneously proffered and withdrawn, i.e. an ironic fiction. The principal devices whereby Musil »stikes through« the illusion of reality are a) the foregrounding of the narrator, whose extensive commentary and long passages of indirect dialogue make him an obtrusive presence in the narrative fabric of Ulrich's world;[5] b) the use of the conditional subjunctive, the grammatical mood of unreality;[6] and c) his elaborate similes, which serve to

---

[5] Peter Nusser corroborates this point, finding that the narrator's game of hide-and-seek, his shifting of tenses and perspectives is a device that Musil introduces, »weil er die Sicherheit der Erzählung zerstören will, um den Leser zum experimentierenden Denken, zum Möglichkeitsdenken zu erziehen. Er wechselt den Standort, um zu vermeiden, daß der Leser einen geschilderten Teilausschnitt der Wirklichkeit mit der ganzen Wirklichkeit verwechselt.« P.N., *Musils Romantheorie* (Paris, The Hague: Mouton, 1967), p. 71. Philip Payne writes that the narrator's voice is a device of self-conscious fictionality that »reminds us . . . this is fiction, not life but words,« P.P., »Robert Musil's Reality,« *Forum for Modern Language Studies*, 12 (1976), p. 316. Cf. also Wilhelm Grenzmann, »*DMoE*: Zur Problematik des Romans« in *Robert Musil: Leben, Werk, Wirkung*, hrsg. von Karl Dinklage (Reinbek bei Hamburg: Rowohlt, 1960), pp. 58–61; Ulrich Schelling, »Das Analogische Denken bei Robert Musil,« in *Robert Musil. Studien zu seinem Werk*, hrsg. von Karl Dinklage zusammen mit Elisabeth Albertsen und Karl Corino (Reinbek bei Hamburg: Rowohlt, 1970), p. 178; Claude David, »Form und Gehalt in Robert Musil's *MoE*,« *Euphorion*, 64 (1970), p. 227.

[6] As Albrecht Schöne points out, the *conjunctivus potentialis* underscores the spirit of possiblity and hypothesis in Ulrich's view of reality. But it is probably

foreground the text's ›literariness,‹ i.e. these similes attract attention to themselves, to their artificiality and the act of representation.[7]

The suspension of realistic illusion by balancing it against acts of representation that betray their status as fiction reveals what I would like to call a strategy of dual reference. Its first aspect is that of ordinary referentiality, the way in which one normally expects a novel to reconstitute a familiar reality in a recognizable manner, in this case 1913 Vienna. This ploy is basic to the style of nineteenth-century realism. However, as Robert Alter has persuasively argued, there is a novelistic tradition that runs counter to the nineteenth century's proclivity to illusionism. Whereas the realist novel seeks to conceal its condition of artifice and produce an unbroken illusion of reality, the other mode of representation, that of the »self-conscious novel,« purposely exposes the contrivances that go into the making of fiction. Prominent examples of this tradition, as Alter demonstrates in detail, are *Don Quixote*, *Tom Jones*, and *Tristram Shandy*.[8] It is to this tradition that *Der Mann ohne Eigenschaften* belongs inasmuch as it shares with its precursors the second aspect of reference that extends, complicates, and enriches mimesis. It is the device of self-reference that permits the novel to

---

also that this use of the subjunctive folds back onto the author's view of the novel itself. Narration in the indicative helps to seal the illusion of a fictive reality, lends to it a declarative certainty. Musil's ubiquitous subjunctives, especially when in the mouth of the narrator, undermine the sense of realism that is implicit in the indicative. Schöne seems close to this idea when he writes, »Musil schreibt ein Kapitel seines Romans und denkt dabei, es könnte ebensogut anders sein.« However he stops short of the conclusion that I am proposing in this study, namely that Musil intentionally ironizes the fictional world that he invents. Cf. A.S., »Zum Gebrauch des Konjunktivs bei Robert Musil,« *Euphorion*, 55 (1961), p. 203.

[7] Robert Alter points out in a different context that »an obtrusive simile is one of the most convenient ways for the literary artificer to flaunt his artifice while using it to render his subject.« R.A., *Partial Magic. The Novel as a Self-Conscious Genre* (Berkeley, Los Angeles, London: University of California Press, 1975), p. 132. Musil's narrator implies a similar point when he describes the *Gleichnis* as possessing a »glasige Atmosphäre von Ahnung, Glaube und *Künstlichkeit*« (2: 582). My emphasis.

[8] Alter defines the self-conscious novel as one »that systematically flaunts its own necessary condition of artifice, and that by so doing probes into the problematic relationship between real-seeming artifice and reality .... The self-conscious novelist is acutely aware that he is manipulating schemata, devising ingenious cryptograms, and he constantly invents narrative strategies for sharing this awareness with us, so that he simultaneously, or alternately, creates the illusion of reality and shatters it.« R.A., »Mimesis and the Motive for Fiction,« in *Images and Ideas in American Culture. The Functions of Criticism. Essays in Memory of Philip Rahv*, ed. Arthur Edelstein (Hanover, New Hampshire: Brandeis University Press, 1979), pp. 110–11.

comment on its own condition of artifice and its relation to reality and truth.

This level of self-reference, or metafiction, is joined with Musil's concept of irony, a stylistic device that for him is the »Form des Kampfes« of *Der Mann ohne Eigenschaften* (7: 941). Irony is his principal weapon in the struggle for authenticity and originality. This irony is especially clear in the thematic recurrence of books and writing. They are the controlling metaphor for the »functional identity« of the author and protagonist: Ulrich's attempt to overcome a way of life ordered like a fictional text, and Musil's struggle against the limits of representation toward original creativity. The fixing of reality in print on paper is emblematic for the hypostatization and falsification of authentic reality, the reduction of truth's ephemerality to the immutable granite of the written word. The central irony is of course that Musil's novel is a written artifact. The scheme of self-reference aims at calling the reader's attention to this fact. Musil's radical probing of his own methods is the mark of his artistic integrity.

II

Ulrich is »der Mann ohne Eigenschaften,« but his ambitions were originally otherwise. He wanted to become a man of distinction, which is to say he wanted to appropriate for himself those characteristics – »Eigenschaften« – that would distinguish him in the eyes of his peers. His first attempt to garner a set of admirable characteristics takes place under the influence of Napoleon's image. Ulrich joins the military with the idea of becoming a hard-riding, duel-fighting, womanizing man of adventure. The clichés of his chosen life-style satisfy him for a while, but when he makes a play for the wife of a superior officer and receives a harsh reprimand, Ulrich decides to discard the man-of-adventure role. He makes a fresh bid for distinction in the brave new world of technology, trading in the spurs of the cavalry officer for the engineer's slide-rule, pipe, and sports cap. But Ulrich is once again in for disappointment when his professional colleagues do not live up to the dramatic image he had invented for them. Instead of dynamic creators and bold dreamers, the builders of mighty engines turn out to be business-like models of mechanical efficiency in professional life and dullards in personal life. So Ulrich peels off the set of characteristics that constitute the life-style of the engineer and turns finally to the austere beauties of theoretical mathematics, mother of sciences.

He sees math and science as the heights of modern imagination: »Es geht in der Wissenschaft so stark und unbekümmert und herrlich zu wie in einem Märchen« (1: 41). Ulrich's passion for the theoretical sciences, a visionary realm as unbounded as the fantasy of fairy tales, marks his utopian turn of mind. His feeling that scientific theory and fairy tales share a fundamental trait distinguishes him from the bulk of his factually-minded colleagues, and Ulrich eventually feels the need to separate himself from their limited vision and aspirations and move toward the spiritual territory ahead.

At the age of thirty-two, with various successes behind him but no fixed place in society, Ulrich determines to take a vacation from life, »um eine angemessene Anwendung seiner Fähigkeiten zu suchen« (1: 47). He has found no satisfaction in any of the three attempts to cover himself with the »Eigenschaften« that would identify him in his own and in the world's eyes as a man of distinction. His uneasiness with the role-playing of his professional lives is the beginning of his »Auseinandersetzung mit der Wirklichkeit.« He senses that the »Eigenschaften« that make up a man's character are imposed from the outside and are not integral to authentic selfhood. The individual is born into a monstrous interlocked network of cultural systems – moral, religious, political, literary, and philosophical – that imprint their own laws – »Eigenschaften« – into the malleable stuff of the human self.

Musil illustrates the temporal dimension of this process when Ulrich moves into his Viennese manor. It is a hunting-palace of bygone years that bears the stamp of successive architectural styles from the seventeenth, eighteenth and nineteenth centuries superimposed one on the other. It reads like a palimpsest of the Austrian cultural heritage and represents the burden of the past on Ulrich. The past has shaped the world he inhabits and deposited the layers of cultural alluvia that form the bedrock of his contemporaneous reality. Ulrich's task is in large part to free himself of the oppressive weight of this sedimentation by recognizing that it is in fact an accretion that conceals the true fundament of the intrinsically human. He makes an initial gesture in this direction when he entertains thoughts of setting up house-keeping in the manor with furnishings of his own contrivance, a project he identifies with the »Ausbau seiner Persönlichkeit« (1: 20). But his ideas lack an organizing principle and so, at least for the time being, he admits partial defeat: »um sich von außen, durch die Lebensumstände bilden zu lassen, er überließ an diesem Punkt seiner Überlegungen die Einrichtung seines Hauses dem Genie seiner Lieferanten, in der sicheren Überzeugung, daß sie für Überlieferung, Vorurteile und Beschränktheit schon sorgen würden« (1: 21).

In his vacation from life, Ulrich has not entirely broken with the habits of his past. Bonadea, an idealistic family woman and one of

Ulrich's mistresses, is the object of his continued womanizing. Her double life is typical of Musil's characterization of Kakania as a society that thrives on illusion. Bonadea perceives herself as being »hochanständig« and believes that »great ideas« are her natural element: »Sie war imstande, ›das Wahre, das Gute und das Schöne‹ so oft und natürlich auszusprechen, wie ein anderer Donnerstag sagt« (1: 42). But her major failing is her erotomania, which she has managed to reconcile with her role of an »impeccably virtuous« wife and mother by inventing the story that her husband, whom the narrator characterizes as »flausenlos, gutmütig und lebensfroh« (1: 43) is actually a ruthless beast of a man, and by convincing herself that through some quirk of physiology her body is hypersensual.

Musil constructs this figure according to his »*oft zu gebrauchende Darstellungsart.* Einen Menschen zusammensetzen aber mit aufgedeckten Karten! aus den fixen Ideen und zwangsläufigen paar Ideeverknüpfungen . . .« (5: 1820). The trump card in Bonadea's suit is the centrality of outward appearances that mask an inner void. She is, for instance, careful to dress herself in observance of the standards of breeding and good taste that Kakania deemed fitting for a matron of her prominence and cultivation. Her willing and even enthusiastic submission of herself to changing fashions and to the security that a conventional appearance generates gives the narrator occasion to reflect on the arbitrariness of fashion in particular and on social codes in general. Like Keller's poor tailor and Zuckmayer's unemployed ex-convict, the image that her clothes project fill Musil's Bonadea with meaning: »Dann geschieht nicht weniger, als wenn in einen krausen Linienzug auf einem Stück Papier der Sinn eines großen Worts hineinfährt« (2: 526).

In fashion, in language, and in general, meaning is not immanent to things but is invested in them by tacit collective agreement. Bonadea's little masquerade is a parable of the general problem of how meanings and values are invented to hold an order of things in place:

Mit großer und mannigfaltiger Kunst erzeugen wir eine Verblendung, mit deren Hilfe wir es zuwege bringen, neben den ungeheuerlichsten Dingen zu leben und dabei völlig ruhig zu bleiben, weil wir diese ausgefrorenen Grimassen des Weltalls als einen Tisch oder einen Stuhl, ein Schreien oder einen ausgestreckten Arm, eine Geschwindigkeit oder ein gebratenes Huhn erkennen. . . . Aber wenn man näher hinsieht, ist es doch ein äußerst künstlicher Bewußtseinszustand, der dem Menschen den aufrechten Gang zwischen kreisenden Gestirnen verleiht und ihm erlaubt, inmitten der fast unendlichen Unbekanntheit der Welt würdevoll die Hand zwischen den zweiten und dritten Rockknopf zu stecken. Und um das zuwege zu bringen, gebraucht nicht nur jeder Mensch seine Kunstgriffe, der Idiot ebensogut wie der Weise, sondern diese persönlichen Systeme von Kunstgriffen sind auch noch kunstvoll eingebaut in die moralischen und intellektuellen Gleichgewichtsvorkehrungen der Gesellschaft und Gesamtheit, die im Größeren dem gleichen Zweck dienen. (2: 526, 527)

Ulrich's awareness of this »Verblendung« has gradually been growing, and the end of his trivial romance with Bonadea proves to be the decisive moment in his relation to the tricks and illusions of everyday reality. His dalliance with her, his passive support of her ludicrous self-deceptions, and the whole silly business of furtive encounters with a married woman no longer seem worth the effort. He offends her and lets her storm off in a huff. After she has gone he gazes idly at the elaborate patterns of his pseudo-Baroque chamber and has a brief moment of mystical lucidity. He suddenly realizes that the design of his life is neither Nature nor Necessity but only a clattering assemblage of habit, convention, and unexamined presupposition.

The tiff with Bonadea has precipitated an important moment in Ulrich's mental life: »Im Grunde gehörte gar nicht viel dazu; ein Firnis war abgefallen, eine Suggestion hatte sich gelöst, ein Zug von Gewohnheit, Erwartung und Spannung war abgerissen ...« (1: 128). The three interlinked guarantors of a sturdy, firmly anchored reality - »Gewohnheit, Erwartung und Spannung« - have become thin to the point of transparency for Ulrich. Emotion and thought reveal themselves to be habits of feeling and habits of intellection that impose old patterns on new experience. Ulrich's romance had little or nothing to do with deeply felt emotion: »man liebt weil und wie es die Liebe gibt,« (2: 364), as he later reflects. Romance is a habitual way of relating between the sexes, a ritual whose occurrence generates a set of expectations - »Erwartung« - that can only find fulfillment within the narrow limits of its own self-definition. Habit and expectation disallow the unique and the unprecedented by channeling human experience into categories of the familiar and the routine. They encircle the chaotic disparity of things, drawing them up and binding them together in an elastic tautness, a »Spannung« that seems to grip the world in a secure noose of calculability and regularity. Ulrich has broken the surface tension of daily reality and found that the seeming order of things and the apparent regularity of human experience are the products of fictions invented to conceal the chaos of true reality. Bonadea's delusions about herself are a case in point. She lives by imitating images that have been projected for her by the values of her repressive, disintegrating culture. The imitation of images is Kakania's way of setting together the »Eigenschaften« that are supposed to provide identity and a sense of security. Since the same images recur over and over, reality falls into patterns of redundancy that Musil encodes as »Seinesgleichen geschieht.«

A simple example of the Kakanian mania for imitating images can be drawn from Ulrich's visit to Graf Stallburg. This venerable old nobleman is the very picture of traditional Austrian aristocracy, »und mit einem raschen Blick überzeugte sich Ulrich, daß Se. Exzellenz wirklich jenen eisgrauen, kurzen, am Kinn ausrasierten Backenbart trug, den alle Amtsdiener und Eisenbahnportiers in Kakanien besaßen. Man hatte geglaubt, daß sie in ihrem Aussehen ihrem Kaiser und Könige nachstrebten, aber das tiefe Bedürfnis beruht in solchen Fällen auf Gegenseitigkeit« (1: 84f). Graf Stallburg, Kaiser Franz Josef, scores of railroad porters, and droves of civil servants are all parodies of each other.

Elsewhere the narrator identifies this characteristic fondness for imitation as a »gewißer Hang zur Allegorie« in everyday life (2: 407). Even the most ordinary daily activity is never just what it is; it always takes on a supplemental, standardized meaning imposed on it by the images that it replicates:

> Im Kino, auf dem Theater, auf der Tanzbühne, im Konzert, in Auto, Flugzeug, Wasser, Sonne, Schneiderwerkstätten und Kaufmannsbüros entsteht fortwährend eine ungeheure Oberfläche, die aus Ein- und Ausdrücken, Gebärden, Gehaben und Erlebnissen besteht. (2: 408; cf. 1: 285)

The salesmen of image generate an expansive blanket of pseudo-reality designed to flatter the culture's vision of itself. These images come from the movies and theater, from fashion designers, technocrats and merchants. It is they, among others, who draw up the blueprints for the average desires, attitudes and emotions of daily life. The process of image-mongering, whether it produces the newest hat, the most popular romantic cliché or the latest intellectual trend, is the »Fabrikationsgrundsatz« for »die Herstellung des Lebens« (2: 410).

Ulrich repudiates the principle of life that is based on manufacturing and imitating illusions, yet he becomes involved in the »Parallelaktion,« Kakania's grandest parody. The Parallelaktion, as its name implies, is a game of mimicry, and it occupies the best and brightest minds of Kakania. It is also the context within which the theme of imitation begins to emerge in tandem with the theme of books and writing. In a note on the novel Musil writes: »Schreiben ist eine Verdoppelung der Wirklichkeit. Die Schreibenden haben nicht den Mut, sich für utopische Existenzen zu erklären« (1594*). Just as the Kakanians habitually copy the images around them, so also can writing double reality, and such a duplication is by no means desirable when the reality is as dilapidated as that in Kakania. It is the kind of writing that appears in newspapers and magazines, and the kind of writing turned out by many celebrated intellectuals. One of these big names in Kakania is Paul Arnheim, who will be discussed shortly.

The promoters of the Parallelaktion intend it to project the »true« Austria to the world. When the reader first meets Graf Leinsdorf, the originator of the Parallelaktion, his secretary is reading to him a passage from Fichte that, appropriately, is concerned with the necessity of ethical »Vorbilder,« images to be imitated (1: 87). Leinsdorf's Parallelaktion is the Austrian imitation of the German plan to celebrate Kaiser Wilhelm II's thirty years on the throne with a jubilee. Leinsdorf intends to emulate the Germans by organizing an even more splendid celebration of Franz Josef's seventieth year of imperial dignity in the Hapsburg realms. Leinsdorf is searching for an idea that will demonstrate the true Austria to the entire world. His banker, Direktor Leo Fischl, asks Ulrich what is to be understood as the true Austria. Ulrich replies that it is the »PDUG.«»›Ich schwöre Ihnen,‹ erwiderte Ulrich ernst, ›daß weder ich noch irgend jemand weiß, was der, die, das Wahre ist; aber ich kann Ihnen versichern, dass es im Begriff steht, verwirklicht zu werden!‹« (1: 135). Leinsdorf's project is a good example of Ulrich's »PDUG,« the »Prinzip des unzureichenden Grundes,« which posits that whatever has insufficient reason to exist will come into being anyway. A non-idea that immodestly aims at reflecting the ›truth‹ of Austria has insufficient grounds for existence: the idea, which has not yet come into being, is predicated on knowing the truth, which nobody knows. Yet, as Ulrich points out, the »PDUG« will prevail, and Leinsdorf's non-idea will become reality.

The first major step toward reifying this non-existent thing demonstrates the hold that writing has on reality. A journalist accidently catches wind of Leinsdorf's proposed scheme, assigns a name to it – »Österreichisches Jahr« – that invests it with the aura of dignity, importance, and reality that emanates from whatever appears in newsprint. The Parallelaktion has become a »pseudo-event,« an occurence that exists not by virtue of its authentic and independent presence outside of writing, but is instead artificially generated by the expectations that the media arouse in the public.[9] The narrator notes that neither Leinsdorf nor the journalist know what they are talking about, which is hardly surprising since what they are talking about does not

---

[9] The term »pseudo-event« comes from Daniel Boorstin, who treats in American culture the same phenomenon to which Musil alludes. A pseudo-event exists when the press and other media publicize some allegedly momentous occurence in advance. The event then becomes the image that the media projected for it *because* they projected that image. Boorstin stresses the disturbing frequency with which the contrived images overshadow the real thing. See D.B., *The Image, or What Happened to the American Dream* (New York: Atheneum, 1962), pp. 744.

exist. But because it appears under the authority of print, and because it has a name, no matter how vague, it instantly becomes the real and fascinating object of public attention. This authority of the written word serves an important function in the novel. Even though he never appears in person, Ulrich's father asserts his considerable authority in the form of writing, in letters, in telegrams, and even after death by means of his will. This »father« is the »already-written« that seeks throughout the novel to dominate Ulrich. It is a seminal form of Ulrich's »Prinzip des unzureichendes Grundes.« For instance, in a peevish, pompous letter the father commands Ulrich to call on a certain imperial dignitary. Obeying this dispatch from above, Ulrich meets Graf Stallburg, who introduces him to the Parallelaktion. Although Ulrich has no intention of participating in Stallburg's project, the father's letter has already set into motion a chain of events that will ultimately lead to his involvement in it.

One day as Ulrich is typically submerged in his private world, pondering the relation of »Geist« to its concrete manifestations, he happens onto the scene of an arrest and then is himself arrested for allegedly interfering with police efforts to bring a belligerent drunk under control. At the police station Ulrich sees that he is in for a bit of unpleasantness. In order to extricate himself he explains to the desk sergeant that he is a good friend of Graf Leinsdorf and secretary to the great patriotic undertaking of which people have been reading in the papers. The truth is that Ulrich has never met Leinsdorf and has no intention of becoming secretary to the Parallelaktion. Ulrich's story ought to be insufficient grounds for the production of reality, but the »PDUG« once again asserts its awesome power to shape the course of human affairs. Because aristocratic connections are not taken lightly in Kakania, the desk sergeant passes the problem to central headquarters where Ulrich eventually ends up in the office of the Polizeipräsident, a personal friend of Graf Leinsdorf. The Graf himself had been at the police station some hours previously making inquiries regarding Ulrich's unlisted address. The Polizeipräsident informs Ulrich that he is expected to appear at Leinsdorf's on the following morning and that the police have no intention of interfering with this important meeting. In this way Ulrich finds that his father's letter and his own little story hold him tightly in their ridiculous grasp. He feels duty-bound to call on Graf Leinsdorf, and on the next day life imitates fiction when the Parallelaktion gets a new secretary.

Ulrich's duties within the Parallelaktion introduce him to his principal adversary in the novel, Dr. Paul Arnheim. Musil's notes inform us that Arnheim was modeled on the real-life figure of Walther Rathenau

(5: 1938), which accounts for the moment of the real in Musil's formulation of a »realer Idealismus.« The second category, »Idealismus,« leads back to the self-referential problematics of writing. Just as Arnheim is a fictional construct in Musil's novel, so also is his image in Kakania a fiction produced by writing. He is the product of the media and public expectations. Musil invents a biography for Arnheim that presents him as the son of a self-made Prussian tycoon who built up a financial empire from humble beginnings in a garbage collection business. It is at least literally true and probably figuratively true also that the younger Arnheim is heir and administrator to an empire of garbage. He is a scholar, financier, writer and apologist for the »Vereinigung von Seele und Wirtschaft oder von Idee und Macht« (1: 108). Arnheim is the object of Ulrich's special contempt not just because he is manipulating the Parallelaktion out of a secret interest in Galician oil fields, but especially because his bogus intellectual project is nothing but another example of fiction that supplants truth. It is particularly disgusting in Arnheim's case because he is intelligent enough to know better.

Ulrich objects to Arnheim as a writer, a »Großschriftsteller« who is not in the service of ideas but is instead in the business of satisfying the public demand for greatness. His writings are an expression of the public's need for a locus upon which to project its version of traditional values in union with a business-is-business mentality. Arnheim takes the chaotic present and wraps it in a package of noble-seeming ideals that will appeal to the intelligentsia's image of itself. His success is due in large part to his press coverage. Publishers, the press, and critics all automatically sieze on a figure in whom they see their own minds and vested interest reflected, and »groß ist nun, was für groß gilt; allein das heißt, daß letzten Endes auch das groß ist, was durch tüchtige Reklame dafür ausgeschrien wird . . .« (2: 433). Arnheim's own writings and the publicistic writings about him give seeming form and substance to popular illusions. They transcribe the age's vision of itself and proliferate a massive self-deception.

Ulrich sees through Arnheim's image, recognizing that he does not offer creativity and originality, but only more of the same, »Seinesgleichen.« Arnheim promotes a self-serving bourgeois spirituality painted in the faded colors of a once brilliant tradition. Its historical credentials give to his philosophy a counterfeit patina of nobility and human excellence. His intellect plays itself out within the boundaries of convention, good taste, and self-delusion. Arnheim is a man of distinction, a man with the »Eigenschaften« that belong to his era: learning, property, social grace, respect for tradition, order, and progress. His image is the age's duplication of itself.

Moosbrugger, the pathological killer, is a similar duplication of the age, a sort of inverted Arnheim. Like the »Großschriftsteller«, Moosbrugger is a man with »Eigenschaften,« only all of them are bad. He is ignorant, poor, vicious, and criminally insane. Both Arnheim and Moosbrugger are constructs of the age, but at extreme ends of the scale. They are the points in historical space where the age's characteristics appear in their densest profusion. Arnheim's admirers follow him in the papers, flattered to see their own images in his. Splashy headlines and lurid details of Moosbrugger's crime and trial create for him a following of sorts also. The public's morbid fascination with the killer points toward a kind of identification with his brutal nature and is a prefiguration of World War I. This »krankhafte Komödiant« (2: 652) acts out the aggressive, destructive impulses that would soon devastate European civilization: »wenn die Menschheit als Ganzes träumen könnte, müßte Moosbrugger entstehn« (1: 76). If Arnheim is a collective daydream, Moosbrugger is a collective nightmare.

Neither Arnheim nor Moosbrugger demonstrates the power of individual imagination that distinguishes Ulrich from them. Each of the two displays a tendency to the slavish imitation of literary models, whether it is Arnheim sententiously quoting Goethe or Moosbrugger mindlessly parroting the language of the law (1: 72). They reflect something of what Musil had in mind when he suggested in his diary: »einen Menschen ganz aus Zitaten zusammensetzen!« (T,I: 356). Constructing a figure entirely from words and phrases gathered from other sources would mean that the figure is absolutely derivative, a parody of the already-written. It would be a verbal montage that embodies the principle of »Seinesgleichen geschieht« in that it would be limited to that which has been thought, said and done already. Putting together a figure from quotations would be an authorial act of construction parallel to the act of construction whereby the systems, institutions and traditions of culture inscribe character on the individual in the real world. These anonymous forces dictate the characters of Arnheim and Moosbrugger, reducing them to parodies of the features that are latent in the society as a whole. Each is something of a Frankenstein-monster assembled from a variety of spare parts culled from the mental habits of Kakanian culture. The implicit comparison of the artificiality of an author's invented characters and the way that culture ›writes‹ character and reality is a theme that gradually gathers momentum in the novel.

Another mechanism of parody in Kakania is that of the dissemination of knowledge and opinion. Once the Parallelaktion is under way in the salon of Ermelinda Tuzzi – called Diotima – its purpose is to find an idea for the jubilee. General Stumm von Bordwehr, an uninvited

76

participant assigned by the Ministry of War to keep an eye on the proceedings, takes an active hand in trying to solve this problem. Driven by his urge to bring order into civilian affairs and by his desire to place this »erlösende Gedanke« at Diotima's feet, Stumm pays a visit to the Kakanian Hofbibliothek. The objective of his mission is to gather and collate the world's great ideas and then select »den schönsten Gedanken der Welt« for Diotima and the Parallelaktion. But browsing through the stacks of the library he makes the staggering discovery that even if he were to read a book every day he would not be able to finish his search for around 10,000 years. The librarian with him then confides an important secret to him, namely that the librarians are able to maintain order in the system only by *not* reading books. They only read titles and tables of contents, or, at most, bibliographies. He leads Stumm into the secret heart of the library, its catalogue room, where order takes precedence over substance. But once again Stumm is thwarted in his efforts to find the world's greatest idea when he falls into the dreaded scholarly regress of reading books about books, and then books about books about books.

An older, more experienced librarian offers his assistance to the General. During his many years of library service he has seen the people come and go, and he has learned how to give them the books that will satisfy their expectations. The unfailing eye of the old librarian notes that the General's interests resemble those of a lady who recently visited the library. This lady is of course Diotima, and so Stumm comes into possession of the same books that she is reading.

This episode is a parable of the mechanisms that disseminate codified knowledge. The library is an archive of Western ideas and tradition, but because each book is a finished and irrevocable product of the past, its relationship to the present becomes problematical. This point can be illustrated by a small confrontation between Arnheim and Ulrich. The great man points out to Ulrich that history is an orderly thing: »In der Welt*geschichte* geschieht nichts Unvernünftiges.« Ulrich responds with a pointed query: »In der *Welt* aber doch so viel?« (1: 174, my emphasis). Arnheim the writer mistakes the historian's ordering vision for the past itself. History is for him a *written account* of the past whereby its chaos is ordered, codified and filed away. Ulrich does not confuse reality with the written account of reality. He insists on the distinction between the truth and its representation. Stumm's library represents the same ordering reduction of reality into tame written accounts. Books and writing are the emblems for the ossification of human truth and experience into a petrified forest of conceptual knowledge. The first librarian demonstrates that order is strictly a matter of

77

form and cannot guarantee substance and excellence. Whatever truth the library might contain is buried under mountains of paper. The authority of the print itself levels out the authority of truth. The second librarian, who, like the first, knows only the order of the library and not the substance of the thought it is supposed to contain, demonstrates how knowledge finds its way out of the stacks into the world. He knows which books will satisfy the expectations of which customers and earns his tips by circulating the same old stuff – »Seinesgleichen« – among the library users whom he advises. In this way Stumm comes into the possession of the same ideas that are on Diotima's mind. The two will be able to reinforce each other intellectually, but not through any independent thinking and agreement reached in earnest dialogue. Instead, it is simply that the same information, plausibly argued and under the persuasive authority of print and tradition, has been fed into each brain. Diotima also defines a like conformity to the »already written« for the Parallelaktion when she sets up a library that contains all of the published works of the campaign's participants. They will not be able to extend themselves beyond this symbolic fixity.

Musil similarly transforms idea into setting when he situates Stumm, Diotima, Arnheim and Ulrich together for a series of scenes in front of the Hofbibliothek. In the first one, Arnheim pontificates to Stumm concerning the ›death of the soul‹ in modern culture. All the while he poses bombastically with a weighty medieval volume which, so he claims, represents what the Parallelaktion can give to the world: »die Erlösung des deutschen Wesens vom Rationalismus« (2: 569). The controlling images of library and book insinuate the limitations of Arnheim's nostalgic irrationalism. He looks with uncritical confidence to the »already-written« of tradition for the answers to his questions.

The centrality of reading, books, and the library here underscores the homology of form that exists between »reality« and »textuality.« Musil views »Wirklichkeit« as a subreption of the vast, inexhaustible sea of possibilities that precede it. ›The text‹ is likewise a fixing of infinite possibilities into the finite bounds of a book or a library. The underlying mechanism of each is identical: they compel into finite form that which is by nature formless and infinite. This form, this static representation, then comes to appear as truth itself. But the text, as a figural expression of reality, is always a fiction, never identical with the truth and so should not be taken literally (cf. p. 92). An unbridgeable rift always separates the image from the true reality it is supposed to represent. The text, conceived of broadly as the sum of reified presuppositions, conventions, and traditions, defers and replaces truth. Images from the past, e.g. Arnheim's medieval angel, impose themselves on and displace the immediacy of the present. Books, the past, the authority of tradition, the seeming stability of »reality,« and the deceptive security of the fixed text all stand between the individual and the unencumbered, spontaneous experience of true reality. Arnheim's fashionable irrationalism, his intellectual posing under the aegis of Germany's tradition of *Besitz und Bildung*, his nostalgic utopianism all seem persuasive because of the trappings of textuality: form, tradition, fixity. But in its eternal sameness all the dogmatic text can offer is »Seinesgleichen.«

While Arnheim lectures Stumm, Diotima quarrels with Ulrich about the morality of a possible commitment to Arnheim. Their lively discussion extends and enlarges the theme of textuality, adding to it the dimensions of ethics and self-reference. The question is whether »a married woman« – Diotima refuses to admit that she is talking about herself – ought to follow her feelings or whether she should subordinate herself to the standards of moral convention. Ulrich takes his cue from her reference to moral ›law‹ to address the problem of reality. The emblematic presence of the library behind them continues to dominate the setting inasmuch as Ulrich's argumentation turns on reading, writing, novels, and great writers. His point of entry into the problem is the specific question of morality: »Moral ist ein durchaus berechtigter Durchschnitts- und Kollektivwert, den man wörtlich und ohne Seitensprünge zu befolgen hat, wo man ihn anerkennt. Einzelfälle sind aber nicht moralisch zu entscheiden, sie haben genau so wenig Moral, genau so viel sie von der Unerschöpflichkeit der Welt besitzen!« (2: 572). Ulrich conceives of morality as a tacit set of collectively acknowledged conventions that persist only under the imprimatur of average reality; morality is a *Vorschrift*, a text of sorts that is prior to the individual and that reflects collectively habituated experience. This text demands to be followed literally – »wörtlich« – especially when it takes the written form of codified law. But a »Mann ohne Eigenschaften« is willing to deny the authority of the text. He perceives that there are always instances of human reality and experience that do not fall into the prestructured categories of average reality. Because Moosbrugger is something new, the public does not consciously see itself in Moosbrugger's unprecedented madness, and for this reason the psychiatrists and lawyers fail to find a ready-made medical and legal cubby-hole in which to file his disturbing case. The lawyers are a particularly clear instance of minds limited by texts. Their reality extends only as far as the juridical *Vorschrift* that determines their interpretation of human doings. They are legally bound to follow the letter of the law. In the case of Moosbrugger, literal reading takes precedence over justice.

Ulrich expands the metaphor of textuality when he suggests to Diotima that reading literature is an activity parallel to that of interpreting reality. He asks her what it means to read: »Was tun Sie da? Ich will gleich die Antwort geben: Ihre Auffassung läßt aus, was Ihnen nicht paßt. Das gleiche hat schon der Autor getan« (2: 573). Ulrich is warning Diotima not to read too literally because an author can only appropriate a fragment of reality for his text. The reader, in turn, can only assimilate those portions of the text that are within the grasp of his imagination or, as is perhaps more often the case, within the grasp of his expectations. The truth accessible in a text is, then, partial at best. He continues:

> Lassen Sie uns etwa an große Schriftsteller denken. Man kann sein Leben nach ihnen richten, aber man kann nicht Leben aus ihnen keltern. Sie haben das, was sie bewegte, so fest gestaltet, daß es bis in die Zwischenräume der Zeilen wie gepreßtes Metall dasteht. Aber was haben sie eigentlich gesagt? Kein Mensch weiß es. Sie selbst haben es niemals ganz in einem gewußt. Sie sind wie ein Feld, über dem die Bienen fliegen; zugleich sind sie selbst ein Hin- und Herfliegen. Ihre Gedanken und Gefühle haben alle Grade des Übergangs zwischen Wahrheiten oder auch Irrtümern, die sich zur Not nachweisen ließen, und wandelbaren Wesen, die sich uns eigenmächtig nähern oder entziehen, wenn wir sie beobachten wollen. (2: 574; cf. 4: 1193)

An important irony informs this passage. Read simply and literally it is only a matter of Ulrich elucidating his theory of »Auslassen« to Diotima. He reaffirms that genuine life cannot be extracted from texts, that the written expression of thoughts and feelings is a reduction and falsification of the authentic truth. But a reading of this passage that takes note of its irony brings much more information.

It is no accident that Ulrich's comments thematize reading, writing, and »große Schriftsteller.« The scene between Stumm and Arnheim has already established in the reader's mind Musil's often repeated point about the danger of accepting traditional dogma as the structure of authentic reality. The images of the book and the library underwrite the presence of this theme. But the open condemnation of reading too literally, of holding too closely to the *Vorschrift*, leaves the impression that Musil has made an unequivocal rejection of books and all convention and codification. This is a position that would be as dogmatic as the one he opposes. Ulrich's talk with Diotima, and in particular this last long passage, are a corrective to the threat of dogmatism. It is a commentary on the novel-immanent theme of printed authority as well as a self-reflective, ironic commentary on the fact that *Der Mann ohne Eigenschaften* is itself a book.[10] Ulrich grants to »große Schriftsteller«

---

[10] In his diary Musil makes a comment on the *Vereinigungen* that holds true

some access to authentic reality, but this reality becomes radically altered when it is committed to paper. His comment is simultaneously an ironic caveat to the reader not to take the novel he is reading too literally, for the short-comings of »große Schriftsteller« are surely Musil's own limitations. He is intentionally subverting the authority of his own narrative by exposing it as artifice in order to uphold the integrity of his proposition that any representation of reality is at best a critical heuristic postulate about reality and can never make any claim actually to *be* the truth. Musil insists on a conscious awareness of the crucial distinction between an image and the object of representation. It is a point that Ulrich's point about images – texts or representations of any sort – in the fictional world of Kakania, folds back ironically on the text that the novel's reader is holding in his hands.

This ironic moment of self-reflection reveals the sense of the narrator's claim that his text intends at no point »mit der Wirklichkeit in Wettbewerb zu treten« (1: 170). In other words the novel is self-conscious of its fictive mode, its fictionality, and does not wish for its readers to take its insights as universal truths. Musil has supplied the narrative fabric of his fictional world with a system of little rips and tears through which the reader pops out of the illusion back into author's own detached point of vantage. The most important device that the author uses to ironize the illusion of reality is the recurring self-reflexive criticism of books, writing and the power of the word.

The novel's major villains and buffoons are all writers of books: Arnheim, Lindner, Hagauer, Feuermaul, Walter, Meingast, and Ulrich's father. Ulrich, on the other hand, repeatedly asserts that he does not write.[11] Until he was twenty years old Ulrich had been interested in writing and had even composed some poems in secret. But he gave it up »aus Gründen, für die er unter den gegenwärtigen Eindrücken am ehesten irgendein Wort hätte gebrauchen mögen, das nach vielen Anstrengungen ein Münden ins Leere ausdrückt. Denn Ulrich gehörte zu den Bücherliebhabern, die nicht mehr lesen mögen, weil sie das Ganze des

---

also for the *MoE*: »Der Fehler dieses Buches ist, ein Buch zu sein. Daß es ein Einband hat, Rücken, Paginierung. Man sollte zwischen Glasplatten ein paar Seiten davon ausbreiten u. sie von Zeit zu Zeit wechseln. Dann würde man sehen, was es ist« (T, I: 347).

[11] Although *Sprachproblematik* is a topos familiar to Musilforschung, secondary literature around the *MoE* has not taken note of its variant form as problematized textuality. For this reason it is not superfluous to cite the pages where this problematization comes up in one form or another: volume 1: 87, 131f., 206f. 244, 245, 251, 300, 326. 2: 360, 372f., 391, 417, 418, 490, 574, 624, 662 3: 678,, 703, 864, 867, 882, 900, 960f. 4: 1115, 1278, 1282, 1381. 5: 1638f., 1640, 1642, 1673, 1818, 1865, 1898, 1904, 1911, 1919, 1921, 1925, 1993.

Schreibens und Lesens als ein Unwesen empfinden« (3: 867). When asked on separate occasions by Tuzzi, Gerda Fischl, and Arnheim if he does or would write, Ulrich answers decisively and even irritably that he is emphatically not a writer (2: 418; 490; 634). Some few hundred pages later, Ulrich recalls for his sister Agathe the conversation with Tuzzi:

> Ich aber habe ihm zugeschworen, daß ich mich töten werde, ehe ich der Versuchung unterliege, ein Buch zu schreiben; und ich habe es aufrichtig gemeint. Denn das, was ich schreiben könnte, wäre nichts als der Beweis, daß man auf eine bestimmte andere Weise zu leben vermag; daß ich aber ein Buch darüber schriebe, wäre zumindest der Gegenbeweis, daß ich nicht so zu leben vermag. (4: 1278)

Instead of committing his utopian ideals to paper, Ulrich wants to try to live them out with his sister. Writing them down would mean surrendering to the hard and fast world of the journalists, the legislators, and the Arnheims. Such a capitulation of his principles would compromise the deeply unique spark of originality that separates him from the herd, and so destroy exactly that which is most central to his life. Writing is a kind of suicide for Ulrich, a theme that Musil evidently had intended to develop.[12] In Ulrich's mind the fixity of the text is an analogue to the fixity of average reality. A spirited conversation with Clarisse results in a passage that demonstrates his awareness of this

---

[12] It may be that after the failure to sustain a utopian existence with Agathe, Ulrich would have turned to writing. In Musil's sketches toward a conclusion we find notes such as »Buch schreiben, also Selbstmord, also in Krieg Gehn« (5: 1904; cf. 4: 1282, 1381 and 5: 1898, 1905, 1921, 1925), which suggest that Ulrich joins in the madness of average reality and meets destruction. It should be noted that Ulrich's memory fails him in recalling his conversation with Tuzzi. What he actually said was that unless the urge to write siezes him soon, he will kill himself, and not, as he recounts for Agathe, that he would rather kill himself than write. It is also not entirely true that Ulrich has completely renounced reading and writing: a) he writes long diary entries on »Gefühlspsychologie« and b) he reads the mystics. *a.* If it is true, as Martha Musil wrote, that her husband had intended to break up these diary entries into conversations between Ulrich and Agathe, part of the author's motivation could have been to be consistant with Ulrich's repeated claims that he does not write. In any case he does not write for popular consumption and so remains free of the tainted literacy that Arnheim and the others represent (Martha Musil, 1615*; see n. 1). *b.* Ulrich makes a distinction between good writing and bad reading, as a comment to Tuzzi implies: »beinahe kein Mensch liest heute noch, jeder benützt den Schriftsteller nur, um in der Form von Zustimmung oder Ablehnung auf eine perverse Weise seinen eigenen Überschuß an ihm abzustreifen« (2: 417). Ulrich's reading of the mystics (e.g. 3: 753, 4: 1203) presumably falls into a special category because the writers of mystic texts, like Ulrich, are at all points aware of the inadequacy of language.

parallelism. But it is a passage that requires special attention. Clarisse's husband, Walter, interrupts Ulrich's talk with his wife, and the narrator takes it upon himself to report what Ulrich might have said if Walter had not appeared.

> Er hatte etwa sagen wollen: Gott meint die Welt keineswegs wörtlich; sie ist ein Bild, eine Analogie, eine Redewendung, deren er sich aus irgendwelchen Gründen bedienen muß, und natürlich immer unzureichend; wir dürfen ihn nicht beim Wort nehmen, wir selbst müssen die Lösung herausbekommen, die er uns aufgibt. (2: 357f.)

It is significant that the narrator introduces this passage with the equivocal adverb »etwa.« Ulrich neither spoke nor thought these lines; they are, as the narrator explicitly states, an approximation of what he had wanted to say to Clarisse. This point is of no importance in Kakania, i.e. in the fictional world in which Ulrich and the others live and move. But it is decisive for the world in which the reader relates to the novel. The word »etwa« 1) announces the presence of the narrator, 2) demonstrates his power over the figures, and 3) enacts the mode of undogmatic assertion to which Musil's irony lays claim. By foregrounding his narrator, Musil militates against the uncritical reading that allows the act of narration to melt into the background of literary convention. In this passage, as in much of the novel, Musil prefers narrated monologue to quoted monologue. This narratological detour draws the reader's attention away from the figures of fiction to refocus it on the figures of speech and thereby weakens the impression of a realistic illusion. In this particular instance, Musil heightens the sense of an alien intrusion into the world of the fiction by passing on information that is not only second-hand but is also only an approximation of something the protagonist neither said nor even thought. The narrative rhetoric of this passage reveals that it, like Ulrich himself, is the invention of an imagination outside of the fiction.

The content of the narrated passage bears out the reading that its rhetorical strategy suggests. The hypothetical statement that the narrator tentatively attributes to Ulrich's intention proposes that God does not mean the world literally. It is a proposition characteristic of Ulrich's »ironic« or facetious temperament, but it is even more ironic than Clarisse and Ulrich would be inclined to think. The passage casts God in the role of speaker, writer, or, more reductively, in the role of a novelist writing reality. The passage's first level of meaning, the one that occurs in the world of the fiction, is a variation on the utopian theme that concrete reality should not be taken too literally. It is a restatement of the possibilitarian's motto: »Nun, es könnte wahrscheinlich auch anders sein« (1: 16). But at a deeper level of meaning there arises the ironic moment of self-reflection that occurs not in the ficitonal world but between text and reader. If God is the ›author‹ of reality, then so too is the novelist a lesser deity over the lesser reality of his narrative. It makes the real world and the fictional one parallel realms of artifice, contingent upon the perhaps fickle whims of an unknown divinity. There is a double valance to Ulrich's injunction not to take reality literally. Inasmuch as he makes his point by likening reality to a text, we are justified in reading it as authorial irony: Ulrich's reality is, literally, textual, »ein Bild, eine Analogie, eine Redewendung.« Ulrich in his world is asserting that the concretely real is only a metaphor for all the possibilities behind it; Musil in his world is asserting, ironically, that Ulrich, Kakania, and all the other figures in his novel are hypothetical constructs and not doubles for the already fictional figures of life. Fiction merges with reality and reality fades into fiction when their shared underlying mechanism is brought to light.

Musil gives his readers a fair chance to catch and interpret the irony that develops between text and reader, but just to be certain that nobody misses the point, he sends Ulrich back to Clarisse to explain things. The specific ›narrativity‹ of Kakanian reality is evident to him, albeit not in the form of novelistic narrative but as bad theater. Note once again that the narrator reports Ulrich's speech in the subjunctive of indirect discourse, thereby forcing the reader to take into account the mediator as an artificer of worlds: »Das jetzt geltende System sei das der Wirklichkeit und gleiche einem schlechten Theaterstück. Man sage nicht umsonst Welttheater, denn es erstehen immer die gleichen Rollen, Verwicklungen und Fabeln im Leben« (2: 364). He goes on to compare politicians to the authors of box-office hits that are really only showy renderings of the same old tired plots and devices, lacking in imagination and originality.[13]

Ulrich has verified and made explicit the message that was implicit in the earlier ironic passage. Shaping reality is an act of construction like that of shaping art works. The conventions that govern the one find analogues in the conventions that govern the other. There is always the danger of inventing a reality that is trite and cliché-ridden. The scripts of »Welttheater« are parodies, repetition of the same old stuff: »Seinesgleichen geschieht.« Ulrich demands originality, spontaneity, and authenticity of life lived according to ideas and ideals that emerge from

---

[13] This passage is cited in full on page 65. The thought that politicians, the »authors« of reality, are generally just bad artists comes up frequently in Musil (cf. T, I: 984, 825). Nor are the poets excused for similar ethical stupidities (cf. his essay »Über die Dummheit«, 8: 1278).

individual imagination instead of the false ideas and ideals that are the plagiarized redundancies of »Weltgeschichte.«

This ironic self-consciousness and self-critique in *Der Mann ohne Eigenschaften* asserts itself once again when Ulrich returns home after having witnessed the preposterous theatrics of a demonstration against Leinsdorf and the Parallelaktion. He is fed up with the absurdities of so-called reality, but he is also slightly disturbed at his inability to put the world in the same kind of perspective that allows his contemporaries to view these absurdities with equanimity. In this state of mind it occurs to him, »daß das Gesetz dieses Lebens ... kein anderes sei als das der erzählerischen Ordnung!« (2: 650). The irony is unmistakable inasmuch as Ulrich's ›literal‹ existence depends entirely on narrative order.

Ulrich's thoughts on the narrativity of Kakanian life are suddenly interrupted on his walk home when a prostitute confronts him with her painted face, commercial smile, and a proposition formulated in the clichés of her trade language. The woman's outward appearance and smile, as well as her language are all the thinnest pretense, and for a reasonable fee she is willing to entertain her would-be customer in a brief, make-believe love tryst. She is a transparent fiction, an emblem of Kakanian life, whose every detail is calculated according to a narrative order that exists in the pitiful imaginations of her customers. The scene is a translation of Ulrich's discursive insight from the preceding passage into the form of a *Gleichnis*. The figure of the prostitute has clear extra-textual moment of ›realistic‹ reference: she is like someone whom an Ulrich might meet on the streets of a place like Vienna. But the moment of self-reference is also in evidence: she is a two-dimensional figure of pure artifice that embodies the theme of »Seinesgleichen« in the novel.

This encounter is a set piece that demonstrates how art and reality come together for Musil in a positive way. The prostitute appears simultaneously as real-seeming illusion and self-conscious artifice: »unter der Nachtbemalung mochte die Haut eines noch jungen Mädchens mit vielen Sommersprossen verborgen sein« (2: 651). Truth lies concealed beneath illusion. Of course her phony routine does not fool Ulrich, but he is nevertheless slightly touched by the strange mingling of contrivance and authenticity in her. He seems to be faced with the choice of going with her and participating in a sexual charade or playing the righteous burgher and rejecting her offer in accordance with moral convention. But Ulrich picks neither of the two average choices, spontaneously choosing instead to do something original and unexpected. He reaches into his pocket for the approximate price of a visit, presses the

85

money into her hand, and continues on his eccentric way. It is a moment in the novel that is slightly comical, thoroughly and refreshingly free of slushy social criticism, yet suffused with a convincing human sensitivity. In it Musil has found a precise balance between the self-consciousness of fictional artifice and a transitory instant of a humane authenticity that is sober and unpretentious. The prostitute is artificial for Ulrich – only another unhappy case of »Seinesgleichen« in Kakanian life – and she is artificial for the reader – a transparent *Gleichnis* in a novel – but for both Ulrich and the reader this encounter leaves behind it a residue of authentic human experience: »Diese Begegnung blieb noch eine Weile lebendig, als wäre sie ein zartes Idyll von einer Minute Dauer gewesen« (2: 652). Musil's irony does not withdraw the richness of this moment. It only qualifies it and prevents it from lapsing into a sentimental lie. Ulrich's response to the situation is an important development in the novel's thematics of originality. The prostitute's life, like almost everybody's in Kakania is only a weak imitation of an already shabby, imaginary order. Ulrich revolts against this order and is determined to do something original. The narrative thread of life in Kakania is that of custom, law, tradition and *Bildung*.

The principal representative of this authoritarian order for Ulrich is his father. This father, Ulrich's »author«, as it were, is absent during the entire course of the novel, yet the power that this invisible being exercises over his children is pervasive. It presses Ulrich to make a place of importance for himself in society and it holds Agathe in a marriage that she loathes (3: 683). The father is a man with »Eigenschaften.« His industrious efforts and accomplishments in the legal profession have made him prosperous, brought him social prestige, and earned him an appointment to the Imperial House of Lords. Appropriately, the father is a legislator, a writer of the laws that determine the bounds of permissible behavior. It is also significant, as I previously suggested, that the father dominates his children not in person but ›textually,‹ i.e. always in the written form of letters, telegrams and, especially, his will. He directs Ulrich into the Parallelaktion by means of a letter, and even the news of his death comes to Ulrich in a telegram that the father himself composed before he died. This telegram is the conscious attempt of the dead and absent past to gain control of the future (cf. 3: 672). This father is emblematic of all the superordinated structures of oppression that imprison the individual in prescriptive schemata of feeling, thinking and living. He is the lawmaker who writes the text of life.

The father's death is a decisive moment in the novel's development. It calls Ulrich away from the ridiculous reality of the disintegrating

Parallelaktion, and it calls Agathe away from the sterile parody of married life that she is leading with the pedantic Hagauer. After many years of separation, the brother and sister are reunited at the father's provincial villa. To describe the strangely powerful attraction that they feel for each other, Ulrich invokes Plato's story of how the gods split the human being into two halves that must seek each other ever after (3: 303f.). Ulrich and Agathe are two errant halves that have rejoined to form a whole. He is a man of icy intellectuality, at home in the rarified atmosphere of mathematics and the theoretical sciences. She is the »sister,« »ein Gebilde, das aus dem ›anderen‹ Teil des Gefühls ersteht« (4: 1314). Agathe is a *Gefühlsmensch*, but she is not a sentimentalist or dewy-eyed romantic like Diotima and Bonadea. She is articulate, well read and intelligent; she has a good memory and recites poetry, but she does not share her brother's emotional detachment, and the precise world of discursive abstraction is not her element. Upon their first meeting in the villa, Musil ties them figuratively by twinning them in identical Pierrot pyjamas. The costume suggests the completeness of their union, but it is also an ironic gesture from Musil to the reader. Pierrot is, of course, a clown, a stock literary figure, an insinuation of the figurality and fictionality of Ulrich and Agathe.

The father is dead and the children have broken away from their respective places in average reality. The scene is set for an experiment in authentic living, but once again average reality in the form of a written text stands in the way. The father's will can uphold Agathe's bond to Hagauer. So Agathe in her »wildsanfte Entschlossenheit« takes the revolutionary measure of forging a codicil to the will so that Hagauer will be excluded from his legacy. Agathe is denying the authority of the text and of reality. In so doing she becomes a criminal. The authority of the father, the law, tradition and custom are all present in this document. By changing it Agathe is rewriting reality and opening a path »ins Tausendjährige Reich« for herself and her brother. Part III of the novel – »Ins Tausendjährige Reich (Die Verbrecher)« – primarily deals with the utopian experiment of Ulrich and Agathe.

The two ›criminals‹ isolate themselves from their old lives and the »Seinesgleichen« reality of Kakanian society in order to inquire into new, untried ways of experiencing the world and each other. Their flirtation with incest is a sign of the radical seriousness of this undertaking. They are moving toward a heightened physical and spiritual unity that Musil calls »die Utopie des anderen Zustands.« The precise nature of the »Other Condition« is never entirely clear, but it is basically a state of receptivity to experience that is free of the constraint that habit, expectation, and presupposition impose on thinking and feeling.[14] It is the condition in which an individual responds to a given stimulus spontaneously and authentically without being influenced by the patterns of response that belong to past experience. In this way, the unprecedented and unrepeatable aspects of even the most quotidian event become accessible, aspects that otherwise slip through the coarsely woven net of prestructured expectations. The person empowered of the Other Condition is able to drink in a fleeting moment without forcing the schemata of habituated experience on it. Ulrich describes the distinction between prescribed and authentic feeling to his sister: »... unser Fühlen hat seine besondere Gestalt dadurch angenommen, daß wir es in das Bild der Wirklichkeit einordnen, und nicht das Umgekehrte, das Ekstatische tun. Eben deshalb muß in uns aber auch die Möglichkeit liegen, unser Fühlen umzukehren und unsere Welt anders zu erleben!« (4: 1201; cf. 1: 186, 284; 3: 1024; 4: 1129).

The problem of textuality returns once again, this time with regard to the Other Condition. Both the event and the experience of the event in the Other Condition are ephemeral. That which is unprecedented and unrepeatable is necessarily falsified when a representation of it gives it seeming permanence. Nevertheless, representations of experience had in the Other Condition are abundant. In a sketch known as »Die Reise ins Paradies,« Anders, Ulrich's precursor in early drafts of the novel, explains to Agathe that the Other Condition leaves behind it the ossified traces of its presence in various sorts of fixed expressions:

> Man könnte ja versucht sein, in diesem schattenhaften Doppelgänger einer andren Welt nur einen Tagtraum zu sehn, wenn er nicht seine noch warmen Spuren in unzähligen Einzelheiten unseres Lebens hinterlassen hätte. Religion, Kunst, Liebe, Moral ... das sind Versuche, diesem andren Geist zu folgen, die mit ungeheurer Mächtigkeit in unser Dasein hereinragen, aber ihren Sinn und Ursprung verloren haben und dadurch völlig verworren u. korrupt geworden sind. (5: 1644)

One of Ulrich's favorite examples of this corruption is bourgeois morality. He believes that the ethical impulse is native to the Other Condition, but that it is not susceptible of being reduced to a text of prescriptive rules and regulations: »Ich muß Agathe einprägen: Moral ist Zuordnung jedes Augenblickszustandes unseres Lebens zu einem Dauerzustand!« (3: 869; cf. 3: 1028). The reification of any experience that originates in the Other Condition is always only an image, a

---

[14] There is much literature devoted to Musil's »anderer Zustand.« See esp. Elisabeth Albertsen, *Zur Dialektik von Ratio und Mystik im Werk Robert Musils* (München: Nymphenburg, 1968); Ingrid Drevermann, »Wirklichkeit und Mystik,« in Sibylle Bauer und Ingrid Drevermann, *Studien zu Robert Musil*, Literatur und Leben, N.F., 8 (Köln, Graz: Böhlau, 1966).

Gleichnis that hypostatizes the constantly shifting fluidity of the inner life. Once again, ›the book‹ is emblematic for the petrification of insight gleaned the Other Condition. Anders to Agathe:

>»Hunderte von Menschen haben es erlebt, daß sie glaubten, sich eine andre Welt öffnen zu sehn. Genau so wie wir.«
>»Und was ist daraus geworden?«
>»Bücher«
>»Doch unmöglich nur Bücher?«
>»Wahnsinn. Aberglaube. Essays. Moral. Und Religion. Die Dinge.« (5: 1642)

The problem here is one of representation, of mimesis, and it has a direct bearing on Musil's own undertaking. He has posed a problem for himself that he answers by thematizing the use of *Gleichnisse*.[15] During his conversation with Diotima in front of the library, Ulrich sketches out the problem involved in representing reality. He tells her that the physical world behaves with sufficient regularity that it can be adequately represented, especially in the precise language of mathematics; »aber alle anderen Begriffe, auf die wir unser Leben stützen, sind nichts als erstarren gelassene Gleichnisse« (2: 574). These other concepts are beauty, love, morality, law, religion, ideology and the various inner experiences of the Other Condition that can appear in the fossilized form of a ›textual‹ objectification. Ulrich draws his metaphor from the realm of literature. A *Gleichnis* is a literary text. It is »die gleitende Logik der Seele« (2: 593) that is the adequate expression of the inner life because it is tentative, hypothetical and only tries to tell what something is *like* and not dogmatically to embody the final truth of a thing. Musil's frozen »Gleichnisse« are highly reminiscent of Nietzsche's definition of truth as

> Ein bewegliches Heer von Metaphern, Metonymien, Anthropomorphismen, kurz eine Summe von menschlichen Relationen, die, poetisch und rhetorisch gesteigert, übertragen, geschmückt wurden und die nach langem Gebrauch einem Volke fest, kanonisch und verbindlich dünken: die Wahrheiten sind Illusionen, von denen man vergessen hat, daß sie welche sind, Metaphern, die abgenutzt und sinnlich kraftlos geworden sind, Münzen, die ihr Bild verloren haben und nun als Metall, nicht mehr als Münzen, in Betracht kommen.[16]

---

[15] In the text of this chapter I retain the German word *Gleichnis* because Musil uses it in a very broad sense that does not translate well. He includes similes, parables, images, symbols, analogies and so on in the word *Gleichnis*. In other words, a *Gleichnis* is any sign, any figural expression, as distinct from its referent.

[16] Friedrich Nietzsche, »Über Wahrheit und Lüge im außermoralischen Sinn,« in his *Werke in drei Bänden*, hrsg. von Karl Schlechta, vol. III (München: Hanser, 1956), p. 314.

Nietzsche and Musil insist on honoring the bounds of representation, distinguishing rigorously between a sign and its itinerant referent. When the *concept* of a thing replaces the thing itself, truth becomes nothing more than a rhetorical construct, a fiction. What Kakania accepts as truths are illusions that have forgotten they are illusions. It is precisely this critical insight that generates the functional identity between Ulrich and Musil. Ulrich treats appearances as appearances. All of human reality is for him a *Gleichnis* of the truth and never the truth itself. In a like manner, Musil treats his novel as a *Gleichnis*. Critical consciousness means for him *self*-consciousness. His various ironic intrusions into the novel's illusion of reality call attention to its condition of artifice, its *Gleichnishaftigkeit*. Irony enables him to reflect on the world and simultaneously reflect on his reflection of the world. Both Ulrich and his inventor are artists in the Nietzschean sense that treats life itself as an aesthetic phenomenon.

This position does not, however, reduce the project of representation to a fool's errand. It calls instead for a clear understanding of the limitations of representation. The scientist treats an equation that describes a chemical reaction as a hypothetical model of that reaction, a tentative construct that is subject to revision. When a heuristic representation hardens into a dogma, the cause of truth is obstructed until a mind of sufficient imagination comes along to unmask the text as a text.

Copernicus, for instance, was a mind empowered of enough imagination to abandon the »Seinesgleichen« models of the solar system and invent a new one. Musil calls this open-minded creativity »phantastische Genauigkeit,« a condition diametrically opposed to »pedantische Genauigkeit,« »und diese beiden unterscheiden sich dadurch, daß sich die phantastische an die Tatsachen hält und die pedantische an Phantasiegebilde« (1: 247). What Ulrich and Musil demand is no less than a Copernican revolution of the »soul«. Ulrich's exhortation that the Parallelaktion establish a »Generalsekretariat für Genauigkeit und Seele« reflects this demand. The humanist, like the scientist, must offer representations – models, *Gleichnisse* – that hold to the facts. His special problem is that the »facts« of the human psyche are in a state of continual flux. In one of his talks with Agathe, Ulrich illustrates this state of affairs with a passage from *Hamlet* that is quoted in full at the beginning of this chapter:

> Die Wolke des Polonius, die bald als Schiff bald als Kameel erscheint, ist nicht die Schwäche eines nachgiebigen Höflings, sondern bezeichnet ganz und gar die Art, in der uns Gott geschaffen hat. (4: 1434; cf. 4: 1348; 5: 1503)

Ulrich's willful re-interpretation of this Shakespeare passage asserts the capacity of imagination to keep pace with the ceaseless shifting of the inner life. Polonius and Hamlet do not reify any one of their representations. As soon as one image is no longer valid, they discard it and invent a new one. They continually rewrite reality.

For this reason the poet, a scientist of the soul, can best hold to the facts of inventing finely tuned *Gleichnisse*. The figural captures that which is unique and spontaneous in a given moment of authentic emotion and experience because it links together two things that otherwise do *not* share identity. In figurality, it is the tension between identity and difference that is decisive: »Selbst in jeder Analogie steckt ein Rest des Zaubers, gleich und nicht gleich zu sein« (3: 906; cf. 4: 1342ff., 1350; 5: 1834, Nr. 6). The epiphanical instant of shared identity does not lapse into dogmatic assertion because the intrinsic difference between the terms of comparison holds identity in check. The *Gleichnis*, with its »glasige Atmosphäre von Ahnung, Glaube und Künstlichkeit« (2: 582) feels its way along the dark contours of »die Welt des Innern« (4: 1200) and hints at its nature by suggesting what it is *like* connotatively, but never offering a hard and fast denotion of what it *is*. Its self-conscious »Künstlichkeit« withdraws the illusion of absolute truth and permanence from figurality and guarantees it as a form of signification free of hypostasis.

Although it is central to Musil's theory and fiction, the *Gleichnis*–theme has not yet aroused its due share of attention.[17] In the present context it is principally important to elucidate only a portion of this theme, specifically, the way in which the *Gleichnis* enacts in miniature

---

[17] Two book-length studies have been devoted to this topic: Jörg Kühne, *Das Gleichnis. Studien zur inneren Form von Robert Musils Roman »Der Mann ohne Eigenschaften«*, Studien zur deutschen Literatur, 13 (Tübingen: Niemeyer, 1968); Dieter Fuder, *Analogiedenken und anthropologische Differenz. Zu Form und Funktion der poetischen Logik in Robert Musils Roman »Der Mann ohne Eigenschaften«,* Musil-Studien, 10 (München: Fink, 1979). In his discussion of Musil's conception of mimesis, Fuder recognizes the self-conscious fictionality of Musil's analogy use that I emphasize here. His point of departure is Törleß' trouble with imaginary numbers and his comparison of them to a bridge: »Ist das nicht wie eine Brücke, von der nur Anfangs- und Endpfeiler vorhanden sind, und die man so sicher überschreitet, als ob sie ganz dastünde?« (cited in Fuder, p. 171). Fuder's conclusion is, »die Dichtung ist eine fiktive Analogie, die sich vom festen Boden so wegwölbt, als besäße sie im Imaginären ein Analogat« (p. 171). The analogy is »eine Relationsbewegung, deren Abbildungscharakter darin besteht, das Analogat im Imaginären erst herzustellen« (173). Cf. also Karl Corino, »Der erlöste Tantalus. Robert Musils Verhältnis zur Sprache«, *Annali: Studi Tedeschi*, 23 (Naples, 1980), 339–56.

the system of dual reference that governs the novel. In Musil's narrative the *form* of literary expression – the figural – becomes the object of itself. Form becomes content when the narrator, Ulrich, and Agathe reflect discursively on the nature of *Gleichnisse*, while at the same time Musil uses *Gleichnisse* to render them. Viewed in this way the whole narrative world appears to be suspended in mid-air, grounded not in solid, referential reality but in a set of self-referential rhetorical relations. All of Kakania is such a *Gleichnis*, a poetic trope whose only referent is itself; but self-referentiality does not rob the sign of meaning. It establishes the origin of meaning as the imagination in its dialectic with the rest of the world. Figural language does not function according to the *adaequatio* model of truth, which posits the priority of the referent in its isomorphic relation to its sign. When the referent is a fragile, transitory moment in affective reality, figurative language addresses it by setting up a relational pattern of words that is auto-significative yet also evokes a meaning that arises somewhere between experience and imagination. Such a signification is one that is free of the words' denotative values. The *Gleichnis* does not double reality. Its words awaken dormant perceptions and then they fade away, leaving behind them a disembodied thought.

A brief example will help to clarify this matter. In one of their idyllic garden conversations, as Ulrich and Agathe walk and talk together, coming ever closer to a mystical union, the narrator dissolves the discursive content of their exchange into figural language:

> und die Worte, die sie wechselten, bedeuteten eigentlich wenig und wiegten sie bloß in ihr Gehen ein wie das kindlich vergnügte Selbstgespräch eines Brunnens, der lallend vom Ewigen schwätzt. (4: 1335)

The medium of exchange, language, comes undone for Ulrich and Agathe and unites them in a fleeting eternal moment of affective truth. But Musil cannot abandon language; he must try to render this extralinguistic experience into words. He tries to pierce the denotative strictures of ordinary signification and penetrate in a precise way into the affective interior. The sign-referent structure of ordinary language is fine for conventional experience that is calculable and repeatable. The sign is by nature a conventional construct that coincides with a conventional meaning. But Musil is after the unprecedented and unrepeatable. He must use figural language – words in an unconventional, unique configuration – to suggest what the experience is like. In comparing the words of Ulrich and Agathe to the gently rocking murmur of a brook he connotatively evokes perceptions that are convincing in their authenticity and precise in a certain way, albeit unverifiably so. Yet there is no danger of substituting the sign for the referent; the difference between words and a murmuring brook is unmistakable. It is at all points clear that the expression is figurative, and so the language itself fades away, leaving in its place the residue of a unique aperçu.

III

The invention of a *Gleichnis* is an act of imagination, but, ideally, it is not an act of unbridled and irresponsible fantasy. Ulrich, the possibilitarian, regards the whole of reality as an act of quasi-divine imagination, no more than an image, an analogy or turn of phrase. His refusal to take reality »literally« seems to leave him open to the charge of being an irresponsible phantast. Similarly, a novel that claims it does not wish to compete with reality and persists in flaunting the artifice of its fictionality also seems to question the seriousness and worth of the writer's work. But in both instances the reverse is true. It is not Ulrich who is a phantast, but Arnheim, Moosbrugger and the rest of the deluded Kakanians who live and act according to destructive illusions. They accept willingly an inadequate reality. Ulrich's rebellion against illusion is an act of ethical imagination. The vigorous intelligence of Musil's self-conscious style also bears the mark of a radical honesty. As Ulrich denies the fixed text of reality, so also does Musil deny the authority of dogmatic assertion. His novel reflects on human reality yet simultaneously renders an account of its own fallible procedures and the intrinsic limitations of literary representation. Ulrich and Musil plead together for a »phantastische Genauigkeit« of vision that holds to the facts: of life, of representation. It is a vision that rewrites reality as readily and as imaginatively as Hamlet and Polonius reaccomodate their similes for a shifting cloud. It is a plea for a utopian flexibility of mind that will be the subject of this study's final chapter.

CHAPTER IV

THE LAMENTATION OF JOSEF K.:
Conscience and Irony in Kafka's *Prozeß*

> Alle Illusion ist zur Wahrheit so wesentlich, wie der Körper der Seele. – Irrtum ist das notwendige Instrument der Wahrheit. – Mit dem Irrtum mache ich Wahrheit.
>
> Novalis

> Wenn man sich nicht bemüht, das Unaussprechliche auszusprechen, so geht *nichts* verloren. Sondern das Unaussprechliche ist – unaussprechlich – in dem Ausgesprochenen *enthalten*!
>
> Wittgenstein[1]

In one way or another, students of literature generally take the poetic word to be a crucially significant way of knowing the world. Biblical narrative, classical myth, and the whole canon of premodern literary monuments all testify to the mutuality and interpenetration of the poetic and the real, especially for the pre-scientific era. Yet the overall trend of modern thought, and in particular the rise of empirical rationalism, has eroded the bond that once united poetry and reality. The tragic grandeur of an Achilles or the moral anguish of an Abraham have been made to release their grip on the real. Once it has been reduced to ›myth‹ and ›fiction‹ – both popular synonyms for ›falsehood‹ – literature becomes suspect as a path to knowledge. This path is the one followed by Don Quixote. His remote descendant, Josef K., is its inheritor.

It is Cervantes' *Don Quixote*, suggests Michel Foucault, that »is the first work of modern literature because in it we see the cruel reason of

---

[1] Novalis, *Fragmente I*, Vol. 2 of *Werke/Briefe/Dokumente*, hrsg. v. Ewald Wasmuth (Heidelberg: Lambert Schneider, 1957), p. 68, No. 208. Ludwig Wittgenstein, *Briefe*, hrsg. v. B. F. McGuinness und G. H. von Wright (Frankfurt a.M.: Suhrkamp, 1980), p. 78. In this letter of April 9, 1917, Wittgenstein is commenting to Paul Englemann on Uhland's poem »Graf Eberhards Weißdorn.«

identities and differences make endless sport of signs and similitudes; because in it language breaks off its old kinship with things and enters into that lonely sovereignty from which it will reappear in its separated state, only as literature...«.[2] The Knight of La Mancha knows the world as it appears in tales of romance and adventure. He takes up these fictions into his life and imposes them upon the world he inhabits. In seeking to preserve the identities and similitudes that join romance to reality he conceals from himself the true differences between them. The signs and figures that appear in his books no longer – or never did – correspond to any lived experience or any life outside of literature.

Cervantic irony delineates clearly between the imaginary and the real. The imaginary world is that of chivalric romance as reflected in the unhinged mind of the book-bound hidalgo. The real world is that of brute actuality and is reflected especially in the figure of Sancho Panza. Sancho's earth-bound literalness offers to the novel's reader a perspective from which to judge the fantasies of Don Quixote's confused imagination. We see with Sancho the difference between a barber's basin and a knight's helmet, between a Spanish windmill and an evil giant. Broch's Vergil, Musil's Ulrich, and Mann's Zeitblom each perform a similar service. Ulrich and Vergil have minds that are powerful enough to penetrate and critique the fictions and fantasies that confine the feeble imaginations of their contemporaries. These two protagonists are empowered of a profoundly ethical vision that rises to the necessity of discriminating between destructive illusions and authentic human reality. As readers we are permitted to join them in their detached perspective and so enjoy the privilege of knowing what is real and what is not. Similarly, Zeitblom plays a Sancho to Leverkühn's demonic Quixote. With Zeitblom we follow Leverkühn's descent into madness and destruction. Mann, Musil, and Broch offer an ironic perspective immanent to the novel, which maintains for the reader a sense of equilibrium between the real and the imaginary. But the irony of Kafka's narrative world is more frightening than the Cervantic irony of his contemporaries, and his subversion of reality is more complete. His readers must descend with the protagonist into a realm in which madness and sanity seem indistinguishable.

---

[2] Michel Foucault, *The Order of Things. An Archaeology of the Human Sciences* (New York: Vintage Books, 1973), p. 48. Cf. Hegel: »Uns gilt die Kunst nicht mehr als die höchste Weise, in welcher die Wahrheit sich Existenz verschafft« *WW*, 10,1, p. 134.

In Kafka, the reader's point of view and the protagonist's imagination converge in a shared quixotic illusion turned nightmare. There is no Sancho Panza here, which is to say that there is no point of view uncontaminated by the delusions that arrest the imagination of the protagonist. In Josef K.'s world, fiction and reality are made of the same stuff. Kafka has done away with the distinction between fiction – the world of the court – and reality – Josef K.'s quotidian life – and has welded the two into a sinister unity. Reading *Der Prozeß* is like viewing the Spanish plains from the inside of Don Quixote's mind. The Archimedean point of Sancho Panza and his commentary has disappeared. With no firm and incontrovertible sense of what is real, the reader loses his footing in the traditional grounding of interpretation and is as baffled in his confrontation with the novel as Josef K. is in his confrontation with the court.

This chapter reads *Der Prozeß* in a way that attempts to trace the fusion of fiction and reality to its double origin in conscience and language: *in conscience* because the confrontation between Josef K. and the court is a function of the unspoken presence of the consciousness of guilt; and *in language* because Josef K., his personal consciousness, and his whole world are nothing but words, text, ink printed on a page.

The theme of conscience and consciousness pivots on K.'s repeated attempts to interpret the court so as to grasp ›the law‹ that governs its machinations. He searches frantically for a pattern in the scrambled features that make up the surface of the court. He expects that external design will reveal to him an orderly internal structure that lies beneath its visible exterior. K. seeks the law within the court that determines its external appearances. To discover this law would make him the master of the situation and restore to him the sense of reality that was destroyed when the court disrupted the tidiness of his normal life. He continually tries to interpret the signs that outwardly constitute the court, but he always fails to discover the law behind them because he himself – his own conscience – is the authority. The law is not some autonomously existing list of statutes but is instead an integral part of his own being for which he must assume responsibility. K. dies in shame because he is a weakling who persists in concealing from himself this truth.

The theme of language, or more precisely: of fictionality and narrativity, qualifies the purport of the novel in a significant way. K., and with him the novel's reader, never escape the feeling that the court is a monstrous fiction. The world has become unknowable. Its appearances are fiction because they lead to no ›deeper‹ meaning. K. dies like a dog because in his confrontation with the court, with his own guilt, he discovers no truth, no reality, and no order that can endow his life and death with dignity and worth. Literary expression has traditionally been a way of knowing the world and revealing the truth, but if the world has become unknowable – as K.'s experience seems to illustrate – then a shadow falls across the link between the poetic word and true life, and narrative fiction loses its grounding in the traditional values and beliefs that have formed the bedrock underlying the appearances of reality and their representation in prose. Kafka's prose despairs of ›knowing the world‹ in terms of representation and so steps back to a metalevel in order to interrogate the relationship between narrative fiction and represented reality. His novel shifts its vision away from the world as such and refocuses on the autotelic dimension of storytelling, which I will call *narrativity*.

The beginning point of the present commentary on *The Trial* is Kafka's attitude toward the narrativity of writing, the specific place of his novel within the context of this poetics of narrative, and finally the prose realization of his ideas as manifested in a strategy of duplicity in a novel whose signs and similitudes are clear but where meanings seem to hang suspended in a void of undecidability.

I

There is a trend in the recent critical reception of Kafka to situate his work in the context of the wide-spread linguistic skepticism at the beginning of this century.[3] Of particular interest is the work of Walter

---

[3] Beda Allemann, »Wahrheit und Dichtung,« in *Weltgespräch 7*, 2. Folge, hrsg. v. der Arbeitsgemeinschaft Weltgespräch Wien-Freiburg (Wien, Freiburg: Herder, 1969), pp. 32–45; Stanley Corngold, *The Commentator's Despair. The Interpretation of Kafka's »Metamorphosis«* (Port Washington, N.Y.: Kennikat Press, 1973); Hans Reiss, »Franz Kafka,« in his *The Writer's Task from Nietzsche to Brecht* (London: MacMillan, 1978); Walter Sokel, »Kafka's Poetics of the Inner Self,« *Modern Austrian Literature*, 11 (1978), 37–58, and »Language and Truth in the Two Worlds of Franz Kafka,« *German Quarterly*, 52 (1979), 364–84. Cited as Sokel, »Poetics,« and as Sokel, »Language and Truth.« The secondary literature that specifically addresses itself to Kafka's *Prozeß* is as varied as it is extensive, but happily two recent and reliable Forschungsberichte are available. Peter Beicken (1974) offers a useful overview and brief critique of the various trends of criticism and interpretation that have developed around the novel. His account is concise, well organized and annotated, and relatively unbiased in its critical judgment. Theo Elm (1979) offers a review of the literature that is overtly guided by a concept he wishes to promote, namely a ›hermeneutical approach.‹ The present study is in line with Elm's general propositions: the identification of K. with the reader in the ›process‹ of trying to understand the text/court (426–32); and the ethical claims of the novel (432–35). It goes beyond Elm and other similar

Sokel, who has shown that a gradual shift took place in Kafka's narrative »poetics.« In his early phase, Kafka was optimistic about the possibility of achieving in narrative prose a unity between word and world. Many passages from his diary and letters bear witness to this ideal as well as to his frustrated attempts toward realizing it in actual practice. Sokel shows that as Kafka's writing experience progressed he lost faith in the possibility of isomorphy between the poetic expression and the object of its representation. Kafka began to see the poetic utterance itself – the word as mimetic representation – as an obstacle blocking the path of truth. The figurality of language and literature guarantees that the thing represented is always absent, deferred into oblivion by the figure that replaces it.[4] The question of how or whether literature is possible at all is implicit in this skepticism.

Toward the beginning of his activity as a writer, Kafka believed that in states of inspiration or even clairvoyance he was able to pour forth his inner self into a prose form that fittingly embodied it (T, 38f.).[5] In his diary he writes of the »großes Verlangen, meinen ganz bangen Zustand ganz aus mir herauszuschreiben und ebenso wie er aus der Tiefe kommt, in die Tiefe des Papiers hinein, oder es so niederzuschreiben, daß ich das Geschriebene vollständig in mich einbeziehen könnte« (T, 117). It is important to note here that Kafka brackets the empirical world out of consideration and is instead interested in representing his own mental and spiritual experience, the »inner life.«[6] His problem is still one of mimesis, but not in the term's most traditional sense.

studies inasmuch as it tries to identify the hermeneutical function of the novel and narrative in general. Peter U. Beicken, *Franz Kafka. Eine kritische Einführung in die Forschung* (Frankfurt am Main: Fischer Athenäum, 1974), 273–86; *Kafka-Handbuch in zwei Bänden*, hrsg. v. Hartmut Binder (Stuttgart: Kröner, 1979), Bd. II, 420–41.

[4] See Sokel, »Poetics.«

[5] Kafka's writings are cited parenthetically within the text of this chapter. »T« designates the *Tagebücher 1910–1923*, hrsg. v. Max Brod (Frankfurt a.M.: Fischer Taschenbuch Verlag, 1980); »H« designates the *Hochzeitsvorbereitungen auf dem Lande und andere Prosa aus dem Nachlaß*, hrsg. v. Max Brod (Frankfurt a.M.: Fischer Taschenbuch Verlag, 1980); »SE« designates the *Sämtliche Erzählungen*, hrsg. v. Paul Raabe (Hamburg: S. Fischer, 1970); and page numbers without a letter refer to *Der Prozeß. Roman*, hrsg. v. Max Brod (Frankfurt a.M.: Fischer Taschenbuch Verlag, 1980).

[6] Friedrich Beißner's influential views have raised to the level of a truism the notion that Kafka's basic aim was always to give form to his inner life: *Der Erzähler Franz Kafka* (Stuttgart: Kohlhammer, 1952); *Der Schacht von Babel. Aus Kafkas Tagebüchern* (Stuttgart: Kohlhammer, 1963); *Kafka der Dichter* (Stuttgart: Kohlhammer, 1958); *Kafkas Darstellung des »traumhaften inneren Lebens«* (Bebenhausen: L. Rotsch, 1972). Sokel's article does not mention Beißner, but it nevertheless implies an important revision of what has become something of a critical dogma. Sokel himself in his earlier book *Franz*

In Kafka's version of mimesis the object of representation is not an empirical thing or event. It is instead what he described as the »ungeheure Welt« in his own mind (T, 192). Kafka's narrative addresses this inner life and in so doing denies its accustomed obligation to the things of the real world. In daily usage, language names things and orders the material world, but its semantics are at no point adequate to denominate and make systematic the individuality and non-material condition of the inner life. In order to conjure this ghostly realm into visibility, Kafka adopts a narrative strategy of figurality. Since Kafka's ideal during this phase was perfect continuity between his inner world and its external representation, his narrative strategy is best described as »symbolic.«

Kafka judged the short narrative *Das Urteil* to be his most successful attempt at rendering his inner life into an intelligible form. He composed it in a single, inspired sitting throughout the night of 22–23 September in 1912. »*Nur so* kann geschrieben werden,« he wrote in his diary with enthusiasm and satisfaction, »nur in einem solchen Zusammenhang, mit solcher vollständigen Öffnung des Leibes und der Seele« (T, 184). Yet he was not able to repeat his success. Aside from the various external circumstances that hindered his productivity – i.e. the opposition of his parents, the demands of his job, wretchedly unhappy romances, and his perpetual self-doubts – Kafka came to believe that language itself is an intrinsically flawed medium and unequal to the task he had assigned to it. The symbolic or allusive representation of truth in words becomes not only practically but also theoretically impossible.

The signs and figures of fiction emerged for Kafka into what Foucault called the »lonely sovereignty« of literature. The bond of representation between narrative expression and lived reality had dissolved. A late diary passage, from 6 December 1921, reveals the specific character of Kafka's changed attitude toward the once hoped-for unity between narrative figure and represented object:

Aus einem Brief: ›Ich wärme mich daran in diesem traurigen Winter.‹ Die Metaphern sind eines in dem vielen, was mich am Schreiben verzweifeln läßt. Die Unselbständigkeit des Schreibens, die Abhängigkeit von dem Dienstmädchen, das einheizt, von der Katze, die sich am Ofen wärmt, selbst vom armen alten Menschen, der sich wärmt. Alles dies sind selbständige,

---

Kafka – Tragik und Ironie. Zur Struktur seiner Kunst (München, Wien: A. Langen, G. Müller, 1964) had supported a similar hypothesis. On page 9 he postulates that this representation of the inner life is one of three fundamental principles in Kafka's writing. His article on Kafka's narrative poetics is thus a re-evaluation of the artist's ideas and intentions, and their limitations.

eigengesetzliche Verrichtungen, nur das Schreiben ist hilflos, wohnt nicht in sich selbst, ist Spaß und Verzweiflung. (T, 343)

It is here that Kafka comes nearest to Hofmannsthal's famous Chandos Letter. They share the notion that language gives no access to the immediacy, the fullness, and the deep silence of true being. By 1921 Kafka's confidence in the unity of narrative and narrated object had broken down. He no longer saw figurality as the vehicle of transcendence but instead as an ineluctably crippling debility that reduces literary expression to *Spaß* and *Verzweiflung*.

It is easy enough to see why the novelist regarded writing as the cause of despair. Since poetic utterance is necessarily imprisoned in its own figurality it can never assimilate to the true being of that which it wishes to represent. Its mimetic claim becomes the desperate pursuit of a hopelessly elusive object. Yet while the origin of Kafka's despair is self-evident, it comes as a surprise that he couples it with »fun.« This unlikely combination demands clarification. The unexpected presence of fun alongside despair is perhaps reminiscent of the surprise many readers have experienced in learning that Kafka broke down in laughter while reading aloud to friends from *Der Prozeß*.[7] Evidently the despair presented in that novel was also bound up with some kind of fun for Kafka.

His despair over the impotence of the written word, his fun with it, and his amusement at *Der Prozeß* are interrelated. The cause of his despair – the failure of representation to be a reliable double for or index to the truth – opens up to him the opportunity of having fun by playing ironic games with the figural status of fictional discourse, its narrativity. These ironic games will be elucidated at the example of *Der Prozeß* in the following section of this chapter. But before turning to the fun and despair in that novel, it is necessary to make clear some ground rules of irony that are at work in Kafka's game.

In a late diary passage, in fact in its very last entry, Kafka touches once again on his »Spaß und Verzweiflung,« only now despair is very much in the foreground and fun appears in its formal aspect, as irony.

Immer ängstlicher im Niederschreiben. Es ist begreiflich. Jedes Wort, gewendet in der Hand der Geister – dieser Schwung der Hand ist ihre charakteri-

---

[7] Max Brod reports that while reading the first chapter aloud to friends, Kafka was so tickled that he could not even continue reading for a while. *Franz Kafka. Eine Biographie*, 3. erw. Aufl. (Berlin, Frankfurt a.M.: S. Fischer, 1954), p. 217. On Kafka's sense of humor see Gerhard Neumann's comments and helpful bibliography in »Umkehrung und Ablenkung: Franz Kafkas ›Gleitendes Paradox,‹« *DVjs*, 42 (1968), 740–44.

stische Bewegung – , wird zum Spieß, gekehrt gegen den Sprecher. Eine Bemerkung wie diese ganz besonders. Und so ins Unendliche. Der Trost wäre
nur: es geschieht, ob du willst oder nicht. Und was du willst, hilft nur un-
merklich wenig. Mehr als Trost ist: auch du hast Waffen. (T, 365)

This final statement is an especially powerful avowal of Kafka's retreat
from his earlier confidence in the possibility of accurate representation
in literature. He now characterizes words as treacherous deceivers that
turn against the hand that creates them. The »Spirits« guide the stroke
of this hand – Kafka's own as it makes the diary entry – and the words,
which not he but these anonymous Spirits command, rebel against him.
The poetic word does not have the power of the symbol, namely to join
together in a unitary whole the »monstrously uncanny« world inside
Kafka's head with its literary representation. Yet he takes consolation
from a certain thought: »You too have weapons.«

If the unity to which he aspired was not possible, why did Kafka
continue to write? If truth has receded from the grasp of language, then
what is the good of writing, for instance, that truth is inaccessible (»Eine
Bemerkung wie diese ganz besonders«)? Kafka's ironic formulation is
an implicit answer to the question it raises. This response to the crisis of
representation becomes explicit in the words of the philosophical
hound of the late narrative *Forschungen eines Hundes*. In regard to the
possible results of his investigations he postulates: »Und es zeigt sich
dabei nicht die Wahrheit – niemals wird man so weit kommen – , aber
doch etwas von der tiefen Verwirrung der Lüge« (SE, 386). A *lie* is the
specifically linguistic form of untruth and as such is the writer's most
formidable obstacle in the pursuit of knowledge in and through literature. No longer does Kafka seek to embody truth symbolically in narrative. His new strategy is to undo the lies and deceptions of language
and narrative by turning words ironically against themselves. In this
way narrative points not toward some absolute meaning but toward
itself as the purveyor of *Spaß* and *Verzweiflung*.[8] Narrative is not an
open door to the truth, and words are not transparent. They have instead turned out to be opaque objects in the world among its other
opaque objects.

---

[8] In a similar vein Theo Elm suggests that Kafka puts an end to the Enlighten-
ment metaphysics of signification by turning its favored form of expression,
the parable, against itself. This thesis, similar to mine here, is that Kafka's
short prose does not figuratively refer to a ›transcendental‹ meaning but instead enacts the inaccessibility of such meaning. Theo Elm, »Problematisierte
Hermeneutik. Zur ›Uneigentlichkeit‹ in Kafkas kleiner Prosa,« *DVjs*, 50
(1976), esp. 495, 479f., and 498.

101

Before opening up a discussion of Kafka's ironic duplicity in *Der Prozeß*, it will be worthwhile to consider briefly certain relevant features of Kafkan prose. The economy of his unpretentious style testifies to Kafka's distaste for confectionery affectation in narrative. This lucidity of form stands in contradiction to the level of ›meaning‹ in his stories. The contradiction is Kafka's self-conscious tactic. The opaque surfaces of Kafkan narrative serve to make visible the disparity between verbal signs and the things they seem to represent.[9] They do so by calling attention to signs themselves as material things. The seductive intelligibility and simplicity of Kafka's language, the uncomplicated common sense of his diction and syntax, and the seeming ingenuousness of his narrative structure appear to hold the promise of an equally rational and well ordered fictional world. Kafka intentionally and relentlessly thwarts this expectation. The remarkably unsettling effect of his storytelling is due in large part to this unexpected rift between the unambiguous coherence of his language and the uncanny ambiguity of the narrative whole.

The purport of his language would seem to overlap with that of the realist tradition. Kafka's meticulous attention to accuracy of detail and his admiration for prose that is evocative of lived reality testify to a certain shared intention between Kafka and his nineteenth-century precursors such as Dickens and Flaubert. Yet beyond the obvious difference in Kafka's subject matter as opposed to that of the realists, there remains a distinction that is not often enough observed. Realist prose offers an illusion that is ›true to life‹ because its language appears

---

[9] In this regard see Roman Jakobson, who postulates a »poetic mode« of language that he characterizes as the point in linguistic discourse at which the referential function is de-emphasized so as to »focus on the message for its own sake.« »Poetic function is not the sole function of verbal art, but only its dominant determining function, whereas in all other verbal activities it acts as a subsidiary, accessory constituent. This function, by promoting the palpability of signs, deepens the fundamental dichotomy of signs and objects.« Roman Jakobson, »Closing Statement: Linguistics and Poetics,« in *Style in Language*, ed. Thomas A. Sebeok (Cambridge, Mass.: MIT Press, 1960), p. 356. Cf. also Tvetan Todorov: »La seule qualité commune à toutes les figures rhétoriques est . . . leur opacité, c'est-à-dire leur tendance à nous faire percevoir le discours lui-même et non seulement sa signification. Le langage figuré est un langage qui tend vers l'opacité ou, en bref, un langage opaque. Mais alors une contradiction semble se dessiner: d'une part, la function du langage figuré est de rendre présent le discours lui-même; de l'autre, nous savons que le langage littéraire est destiné à nous rendre présents les choses decrites et non le discours lui-même. Comment se fait-il alors que le langage figuré soit le matériau préféré de la poésie?« *Littérature et Signification* (Paris: Larousse, 1967), pp. 116f.

102

to be bound intrinsically to the places, events, and things of the real world. It is writing that seems to be at one with that which it represents. Kafka's style exploits the conventional illusionism that is so firmly entrenched in the reading habits of the realist novel's popular audience. He turns this convention against itself by using the language of the real to invent an impossibly irreal world. In this way Kafka parodies the representational conventions of realism.[10]

Realist prose, grounded in the habitudes of daily and communal speech, disguises itself as the language of reference, as an accurate representation of some plausible state of affairs in the real world. The ideal writer of realist prose is confident in the power of language to mirror the truth of things. He feigns objectivity by effacing the traces of artifice that go into the making of fiction. For him to expose the narrative as a product of contrivance would imply its fallibility and subvert its claim to be a responsible instrument of knowledge. This claim to knowledge is, in turn, the idea that literary mimesis is an isomorphic doubling of the world into words. At bottom, the mimetic project to limn external reality and the earlier Kafkan project to give narrative form to the world inside his head do not differ fundamentally. Each undertaking is mimetic in the term's popularly conceived sense inasmuch as each attempts to represent in narrative an independently existing, extralinguistic reality. In one case it is external reality, and in the other case it is inward reality. Despite important differences, the two aims coincide at a deep level of representational strategy where they are rooted in the common ground of »symbolic« expression, if we understand symbolic as the notion that poetic word and represented world – no matter whether inner or outer – can and do fuse together in unity and coherence. The extraordinary inwardness of Kafka's prose is

---

[10] Kafka's tactic in prose is similar to that of Lewis Carroll's nonsense poetry. When Carroll writes: ›Twas bryllyg, and the slythy toves / Did gyre and gimble in the wabe:/ All mimsy were the borogroves;/ And the mome raths outgrabe.‹ his reader is surprised and amused at how little and how much sense the stanza simultaneously generates. The words, sustained semantically by the framework of the well-known English ballad tradition, resonate with familiarity yet remain lexically out of reach. The familiarity of the ballad form itself – its characteristic diction, cadences, rhyme, and substance – awakens a set of expectations that the reader contributes to the poem's ›meaning.‹ Kafka's prose more subtly relies on corresponding subliminal expectations from the novel tradition: conventions of characterization, personal psychology, plot development, and cause-and-effect relations all belong to the expectations that we are liable to impose on a novel being read. Cf. Eugenio Coseriu, *Textlinguistik. Eine Einführung*, hrsg. v. Jörn Albrecht, Tübinger Beiträge zur Linguistik, 109 (Tübingen: Gunter Narr, 1980), on Kafka pp. 128–32.

certainly a hallmark of his style and of modernism in general, but its prominence should not be allowed to obscure his shift from mimetic figurality to ironic self-reflexivity. A growing linguistic skepticism undermined his confidence in the possiblity of accurate narrative representation to such an extent that his former ideal became not only practically but also theoretically impossible.

Kafka's revised concept of narrative abandons the possibility of the flesh becoming word and takes up a mode of irony that exposes the artifice and fallibility of storytelling. He seizes the language of realism and turns it against itself. The fantastic irreality of his tales militates against the apparent referentiality of the language by foregrounding their condition of literariness, their narrativity. Kafka's aim is no longer to pour forth his inner self into symbolic signs and figures. He begins instead to probe the disturbed relationship between reality and literary expression, to show how the seemingly transparent language of realism congeals into an impenetrably dense verbal surface that calls attention to itself and shows itself in the true form of its separated state, as mere literature, as »Spaß und Verzweiflung.«

II

Der Prozeß is an interesting case in point because it is a work from the middle period of Kafka's writing and demarcates his turn toward self-reflexive irony. He started composing the novel in August of 1914 and eventually abandoned his efforts around the beginning of 1915.[11] As he was beginning the project he expressed in a diary entry the fear that his ability to represent his »dreamlike inner life« may have left him forever (T, 262). This concern makes explicit his continued ambition to pour forth into symbolic narrative an unmediated vision of his inner self and thereby achieve a full unity of art and truth.

On the 18th of December, or about the time the novel was nearing its inconclusive end, Kafka made a startling diary entry that is in effect a recantation of his former ideal of representation. He recounts a con-

---

[11] Binder judges that Kafka must have begun writing *Der Prozeß* in the second week of August. He dates the termination of Kafka's efforts somewhere between late December and mid-January, 1915. He estimates that the final chapter, K.'s death scene, must have been written in this same short span between December and January. Hartmut Binder, *Kafka-Kommentar zu den Romanen, Rezensionen, Aphorismen und zum Brief an den Vater* (München: Winkler, 1976), pp. 161, 182.

versation in which he assures Max Brod that he – Kafka – will be able
to lie on his deathbed with satisfaction:

Ich vergaß hinzuzufügen und habe es später mit Absicht unterlassen, daß das
Beste, was ich geschrieben habe, in dieser Fähigkeit, zufrieden sterben zu
können, seinen Grund hat. An allen diesen guten und stark überzeugenden
Stellen handelt es sich immer darum, daß jemand stirbt, daß es ihm sehr
schwer wird, daß darin für ihn ein Unrecht und wenigstens eine Härte liegt
und daß das für den Leser, wenigstens meiner Meinung nach, rührend wird.
Für mich aber, der ich glaube, auf dem Sterbebett zufrieden sein zu können,
sind solche Schilderungen im geheimen ein Spiel, ich freue mich ja in dem
Sterbenden zu sterben, nütze daher mit Berechnung die auf den Tod gesammelte Aufmerksamkeit des Lesers aus, bin bei viel klarerem Verstande als er,
von dem ich annehme, daß er auf dem Sterbebett klagen wird, und meine
Klage ist daher möglichst vollkommen, bricht auch nicht etwa plötzlich ab
wie wirkliche Klage, sondern verläuft schön und rein. Es ist so, wie ich der
Mutter gegenüber immer über Leiden mich beklag[t]e, die bei weitem nicht so
groß waren, wie die Klage glauben ließ. Gegenüber der Mutter brauchte ich
allerdings nicht so viel Kunstaufwand wie gegenüber dem Leser. (T, 279)

Sokel has also singled out this passage as evidence for Kafka's changed
attitude toward writing.[12] No longer does Kafka see the strength of his
narrative in terms of filling every word with himself (T, 24f) or of
giving to his »dreamlike inner life« its commensurate literary form.

His writing has now become an exercise in controlled duplicity. This
crucial shift has occurred precisely during the period in which he was
composing *Der Prozeß*. Even though this passage makes no mention of
the novel, one of the death scenes to which he refers must be that of
Josef K.

---

[12] »Such artful deceit and clever contriving for aesthetic effect, while attesting
to Kafka's subtle mastery of the art of fiction, glaringly contradict his ideal of
the writer's absolute faithfulness to and unity with the feeling permeating his
work and embodied in his character. The bifurcation of perspectives of author and character, and thus of author and reader gives the lie to the presence
of the writer's ›truth‹ in his text.« Sokel, »Poetics,« p. 52. For a related view
see Peter Beicken, »*Berechnung* und *Kunstaufwand* in Kafka's Erzählrheto-
rik« in *Franz Kafka*, Eine Aufsatzsammlung nach einem Symposium in Philadelphia, hrsg. u. eingel. v. Marie Luise Caputo-Mayr, Schriftenreihe Agora,
29 (Berlin, Darmstadt: Agora, 1978), 216–34; and »Kafka's Narrative Rhetoric,« *Journal of Modern Literature*, 6 (1977), 398–409. Beicken's reading of
this passage is in my estimation off the mark because he applies it to both late
and early works. Horst Turk's Lacanian reading of *Der Prozeß* also limits its
findings by regarding the novel too much in terms of Kafka's personal subjectivity. See H.T., »»betrügen . . . ohne Betrug‹. Das Problem der literari-
schen Legitimation am Beispiel Kafkas,« in *Urszenen, Literaturwissenschaft
als Diskursanalyse und Diskurskritik*, hrsg. von Friedrich A. Kittler u. Horst
Turk (Frankfurt am Main: Suhrkamp, 1977), 381–407.

On the 6th of August Kafka doubted his ability to achieve the yearned-for symbolic unity in the work ahead of him; on the 19th of December, toward the end of his frustrated work on the novel fragment, he claims to find his fullest literary satisfaction not in perfect oneness but in cunning duplicity. He exploits »mit Berechnung« his readers' habit of projecting themselves into the protagonist. This deceit is for him »im geheimen ein Spiel.« This calculated playfulness recalls the »fun« in his »despair.« But the game he is playing is not trivial. A stray aphorism helps to understand precisely the character of Kafka's interest in duplicity:

> Geständnis und Lüge ist das Gleiche. Um gestehen zu können, lügt man. Das, was man ist, kann man nicht ausdrücken, denn dieses ist man eben; mitteilen kann man nur das, was man nicht ist, also die Lüge. (H, 249)[13]

Kafka develops this dialectic of *Geständnis* and *Lüge* in the structure of *Der Prozeß.* He embeds into the novel a series of »mirrors,« as it were, that reflect the fictional status of the narrative. These self-reflexive, metafictional devices are the playful vehicle of *Geständnis* because they confess to the reader that the novel's signs, figures, and images are mere fictions – *Lüge.* These mirrors of narrativity are representations – paintings, descriptions, scenarios and, especially, the prison chaplain's parable of the law – that Kafka nests into the text of the novel, which is itself a representation. K.'s confrontation with the court is identical with his attempt to decipher these representations. He takes them to be manifestations of the court's inner law and assumes that these surface features are continuous with the truth that lies beneath and beyond them. He always fails because the law always eludes the categories he tries to impose on it.

K.'s problem as a seeker of the law is analogous to Kafka's problem as a writer and the reader's problem as an interpreter.[14] From all three points of view, representation has become something that is autonomous. It has lost its traditional tie to the truth that it is supposed to embody or re-present. Kafka's comments on the despair of writing, Josef K.'s experience with his court, and the reader's vain attempts to wrest some kind of objective meaning from the novel all point toward

---

[13] »Wahrheit ist unteilbar, kann sich also selbst nicht erkennen; wer sie erkennen will, muß Lüge sein« (H, p. 36, No. 80). »Kannst du denn etwas anderes kennen als Betrug? Wird einmal der Betrug vernichtet, darfst du ja nicht hinsehen oder wirst zur Salzsäule« (H. p. 40, No. 106; cf. also H. pp. 53, 69, 73).

[14] For parallels between K. and the reader see esp. Theo Elm, »Der Prozeß,« pp. 426–32.

the aporia of literature as represented reality. The rift between narrative representation and the putative *object* of representation means a crisis of narrative art. Yet the failure of representation – or more precisely, the awareness of its inherent limitations – need not mean the failure of art itself.

Kafka's disclosure of the rupture between truth and representation is simultaneously the opening up of a space from which something else can emerge. Narrative signals this event by means of a poetic articulation. This articulation is neither a representation nor objectification of that which it addresses. Instead it is something more along the order of a gesture or a hint that intimates the presence of this emergent truth. »Articulation,« »gesture,« and »hint« are not very felicitous designations for what happens, but they are probably no worse than Kafka's own descriptions of the situation in his »Oktavheft« of 1917:

> Die Sprache kann für alles außerhalb der sinnlichen Welt nur andeutungsweise, aber niemals auch nur annähernd vergleichsweise gebraucht werden, da sie, entsprechend der sinnlichen Welt, nur vom Besitz und seinen Beziehungen handelt. (H, 34, No. 57)

The linguistic-philosophical context of this comment is a view of ordinary language that authorizes a speaker to call the things of the empirical world by their conventional names. The word »book« *belongs* properly to its empirical signandum. It is a system of communication geared to passing along facts and information. But there are no signs that belong to that which is not part of the sensory world. Traditionally, figural language has been called upon to render the spiritual half of being. It is startling that Kafka rejects even this means: language can never be used, not even approximately, in the manner of a metaphor or simile – i.e. *vergleichsweise* – for whatever is not sensory. Yet the disqualification of literal and figurative language does not entirely preclude approaching the spiritual through the medium of language. Kafka suggests the obscure third possiblity of using language *andeutungsweise*, as hint, gesture, intimation, or articulation.

If Kafka is to be taken at his word, then his emphatic rejection of figural representation as an adequate means for giving form to the spiritual has important implications for the reading of his works. Symbol and allegory, metaphor and metonymy suddenly collapse together as representational strategies for naming the ›other‹; as tropes they all function *vergleichsweise* in one way or another. Kafka is suggesting that this ›other‹ cannot be named or represented at all. The alternative that he offers is *Andeutung*, a vague term that resists precise translation. The sense of his proposition is that language can imply or indicate the

107

presence of a thing or event for which there exists no proper name and no basis for linguistic comparison. In remaining true to this insight Kafka honors the limits of representation. Poetic utterance becomes a gesture, an articulation that encircles some unmapped territory of being in order to reveal its presence only as a rent place in the fabric of language and narrative. The embrace of poetic language does not violate the integrity of the silence whose dark contours it presses against. Kafka gives this thought its finest expression in *Josefine, die Sängerin oder das Volk der Mäuse*. The story's narrator discloses the heart of the matter with this subtly profound query: »Ist es ihr Gesang, der uns so entzückt oder nicht vielmehr die feierliche Stille, von der die schwache Stimme umgeben ist?« (SE, 196).

The relation of song to silence, of narrative to ›other‹ is similar in Kafka's *Prozeß*. Its irony makes sport of the signs and similitudes that seem to promise K. a way of grasping the law or defeating the court. Yet the grotesquely comical despair of K.'s situation is fraught with the gesture that articulates the novel's true purport: conscience. Conscience is not a thing that can be represented, yet it emerges from the seeming void that appears when representation and ›objective truth‹ cleave and drift apart.

In his study of Kafka, Heinz Politzer struck very near the distinction between representation and articulation that I am trying to draw here. He compares Kafka's reserved silence with Franz Werfel's promiscuous metaphorizing. In a poem called »Schlaf und Erwachen« Werfel attempts to represent the modern experience of fear and isolation. Politzer points out that it is similar in its themes and tonalities to the general tendencies of Kafka's work. Yet a decisive difference separates the two artists. Werfel gives to this experience a name; he calls it a »Gottesfinsternis.« By Kafkan standards he has said too much. He has reduced an ineffable enormity down to a manageable size, made it to seem less terrible than it is, and offended precincts best treated in observance of what Hofmannsthal once referred to as the »Anstand des Schweigens.«[15]

Kafka, notes Politzer, »bildete diese Finsternis in Schweigen.«[16] Kafka does not try to represent the unrepresentable. Rather than violate the stillness of its presence he attempts to draw our attention to it by means of subtle indirections. Politzer elaborates:

---

[15] In his »Ad me ipsum.« Hugo von Hofmannsthal, *Reden und Aufsätze III 1925-1929, Buch der Freunde, Aufzeichnungen 1889-1929*, hrsg. v. Bernd Schoeller und Ingeborg Beyer-Ahlert in Beratung mit Rudolf Hirsch (Frankfurt a.M.: Fischer Taschenbuch Verlag, 1980), p. 601. Cited as Hofmannsthal.
[16] Heinz Politzer, *Franz Kafka, der Künstler* (w.p.: S. Fischer, 1965), p. 42. Werfel's poem is quoted in full on p. 41 of Politzer's book. Cited as Politzer.

In eindrucksvolle Bilder gebannt, entlädt sich diese Spannung zwischen dem Einzelnen und dem All plötzlich, wobei dem Leser seine eigene Situation und die des Menschen schlechthin blitzartig erhellt wird. So verraten diese Bilder ein Unaussprechliches, ohne es doch auszusprechen. Ludwig Wittgenstein mag ähnliche Erfahrungen im Sinne gehabt haben, als er in seinem *Tractatus Logico-Philosophicus* anmerkte: »Es gibt allerdings Unaussprechliches. Dies *zeigt* sich, es ist das Mystische.« Wittgenstein selbst unterstrich das Wort »zeigt,« wohl um seinen Lesern aufs nachdrücklichste vor Augen zu führen, daß das Geheimnis erscheinen könne, ohne sich der Logik und Grammatik zusammenhängender Sprechweisen unterwerfen zu müssen.[17]

Politzer's point is well taken. It helps to elucidate what is at work in the narrative of *Der Prozeß*. Kafka articulates the presence and power of conscience as it pervades and suffuses the narrative from which it a-rises. He provides it with a space in which it can show itself.[18]

Der Prozeß defines with its irony the limits of the concept of representation and at the same time articulates by a *via negativa* the dimension of conscience.

The visible circumstances of Josef K.'s story is first of all the unexpected confrontation of two worlds. K. finds himself caught between two apparently irreconcilable realities. The first is his workaday world, with its regular banking hours, evenings at the usual *Bierstube* with the usual fellows. The president of the bank in which K. is an officer thinks highly of him, but there is also an ill-concealed hostility and competition between K. and his immediate superior. The local district attorney is K.'s special friend and is representative of the class of people with whom K. would like to be associated. He is a bachelor with no close ladyfriend, but he does regularly – and apparently rather dispassionately – satisfy his libidinal urges on weekly visits to a certain waitress he knows. The upshot of these mundane details is that Josef K. comes across as a sturdy up-and-coming young businessman, perhaps efficient in professional life but with a personal life that is dull and stunted. He

---

[17] Politzer, 37.

[18] On many other points I am at odds with Politzer. In his comparison of Kafka with Werfel, Politzer goes on to suggest that the only insight Kafka was ever able to establish was that the incomprehensible is incomprehensible: »Was er dem Schweigen und der Finsternis, die um ihn wuchsen, entrang, war lediglich die Einsicht, ›daß das Unfaßbare unfaßbar ist, und das haben wir gewußt‹« (p. 42). I disagree with this orthodox reading of Kafka. In stressing the nonobjective, ethical dimension of *Der Prozeß*, the present study is trying to find a way out of the aporia that Kafka criticism has talked itself into. A provocative study that is in this and other regards similar to mine, and which appeared after I completed my manuscript is Susanne Kessler, *Kafka – Poetik der sinnlichen Welt. Strukturen sprachkritischen Erzählens*, Germanistische Abhandlungen, 53 (Stuttgart: Metzler, 1983), esp. 53–126.

has no binding emotional ties to any men or women, and he professes no religious convictions or intellectual commitments. His humdrum life lacks depth yet he is for all appearances satisfied with himself because his external circumstances, like his bedroom, are »in großer Ordnung« (10).

But on the morning of K.'s thirtieth birthday he awakens to the presence of something unprecedented and unexpected: »Die Köchin der Frau Grubach, seiner Zimmervermieterin, die ihm jeden Tag gegen acht Uhr das Frühstück brachte, kam diesmal nicht. Das war noch niemals geschehen« (7). In her place is an unknown intruder who informs him that he is under arrest. Another reality, that of the inexplicable court, has breached the orderly continuity of K.'s everyday life.

The average reality of Josef K. is directed toward his material wellbeing. It hinges on earning money, getting ahead in business, knowing the right people, and satisfying his need for companionship at its most uncomplicated and least rewarding level. Everything that happens to him in this world is familiar and predictable. The new reality is unfamiliar and unpredictable. It is the world of a court that, strangely, has gone unnoticed during all of the protagonist's thirty years.

One of Kafka's best readers, Ingeborg Henel, has perceptively noted that it is typical of Kafka that the protagonist's counterworld – in this case K.'s court – is to be understood as a projection of the protagonist himself.[19] K.'s awakening, which coincides with the appearance of the court, marks the beginnning of a conflict that reveals the unspoken presence of conscience.

It is Kafka's irony that grounds the possiblity for conscience to present itself. A jotting from Goethe's diary describes the technical situation with exemplary lucidity:

Betrachtung über den Reflex von oben oder außen gegen das Untere und Innere der Dichtkunst, z. E. die Götter im Homer nur ein Reflex der Helden; so in den Religionen die anthropomorphistischen Reflexe auf unzählige Weise. Doppelte Welt, die daraus entsteht . . . .[20]

Josef K. inhabits just such a double world, and Goethe's observation provides a way of opening it up. Goethe offers two distinct mechanisms of reflection: 1) from above toward below, and 2) from the outside

---

[19] Ingeborg Henel, »Die Deutbarkeit von Kafkas Werken,« *Zeitschrift für deutsche Philologie*, 86 (1967), 256, 262. Cf. also Wilhelm Emrich, *Franz Kafka* (Bonn: Athenäum, 1958), pp. 264–65. Cited as Emrich.

[20] Johann Wolfgang von Goethe, *Tagebücher I*, Vol. 11 of his *Schriften in 22 Bänden*, II. Abt. (Schriften), hrsg. v. Gerhart Baumann (Stuttgart: Cotta, no date), 858. Entry of November 16, 1808. Cf. Hofmannsthal, 614.

toward the inside. In Kafka's *Prozeß* both directions of reflection are present. The court »above« reflects K. »below,« in the same way that the Olympian gods reflect the Homeric heroes. Both the »above« and the »below« occur within the given framework of the fictional world. The second possibility is that of irony. It is the reflection of reality outside of the fictional world on the inside of the narrative. Kafka achieves this end by reflecting in his novel the narrativity of Josef K.'s existence. Let me illustrate both of these modes of reflection in more detail.

Within the framework of the fictional world K. and the court reflect one another mutually. The court and the figures associated with it constitute the ramified images of K. and his normal life. A simple example for this phenomenon is the perniciously accomodating women of the court, especially Leni. They reflect his thwarted desire for Fräulein Bürstner. Taken together, the scenes and figures of the court comprise an elaborate double for K.'s hopes, fears, desires, and bad conscience. There are many signs that point toward the fundamental unity of K. and court. After his »awakening« and arrest K. bites into a breakfast apple that is so obvious an allusion as to border on parody. He has eaten of the tree of knowledge and knows the difference between good and evil. In spite of his protestations to the contrary, K. knows that he is guilty, and he knows that the trial is *his* trial in a radical sense. Yet he refuses to admit to himself that his own conce is the final authority in his confrontation with the court.

A good deal of the novel is invested in unmasking the complexities of K.'s self-deception. For instance, after the warders arrest him he watches carefully to see if they will remember to make him take »the bath« before his preliminary hearing. K. is secretly delighted when they »forget« to do so (14). Of course K. has no way of knowing that any ceremonial bath is part of official procedure, which means that if any bath is actually prescribed by the court it is only because K. himself says it is. Similarly, it is under the authority of K.'s accusation that the court punishes Willem and Franz for petty offenses committed during K.'s arrest. K.'s half-conscious desire to be revenged on them finds fulfillment in the whipping scene in the storeroom of his bank. When Franz's cries of pain and fear attract attention, K. offers to co-workers the comically weak explanation that they should pay no attention because the noise is only a dog »shrieking« in the courtyard: »es schreit nur ein Hund auf dem Hof« (77). The ›shrieking dog‹ image anticipates Block's doglike groveling to Huld as well as the novel's final scene in which K. will die »like a dog.« The return of this image serves to underscore the ultimately shared identity of K.'s own will with the deeds of the court.

There are other indications of this shared identity. When K. is lost among the tenement staircases while looking for the court's assembling place, he recalls »den Ausspruch des Wächters Willem, daß das Gericht von der Schuld angezogen werde, woraus eigentlich folgte, daß das Untersuchungszimmer an der Treppe liegen mußte, die K. zufällig wählte« (35). And so it does. During his hearing he insists that the proceedings against him exist only if he authorizes them: »es ist nur ein Verfahren, wenn ich es als solches anerkenne« (39). Again he is right and proves it by conscientiously and without prompting from the court always returning to attend to his trial. His arrest hinders him in no way from his daily activities and no hearings are forced on him. He returns again and again because he wants to. The prison chaplain emphatically points out to him that the court receives him only when he comes to it himself and it leaves him alone when he chooses to ignore it. K. can no more ignore the court than anyone else can ignore a bad conscience.

It has become a commonplace of Kafka criticism to note that the protagonist's perspective determines the reader's perspective and that the protagonist's subjectivity is at the center of the narrative's fictive reality.[21] It has seemed to most critics that individual consciousness dominates the shape of reality in Kafka's works, and there is surely a good deal of truth to this view. On the other hand, what Goethe has called the reflection of reality from the outside toward the inside of the fiction also has a bearing on the matter that has not as yet been reckoned with. Kafka's narrative irony takes reality a step further than consciousness. It reveals the stuff of which K., his alleged consciousness, and the whole novel are made: narrative fiction. This point returns us to the question of Kafka's controlled duplicity and to his oblique »Geständnis« that all fiction is »Lüge,« a simultaneous exercise in »Spaß und Verzweiflung.«

Kafka's confessional fun begins with K.'s arrest in his bedroom and the subsequent hearing in Fräulein Bürstner's bedroom. While K. is still waiting in his bed for breakfast, he notices that the old woman in

---

[21] It was Beißner who originally delineated this phenomenon and dubbed it »Einsinnigkeit.« Friedrich Beißner, Der Erzähler Franz Kafka (Stuttgart: Kohlhammer, 1952), pp. 21 ff. It has subsequently been picked up, modified and refined by various other critics. See esp. Martin Walser, Beschreibung einer Form. Versuch über Franz Kafka (München: Hanser, 1961); Winfried Kudszus, »Erzählperspektive und Erzählgeschehen in Kafkas Prozeß,« Deutsche Vierteljahrschrift 44 (1970), 306–317; Jörgen Kobs, Kafka. Untersuchungen zu Bewußtsein und Sprache seiner Gestalten, hrsg. v. Ursula Brech (Bad Homburg: Athenäum, 1970); for a critique see Peter U. Beicken, »Erzählweise,« in the Kafka-Handbuch in zwei Bänden, hrsg. v. Hartmut Binder, II (Stuttgart: Kröner, 1979), 36–45.

the apartment across the street is watching him with unusual interest. Before long she has pulled an old man to her side, and with the arrival of a third, younger man, K. begins to feel himself the object of unwarranted public attention. These voyeurs follow the action of the drama unfolding in Frau Grubach's boarding house from K.'s room into the living room and on into Fräulein Bürstner's bedroom. K. himself voices the metaphor that the proceedings around him are a »Komödie« (10) and that the »Zuschauer« (17) peeping at him through the windows give to the scene an air of theatricality and to him a feeling of being put on show, being placed to »Schaustellung« (12).[22]

The suspicion that Kafka possibly intends for this scenario to be taken ironically, or at least that he does so himself, gains plausibility during the hearing scene. The court has commandeered Fräulein Bürstner's room in her absence for its own purposes. The »Aufseher« sits at her nightstand, which he has moved into the center of the room. It is supposed to represent a »Verhandlungstisch.« On its top are some miscellaneous objects: a book, a pin cushion, and a candle with a box of matches. As he interrogates K., the inspector is strangely absorbed in arranging these objects on the tabletop. He sets the candle into the center of the table and carefully groups the other objects around it. His preoccupation with this private game is inexplicable both to K. and to the novel's reader. But an eye for irony suggests a possible significance for this apparently aimless fidgeting.

It is not a hearing that is being held, but the representation of a hearing. The court is only a bedroom, and the tribunal table is only a working girl's nightstand. Across the way an eager audience watches the scene as if it were a theatrical performance. The top of the table represents the scene in miniature. The candle stands in the middle of the table as K. stands in the middle of the room. Grouped around this candle are various arbitrary objects, including a book. And when the image of a book occurs in a book, ironies are likely to be at work. Grouped around K. are three sets of individuals corresponding roughly to the tabletop objects: the inspector seated at the nightstand (book), the two warders seated on a trunk (match box), and three court lackies

---

[22] This theater metaphor expands when later that evening K. re-enacts for Frl. Bürstner, who has come home late because she was at the theater, the drama that took place in her room. In the novel's final chapter, K. complains that the court has sent broken down old actors to fetch him. See esp. James Rolleston, *Kafka's Narrative Theater* (University Park and London: Pennsylvania Univ. Press, 1974), 73ff.; and Henry Sussman »The Court as Text: Inversion, Supplanting, and Derangement in Kafka's *Der Prozeß*,« *PMLA*, 92 (1977), 42–43.

standing in a corner like so many pins poking out of a cushion. The inspector's deliberate but apparently arbitrary fiddling with indifferent objects as if imaginary props on a makeshift stage suggests Kafka's own fiddling with words and images on a blank sheet of paper. The presence of the book among the objects strengthens this suggestion.

The ›scene‹ on the nightstand is an oblique commentary to the scene in the novel. The trifles on the tabletop, set into deliberate configuration by the inspector, have no evident meaning for anyone other than their manipulator. They are opaque objects on an imaginary field of play and are primarily exactly and only what they are: a book, a pin cushion, and a candle with matches. Any ›deeper‹ meaning must come as a supplement from the outside. The sense of this oblique commentary is, then, not to let some immanent meaning shine through the figures in the bedroom hearing scene but instead to reveal these would-be symbols for what they are: word-objects that are as intrinsically opaque as the assemblage of knick-knacks on Fräulein Bürstner's nightstand. This tabletop doubling of the hearing scene does not interpret in the ordinary sense of drawing forth a hidden meaning. Instead it accounts for the specific nature of the scene's inexplicability.

Kafka is at pains to remind his readers that Josef K. lives out his fate not in the real world but on the reflecting distorting surface of fiction's mirror. The writer is having fun with his protagonist's fictional status in a scene in which Josef K. unknowingly stumbles on the mystery of his origin. One evening when he is working late at the office, K. hears muffled sobs from behind a storeroom door. He investigates and discovers his two warders, Willem and Franz, about to be beaten because K. has accused them of stealing his breakfast and trying to pilfer his underwear. This storeroom is the bank's repository for »unbrauchbare, alte Drucksorten« and its floor is littered with »umgeworfene leere irdene Tintenflaschen« - ink bottles and printed matter - exactly the stuff of which K. and his whole unsettling world are made.

Josef K. seems here to be an avatar of Don Quixote, who near the end of his chivalric adventures visits a printing shop in Barcelona (Book II, Chapter 62). He watches the printers busily drawing and correcting proofs, setting type, making revisions, and performing all of the tasks that bring about the finished product of a book. »At such a moment,« remarks Robert Alter, »we can hardly forget that Don Quixote is no more than a product of the processes he observes, a congeries of words set up in type, run off as proof, corrected and rerun, bound in pages and sold at so many reales a copy.«[23]

---

[23] Robert Alter, *Partial Magic. The Novel as a Self-Conscious Genre* (Berkeley, Los Angeles, London: Univ. of California Press, 1978), 4-5.

It is just such a moment when K. discovers his warders and their Whipper among empty inkpots and uncorrected first impressions of old forms. Fearful that Franz's moans will attract attention, K. slams the storeroom door, makes excuses for the noise to his co-workers and goes home to forget about the incident. But he cannot forget. On the next night he works late again, and before leaving, a sense of uneasiness prompts him to look again into the storeroom. To his horror he finds that nothing has changed. The overturned inkpots, the old proofcopies, the Whipper and the two naked warders are all exactly as he had left them twenty-four hours before. K. slams the door in terror and runs to two office boys, who – significantly – are running a copy machine. He orders them to clean out the storeroom at the next possible opportunity. Franz, Willem, and the Whipper are not heard from again in the novel. Evidently, getting rid of the inkwells and old proofs has put an end to them.

Kafka's skepticism about the ability of empirical words to recuperate non-empirical realities overlaps with Josef K.'s problem. K. is seeking the authority that governs the court. What I am calling »conscience« is only a makeshift shorthand notation for that which Kafka attempts to articulate in the novel. The truth of the matter is not to be sought in the representations themselves but instead in the silence that enfolds them. Josef K. attempts to read and interpret the surface features of the court in the vain hope that these features are representations that are continuous with the power from which they emanate, »the law.« Scene after scene in this novel dramatizes the rift between signs and the truth they are supposed to represent. It reveals the deceptive similitudes for what they are, »Spaß und Verzweiflung.« Because it is a major theme in the novel, it will be worthwhile to pursue its presentation in some detail. The principal scenes that come into play here are: 1) K.'s ›misreading‹ of his first hearing, 2) his encounter with the judge's portrait in Huld's study and Leni's commentary on it, 3) Huld's account of court procedure, 4) Titorelli's portrait of Justice and his explanation of it, and 5) the prison chaplain's parable »Vor dem Gesetz.«

K's first hearing before the investigative commission assigned to his case marks the point in the novel at which K.'s hermeneutic quandary becomes thematic. The setting of this scene provides an abundance of precise, realistic detail that seems gravid with hidden meaning. These tantalizing details provoke an interpretive response both in K. and in the novel's reader. It is conspicuous, for instance, that the hearing is set for a Sunday, that the court is somewhere in a lower-class district on the city's edge in a tenement, that the entrance to the courtroom is reached through the living room of a woman's apartment. K. knows neither the

115

time nor the precise location of the hearing, but they turn out to be when and where he expects them. While looking for the proper room he invents the silly excuse for poking around that he wants to find a cabinetmaker named Lanz. When he asks a certain woman washing clothes in her living room, she sends him through an open door into the adjoining room, which turns out to be a hall in which many people are gathered. K. assumes that he has mistakenly stumbled into some sort of large meeting, returns to the living room and insists that he wants to find the »Tischler Lanz.« The washer woman simply answers »Ja,« sends him back in and shuts the door behind him. In this typically Kafkan confusion the woman explains nothing to the mystified K., and the narrator explains nothing to K.'s companion in puzzlement, the reader. There is no solid ground upon which to base interpretation.

A little child leads the way for K., and as they move through the crowd he notes that everybody is wearing black. K. also notes that the people are evidently divided into two groups, »möglicherweise zwei Parteien« (37). K. carefully takes note of the seating arrangements, of variation in applause and murmurs in the crowd. On the basis of his close reading of these signs he attempts to manipulate what appears to him to be the internal dynamics of an ideological schism within the court's organization. He rails against the injustice of his arrest and against corruption within the court, thinking that one of the two apparent parties will rally behind him. But to his great consternation »die zwei Parteien, die früher so entgegengesetzte Meinungen gehabt zu haben schienen, vermischten sich ... »(43). Confusion becomes chaos when a loud squawking from the back of the room interrupts K.'s oration. The squawker is a man who is sexually molesting the woman from the apartment. Uncontrolled erotic desire – a refracted image of K.'s desire for Fräulein Bürstner – has irrupted into the scene and made a shambles of the order that K. believed he had brought to his situation. Strangely, this lurid interlude seems to be a matter of little concern to the people assembled to hear Josef K.'s case, for no one moves to restrain the molester. Josef K. feels otherwise and is virtually overcome by the need, »dort Ordnung zu schaffen« (44) and thus to restore his command of the situation. But the people between K. and the molester physically prevent him from interfering. In his tussle with the crowd on the floor, K. suddenly notices that everyone present is wearing an insignia on his coat lapel concealed beneath his beard. He forgets about the woman being abused in the back of the room as he angrily denounces the court for having deceived him. K. feels as if he has been tricked into addressing one of the two seeming parties, but in reality he has yielded to his own interpretive impulse and made mistakes for which he alone is accountable. He fails to recognize his responsibility and in a gesture of anger and contempt he calls the members of the court »Lumpen« and tells them that they can keep their interrogations and hearings to themselves.

It is a telling circumstance that K. returns voluntarily to his trial even though no messages come to him from the court after the first hearing. He knows where his responsibility lies even if he will not consciously admit it. On a Sunday he seeks out the woman and her apartment once more, but when she lets him into the assembly hall K. finds only a pile of books. Once again the image of the book appears. It first comes up in Chapter I as the warder Willem sits reading a book by an open window in Frau Grubach's living room; turns up conspicuously on Fräulein Bürstner's nightstand; and in Chapter VIII Kaufmann Block kneels at a lightless window reading from the »Schriften« that Huld has loaned to him. Fictional figures reading fictional books give us reason to pause and think about where all this fictionalizing must end. The pile of books that K. finds instead of the crowd of people he had hoped to find is an effective bit of irony. Kafka has collapsed the entire assembly down to a heap of books on a table. The novelist is at work here, subtly making his role as artificer known. He has revealed K.'s previous hearing, and for that matter the whole novel, as »Lüge.«

These books attract Kafka's curious puppet. He wants to examine them more closely but the woman says it is not allowed because they belong to the »Untersuchungsrichter.« As she and K. become friendly the woman relents and takes him to the forbidden books. K. opens a battered old volume to find a clumsy scene of erotic embrace depicted in it. This book functions first of all to remind us that we, like Josef K., are holding a book in our hands, trying to interpret figures and images. But the specific image in this book offers a commentary on the action within the novel. When K. looks into the judge's book and sees a lewd scene, what he really sees is the image of his own desire. The scene between the squawking molester and the washer woman has turned up in a book and turned out to be fiction. When K. reads the book and when he ›reads‹ the court he fails to understand that what he finds reflected there is his own face. Doubling, the mutual reflection of two seemingly distinct worlds, is the literary mechanism that defines the unity of K. and his court.

This mechanism becomes functional again during K.'s visit to his lawyer, Huld. At his uncle's insistence, K. has called on Huld to consult about his trial. But while the uncle, Huld and an anonymous court official discuss the case, K. slips out of the conversation in order to pursue Leni, Huld's attractive young live-in nurse. She takes him into

117

the lawyer's study so that they can be alone together. Here a large portrait of an *Untersuchungsrichter* arrests K.'s attention. It portrays a man in judge's garb seated on a gilded throne at the head of yellow-carpeted stairs. This judge is not seated at rest but instead presses his left arm against the chair's arm and back while gripping the chair's other arm with his right hand, »als wolle er im nächsten Augenblick mit einer heftigen und vielleicht empörten Wendung aufspringen, um etwas Entscheidendes zu sagen oder gar das Urteil zu verkünden« (93–94).

Kafka's narrative ploy here is similar to that of the previous scene. He has implanted a representation into his novel as a reflecting device. This time it is a painting instead of a book. As in the previous instance, K. takes it as a clue to the true nature of the court, a sign that will lead his interpreting mind beyond the merely symbolic surface of the sign to a deeper, hidden meaning. The narrative mode that renders K.'s observation of the painting deserves analysis. It begins with an objective, declarative description of the painting – »Es stellte einen Mann in Richtertalar dar ... « – but soon shades over into the subjunctive of K.'s subjective perception (»als wolle«), and ends with the purely subjective speculation on K.'s part as to what the judge is about to do. This subtle shift of perspective insinuates the mind of the reader into K.'s mental set. Together, the reader and K. respond to a conditioned interpretive impulse and try to establish a symbolic connection between *signum* and *res*, representation and court authority.

K. and Leni enact this drama of interpretation. She claims to know the judge personally and tells K. that this depiction bears little resemblance to the truth. He is not a high official at all, she says, and his enthronement on an elevated dais is nothing more than a testament to his vanity and to the artist's fancy: »›Das ist alles Erfindung,‹ sagte Leni. .. , ›in Wirklichkeit sitzt er auf einem Küchensessel, auf dem eine alte Pferdedecke zusammengelegt ist‹ « (94). Leni's commentary seems to settle the matter authoritatively in illustration of Foucault's thesis that the cruel factuality of identities and differences has made a mockery of the claim of signs and similitudes on truth.

But the situation is even more desperate than it appears at first glance. If we press the logic of Kafka's presentation a little further, Leni's commentary is only another representation of the court, a narrative representation as badly in need of interpretation as is the painting. K. and the reader find themselves confronted with two mutually exclusive versions of the judge and the court. Kafka has cunningly withheld all first-hand knowledge of the court and its judges. There is once again no solid foundation upon which to base interpretation. This insight points toward the conclusion that undecidability itself is the message.[24] The stalemate conflict of interpretations implies the final undecidability of the entire novel inasmuch as the text of the novel is also an opaque surface composed of signs with no verifiable link to any substantial reality beyond the representation itself. Yet there is more truth at work here than the assertion that representation cannot grasp the beyond.

The way to establish a sure footing on some hermeneutical terra firma is to take into account Kafka's self-conscious narrative trickery. He intentionally exploits the finely tuned exegetical attention of his reader in scenes such as the one in Huld's study. This manipulation proceeds according to the scheme that underlies his death scenes: »ich ...nütze...mit Berechnung die... gesammelte Aufmerksamkeit des Lesers aus, bin bei viel klarerem Verstande als er...«. He asserts that these scenes are for him »im geheimen ein Spiel« (T, 279), and it is reasonable to infer that his intention in these death scenes applies to other types of scene as well. K.'s encounter with the judge's portrait is a case in point. The reader's general sympathy with K.'s plight, aided by the subtle shift in perspective and unreflected habits of interpretation, leads the reader to identify closely with K. The conspiracy of these circumstances amounts to a hermeneutical trap. Kafka is inviting us to repeat the mistake that K. has made, first in the assembly and then again with the book, namely to construe surface features so as to reveal depths of meaning concealed behind symbols. As long as we, with K., seek a transcendental signified *beyond* the signs, we are doomed to hang suspended above an abyss of undecidability. When we realize meaning is not beyond but present and apparent, mystification yields to understanding. Put more simply, what K. sees when he looks at the painting in Huld's study is the image of his own ambivalent consciousness of guilt. The wrathful judge is poised above K. - permanently poised - because K. himself is permanently on the verge of acknowledging his guilt and passing judgment on himself, but is always too weak to do so.[25] The judge's awkward posture mirrors K.'s ungainly

---

[24] Theo Elm has observed that this groping into emptiness must be made into a *tertium comparationis*. »Problematasierte Hermeneutik,« 500f. The reader must read this experience in such a way as to take the experience itself and the process of interpretation as the object of interpretation.

[25] I speculate that K. is too weak to come to conscious terms with his guilt for two reasons: 1) In his death scene, K. realizes that it is his duty to take the knife and kill himself, »die Verantwortung für diesen letzten Fehler trug der, der ihm den Rest der dazu nötigen Kraft versagt hatte« (194); and 2) a note from the Oktavhefte lends credence to the supposition that weakness is his failing: »Niemand kann sich mit der Erkenntnis des Guten und Bösen allein begnügen, sondern muß sich bestreben, ihr gemäß zu handeln. Dazu aber ist

balancing act between the subliminal knowledge of his guilt and his desire to be thought innocent. The judge cannot sit in dignified repose because he knows, which is to say K. knows, that justice has not been served. There is a guilty man at large. His regal trappings reflect K.'s vision of the authority of the court, and Leni's version reflects K.'s desire to demean what he perceives as a hostile, alien authority. Furthermore, it is conspicuously K.'s own interpretation that the judge looks as if he were about to utter something decisive or even pronounce verdict. This judge, a double for K., is always only *about* to pass judgment but can never carry through the deed. The painting has captured him in a moment between repose and the completed act. The novel captures K. in an identical moment.

K. remains blind to what is everywhere evident and continues to seek aid in his attempt to unmask the foreign source of authority, or at least to beat it at its own game. He turns to Huld for an account of the court's inner workings, hoping for a glimmer of the objective reality beyond appearances. Huld holds forth at great length on official and unofficial court procedure, and the two defendants – K. and the reader – follow his expatiations for several pages with attentive patience. The convolutions and labyrinthine complexities of his explanation tantalize the listener who clings fast to the hope that he will be able to seize hold of some useful, verifiable piece of information as it floats by in this flood of words. The gist of Huld's narrative is that the court is not responsive to substantive written or verbal communication from the lawyer or his client regarding pertinent evidence. Attorneys are not permitted to witness the proceedings, and they do not have access to court documents or even to the official indictment. The written defense can therefore contain relevant statements only by accident. When relevant points do appear in the attorney's argument they still cannot help the client because the court disregards documents handed in by attorneys. The message to be had in this understated burlesque is that the lawyer, like K.'s other »helpers,« is completely useless.

The impossibility of an exchange of relevant information between lawyer and court illustrates once again the futility of trying to penetrate into the court's interior. Huld's account, like the painting in his study and Leni's commentary to it, is only another representation of the court. Once again the meticulous novelist permits no means to verify

---

ihm die Kraft nicht mitgegeben, er muß daher sich zerstören .... Lieber will er die Erkenntnis des Guten und Bösen rückgängig machen ...; aber das Geschehene kann nicht rückgängig gemacht, sondern nur getrübt werden« (H, 37, No. 86). K. succumbs to precisely this weakness. Cf. also Kafka's letter to Max Brod of November, 1917 (B, 194f.).

the accuracy of Huld's statements. The »Spaß« in this »Verzweiflung« is that Huld's account disqualifies itself. He claims to his patient dupe that he can help him, yet all the while everything that he says points to his impotence. Huld's impotence is K.'s impotence. As long as he seeks authorities outside himself he will remain mystified.

Another figure of seeming authority is the court's hereditary painter and »Vertrauensmann,« Titorelli. He makes impressive claims to the harried protagonist: »Ich allein hole Sie heraus,« and K. turns a willing ear to his advice. Titorelli's long-winded explanation of the three methods of achieving acquittal is similar in its absurdity to Huld's description of court procedure. Once again the joke is on K. because everything that Titorelli says points back to the inescapable conclusion that the only way to be acquitted is to *be* innocent. Thus, no acquittal is possible for K., »der Schuldige« (T, 299). His court is »attracted by guilt«; it comes into being with guilt itself and will disappear only with the extirpation of the guilty party. The best K. can hope for is to hold his court at bay.

Rather than explicate Titorelli's account in detail, I want to turn instead to the painting that K. finds in the artist's squalid attic studio. It is a nearly finished judge-portrait similar to the one in Huld's study. The canvas shows a fat man with a full beard who, like the other judge, is braced to spring up out of his throne. This time K. notices a large but indistinct figure in the middle of the chair's back. Adding a few strokes, Titorelli explains that she is Justice and Victory blended into a single figure. The court's apparent emblem does little to bolster K.'s confidence in the fairness of this judicial system: »Die Gerechtigkeit muß ruhen,« he objects, »sonst schwankt die Waage, und es ist kein gerechtes Urteil möglich« (126). Suddenly K. perceives her as the Goddess of the Hunt.

As in the previous instances, the relationship of representation to truth becomes the center of attention. K. asks Titorelli if he has copied the emblem from the real throne. Like Leni, Titorelli answers, »Das ist alles Erfindung« (126), and explains that this judge is a lowly official who has never sat on a real throne. What is by now a familiar rift gapes open between mimetic illusion and true reality. The painting shows it one way, and Titorelli tells it another way. Neither the pictorial representation nor the narrative account can be submitted to any objective verification because Kafka has withheld the ›original‹ that these are supposed to represent.

It might at first seem that the agreement between the two commentaries of Leni and Titorelli lends a certain amount of credence to their respective stories. But the meticulous Kafka has been careful to undermine their credibility. Leni is a giddy seductress with no sense of loyalty, and the *Fabrikant*--an impartial observer who recommended Titorelli's help to K. in the first place - appended to his recommendation the warning that Titorelli is a known liar (117). Finally, Titorelli's jovial witticism, »Es gehört ja alles zum Gericht« (129), probably ought to be taken seriously, for both he and Leni have suspiciously close ties to the court. Their connections make them potentially useful to K., but these same ties cast more than a shadow of a doubt upon their motives for wanting to help him. Their explanations and advice only amount to more puzzles for the baffled protagonist.

Throughout the novel Josef K. must interpret signs, figures, and fictions of intractable ambiguity. His desperate game of interpretation reaches its parodical extreme in the eighth chapter when the »Kaufmann Block« imparts to K. a superstition that is current among the defendants. It is said that the outcome of a specific trial can be read in its defendant's face, and in particular from his lips. Rumor has it, says Block, that K.'s lips are those of a condemned man. As Block nervously goes on to assert that such court lore is surely nonsense, K. is already reaching for his pocket mirror to have a look at his lips. The image of his silent lips in the glass divulges no secret to him. Block's comical twaddle is as ridiculous as it seems from any ordinary point of view, but if the image is taken literally enough its meaning becomes obvious: the judgment must pass from the lips of the defendant himself. What he sees in his pocket mirror is what he always sees whenever he looks at the court and its representations, a silent image to which no meaning accrues until he himself speaks the truth. The images of the court are always his own image variously reflected.

K.'s failure to understand what he sees is the novel's theme of flawed hermeneutic. This question of interpretation appears in its clearest form in the novel's most imposing chapter, »Im Dom.« The bank has assigned K. to act as a tour guide to local »Kunstdenkmäler« for an important client visiting from Italy. K.'s Italian is weak to begin with, but his problems in understanding properly are compounded when he finds that the client speaks a southern dialect of which K. has no knowledge. His trouble with the Italian is an index to his trouble in general. Thanks to the helpful intervention of the bank president, whose Italian is better, it is arranged that K. will meet the client at ten o'clock in the city's cathedral for a guided tour. K. arrives punctually, but the Italian does not appear, so K. sits alone in the dimly lit cathedral and leafs through the album of the city's sights that he has brought with him. It is a gloomy, rainy day, and soon there is so little light inside the cathedral that K. can scarcely distinguish objects in the aisle near the pew in which he is sitting. He sees a triangle of lighted candles at the main altar in front of him and a single lighted candle on a pillar behind him. But these do not produce enough light for him to see anything.

This candle image recurs several times in the novel and is perhaps one of the few images that offers itself to traditional habits of interpretation. The candle on Fräulein Bürstner's nightstand reflected K. as he stood in the middle of her bedroom during his initial hearing. It subsequently remains associated with K. during the rest of the novel. In Huld's dark bedroom there is a weak candlelight that only partially illuminates the scene. Certain objects of importance – in this case a court official – are not within K.'s field of vision. There is also candlelight in the printing storage room where the Whipper beats Franz and Willem. It is a small enclosed chamber, dimly illuminated by candlelight from within. These spaces stage the scenes of K.'s ›other‹ life and are suggestive of consciousness, the inner light of an interpreting mind. The novel's candle-lit interiors – the storeroom, Huld's bedroom, as well as the bedrooms of Block and Fräulein Bürstner, the cathedral, and the midnight lucubrations of the magistrate assigned to K.'s case – all of these places, together with the stuffy attics of the court, are settings in which the drama of Josef K.'s conscience plays itself out. The puny candle flames that illumine these scenes never produce enough light for K. to see anything clearly. His interpreting mind never manages to enlighten him with regard to his trial and its court.

The image of K. sitting alone in a cathedral dark but for the feeble glow of candlelight, and the loss of objects that recede into the darkness beyond the pale of its faint luminescence, suggest the limitations of K.'s conscious mind. When he pulls out a pocket flashlight, a variation on the candle theme, and steps over to an adjacent side chapel, the purport of this light imagery becomes even clearer. K. climbs a few steps up to a low balustrade, leans over it, and shines his little light on the altarpiece: »Störend schwebte das ewige Licht davor« (175), says the narrator. Since even the mightiest of flashlight batteries cannot boast an »ewiges Licht,« the language of the passage points toward the conclusion that the light K. shines on the altarpiece is more numinous than luminous. He has turned his interpreting mind onto the painting. The first thing he sees, and partly only surmises, is a large armored knight on the edge of the canvas. Rather than explore the entire work with his light, K. holds his beam on this knight and contemplates him at length, wondering what the knight is watching and why he does not approach the object of his attention. When K. finally proceeds to examine the rest of the painting, he takes it to be an entirely conventional deposition of

Christ and notes to himself that it is of recent origin. Satisfied that he has seen all there is to see, he turns off his light and returns to his pew.

Significant ironies shape this little scene. Because of his reputation for having a knowledge of art history, K.'s bank has asked him to accompany the Italian client on a tour of the city's art treasures. Given this set of circumstances, Kafka could just as well have set this scene in a museum or an art gallery or a palace, yet he has conspicuously chosen to situate his protagonist in a cathedral. The first generation of Kafka critics pounced on this image to authenticate their reading of Kafka as a religious allegorist. While the element of the religious must not be overlooked, neither should it be allowed to overpower the text in acts of illicit allegoresis. Kafka's diaries and letters demonstrate that he had no special interest in a traditionally theological or narrowly religious frame of reference. *Der Prozeß* has as its central image a court, not a church. But even if organized religion and academic theology were of no special interest to Kafka, his *Oktavhefte* show that what he called »the spiritual« – *das Geistige* and not *das Geistliche*--was a matter of great consequence to him. Viewed from this perspective, that which is »religious« definitely belongs within the scope of Kafka's writing, though probably in unexpected ways. In *Der Prozeß* the image of the cathedral belongs to this broadly conceived sense of spirituality and religiosity.

Kafka sets the scene in this cathedral and sends his protagonist to it out of an interest in art. K. is literally inside a work of human imagination and artistic contrivance in which art has traditionally made its most substantial claims to participation in a reality beyond the here-and-now. This cathedral, like any other temple, is a sacramental artwork, a sign for the unity of man with transcendent divinity. The irony here is that K. is also situated in a *novel*, which is likewise a work of human imagination and artistic contrivance. As works of art, narratives and temples are indices to the spiritual realm of human experience.

Literature, like Church and Court, is a concrete institution in the material world that attempts to render the invisible but real spiritual world into intelligibility. But because of its concreteness, because it does belong to the here-and-now, literature becomes a prisoner of its own materiality, and its signs begin to mask the very realities that they were supposed to conjure into visibility. It is in this same sense that Titorelli's portraits are pure »Erfindung,« mannered and standardized according to court convention (126) with no resemblance to truth. K.'s response to the altarpiece echoes what he has learned about Titorelli's paintings. After his flashlight examination of the side chapel's altarpiece, K. judges the dead Christ to be a schematically conventional

representation – »in gewöhnlicher Auffassung« – and temporally removed from the truth it is supposed to embody – »es war übrigens ein
neueres Bild« (175). The knowledgeable K. demonstrates here his liberal education in the finer things of life. His response is a typical product
of *Bildung* in the modern Western world. K. experiences the painting,
and the cathedral itself, only as ›art objects‹ concerning which various
facts, figures, and standardized valuations can be uttered. But the dimension of the sacred, that which enfolds and suffuses the artwork
with a meaning in excess of its constituent parts – the same sovereign
stillness that ensconces Josefine's song – precisely this dimension is
inaccessible to the dull and unimaginative Josef K..

»Es gibt nichts als die geistige Welt,« writes Kafka in his *Oktavhef-
ten*, »was wir die sinnliche Welt nennen, ist das Böse in der geistigen,
und was wir böse nennen, ist nur eine Notwendigkeit des Augenblicks
unserer ewigen Entwicklung« (H, 34, No. 54). What Kafka calls the
spiritual was for him a vital and authentic presence, but he was pessi-
mistic about its accessibility. »Es gibt ein Ziel, aber keinen Weg,« he
writes elsewhere in his aphorisms (H, 32, No. 26). Kafka's point is that
the material world and its institutions – church and court at K.'s level,
and the novel or literature itself at the reader's level – exist in a state of
separation from the truer, unrepresentable reality of the spiritual
world. K.'s futile shadow boxing with the court reveals itself as a dark
quixoticism because the objectively material has fully supplanted the
spiritual. The objective reality of his court, in which illusion and reality
are identical, has made K. blind to the truer, more real realm of the
spiritual.

»Siehst du denn nicht zwei Schritte weit?« is the prison chaplain's
impatient rebuke. In order to help the befuddled defendant, the prison
chaplain tells K. the »Türhüterlegende.« It is supposed to clarify for K.
how he has deceived himself of the court. »Before the law« stands a
doorkeeper to whom a man from the country has come. This man seeks
entry into the law. The door is open but the doorkeeper forbids admis-
sion. After many years of questioning and coaxing his doorkeeper, this
man has learned little and achieved nothing. His »Augenlicht« has
become weak (a reprise of the candlelight motif, 182), and he is near
death. The last thing he learns from the doorkeeper is that this door was
intended for him alone.

The parable's basic paradox is that the door is open, yet the man is
not permitted to pass through it. He and his doorkeeper are »vor dem
Gesetz,« i.e. they are physically in front of the edifice that separates
them from the law. This edifice and its door are important images in
the parable and are in need of explanation. What is the sense of this

edifice that prevents the man from passing to the other side? And why the strange contradiction of an open yet impassable door? In order to answer the questions it is necessary, as the chaplain admonishes K., to observe a rigorous »Achtung vor der Schrift« (184).

The phrase »vor dem Gesetz« has a double meaning within the context of the chaplain's remarks. It is first of all the simple location of the doorkeeper and the man. Its other meaning is more literal. The chaplain tells K. that the parable itself is located »in den einleitenden Schriften zum Gesetz« (182), which means that the parable is itself quite literally »vor dem Gesetz.« It is a preface that is supposed to be a sort of entryway into the written text of the law. Both the man from the country in the parable *and* the parable itself are before the law. The story of the man who wants to enter into the law through a doorway is the story of anyone who wants to enter into the text of the law through the parable. In this way the parable as introductory preface to the law becomes an edifice that separates the seeker from the law. But of course a narrative introduction is not meant to obstruct entry but instead to facilitate the passage to understanding. It stands between the seeker and the law but it simultaneously a doorway into what lies beyond. The strange twist here is that the doorway of the parable is open yet impassable. This doorkeeper is the personified reflection of the parable's own stubborn ambiguity, its refusal to yield up a clear, objectively verifiable meaning. The chaplain's long-winded parody-commentary underscores the parable's ultimate undecidability and is an assertion that »the law,« as a transcendent, is out of reach.

The man from the country reflects K., who stands before the court in the same sense that the man stands before an edifice that separates him from the law. Josef K. in his turn is also a figure in a parable called *Der Prozeß*, and in the novel he is denied access to whatever it is that lies beyond the court's imposing and inscrutable facade. Finally, the reader of the novel is a seeker of the law that governs meaning in the narrative. The extraordinary diversity of Kafka-interpretations in the secondary literature bears witness to inaccessibility of »the law« that perhaps lies hidden beyond the novel's puzzling surface of words and figures. At each of these four levels, »the law« – authority – seems to be locked behind a dense surface of opaque representations. Seemingly open doors invite passage into another world beyond appearances. »Gehe hinüber,« enjoins the wise man in Kafka's parable »Von den Gleichnissen,« to which the skeptic replies:

so meint er nicht, daß man auf die andere Seite hinübergehen solle, was man immerhin noch leisten könnte, wenn das Ergebnis des Weges wert wäre, sondern er meint irgendein sagenhaftes Drüben, etwas, das wir nicht kennen, das auch von ihm nicht näher zu bezeichnen ist und das uns also hier gar nichts helfen kann. Alle diese Gleichnisse wollen eigentlich nur sagen, daß das Unfaßbare unfaßbar ist, und das haben wir gewußt. (SE, 411)

This »fabulous beyond« – meaning, transcendent order, the law – lies out of reach, and the words of wise men and novelists are always only *Gleichnisse*, illusions of open doors.

IV

These observations have now come full circle and arrived back at the point from which this chapter departed. Signs and similitudes, the one-time guarantors of the validity of knowledge in the condition of literature, have proved themselves to be mendacious. They have deceived and misled Josef K. in his quest for »the law.« K.'s vexation in trying to read the signs of his trial is a mirror to the reader's tribulation in trying to read the signs of Kafka's vexed novel. Josef K.'s interpretive failures seem to imply a like quandary for exegetes of the novel. Yet the course of this reading has paradoxically affirmed a successful hermeneutic around which the theme of conscience has condensed. It is a productive contradiction: there is a dynamic tension between the novel's nihilistic irony – any irony that denies narrative representation as the vehicle of transcendence – and the spectral entity of conscience that has emerged in the rift between signs and meanings. Are the categories of irony and conscience mutually exclusive, or are they somehow complementary?

The solution to this problem lies in the distinction between representation and articulation. Josef K.'s story is a case study in the aporia of representation. K. consistently repeats the same error, which is rooted in his unexamined assumption that the court in its various guises is an objectification of ›the Law.‹ Wherever he looks he sees what he believes to be the representations of some hidden, autonomous authority. He assumes that this authority lies somewhere behind the surface of things, in an indeterminate ›beyond.‹ This beyond does not exist; it is a supernaturalism. The truth of K.'s trial is to be sought in that which lies nearest at hand, on the specular surface of appearances. K. fails to see this truth because his vision is fixed on an illusory beyond. Behind the mirror is nothing, not even a void.[26] The court does

---

[26] The »void« is a recurring term in the criticism of modernist literature. It generally comes up in reference to the supposedly vacant spot left by the »death of God.« This melodramatic »void« is as much a supernaturalism as was the bourgeois notion of divinity it is supposed to have replaced. It bears the stamp of nostalgia or, at best, trendy nihilism.

not represent an externally autonomous authority because it is already identical with the true authority, which is K. himself.[27] His half-hearted attempts to resist the trial are as futile as trying to run away from his own shadow. K.'s way of dealing with the court is no different from the slapstick routine of a circus clown who, while standing in front of a mirror, casually turns away from his reflection then suddenly jumps to face the glass, trying to catch his own image off guard.

In pursuit of the law, K. runs a gauntlet of mirrors until finally the twin images of K. and court merge into the unified oblivion of death. Because of the special reciprocity between K. and his apparent antagonist, it is tempting to suggest that the court represents K.'s conscience. Yet if the self-cancelling rhetoric of Kafka's presentation is to be thought to its end, then the court must not be read as a metaphor for conscience in the usual force of ›metaphor.‹ At least one objection to this proposition comes readily to mind. It can be argued that a person's conscience is »like« a court, and a figure no less imposing than Immanuel Kant has set a precedent for saying so.[28] But for Kafka ›conscience,‹ ›guilt,‹ ›right,‹ and ›the law‹ belong to a mystical order of being that is necessarily falsified when reduced to a word-image. Language can only be used »andeutungsweise« for the things of the non-sensory world, »aber niemals auch nur annähernd vergleichsweise« (H, 34, No. 57).

This critique of metaphorical signification is abundantly evident in the matter-of-fact concreteness of the language in *Der Prozeß*. Kafka does not try to force his language to perform extraordinary metaphys-

---

[27] Sokel has noted that K. refuses to assume the responsibility for what he already knows is true. I add to this insight the complementary dimension of conscience as something that Kafka invites the reader to perform. Sokel, »Das Programm von K.'s Gericht: ödipaler und existentieller Sinn des *Prozeß*-Romans,« in *Franz Kafka. Eine Aufsatzsammlung nach einem Symposium in Philadelphia*, hrsg. u. eingel. v. Marie Luise Caputo-Mayr, Schriftenreihe Agora, 29 (Berlin, Darmstadt: Agora, 1978), 81–107. Cf. Emrich, p. 275.

[28] *Kants Gesammelte Schriften*, hrsg. v. Königlich Preußischen Akademie der Wissenschaften, I. Abt. (Werke), Bd. 6, *Die Religion innerhalb der Grenzen der bloßen Vernunft/Die Metaphysik der Sitten* (Berlin: Georg Riemer, 1907), p. 438: »Das Bewußtsein eines *inneren Gerichthofes* im Menschen (›vor welchem sich seine Gedanken einander verklagen oder entschuldigen‹) ist das *Gewissen*.« The equivocation of court to conscience would reduce the court to an allegory, but Kafka's hostility to allegory is well known. He wrote this comment to Greta Bloch a couple of months before beginning *Der Prozeß*: »Aber unüberwindbar bleibt für mich der trockene Aufbau der ganzen Allegorie, die nichts ist als Allegorie, alles sagt, was zu sagen ist, nirgends ins Tiefere geht und ins Tiefere zieht,« *Briefe an Felice*, hrsg. v. Erich Heller u. Jürgen Born (Frankfurt a.M.: Fischer Taschenbuch Verlag, 1976), p. 596.

ical feats, for, as Wittgenstein once suggested, nothing is lost if one does not try to utter the ineffable. Instead, the ineffable is contained, ineffably, in that which is spoken. Conscience, the unspoken, emerges from the rift laid open by self-reflexive Kafkan irony. Its presence is entirely silent, negative, conspicuous in the almost palpable stillness with which it pervades the interaction of K. and court, of reader and novel. Kafka brings conscience to articulation by a *via negativa*. Ingeborg Henel does not propose conscience as a touchstone of the novel, but she does offer a keen insight into Kafka's non-objectifying mode of articulation:

> Bei Kafka wie in der negativen Theologie weist das Negative auf ein Positives hin: die Lüge auf die Wahrheit, das Bewußtsein des Gefangenseins auf eine Ahnung von Freiheit und das unausweichliche Schuldgefühl auf die Unbedingtheit des Gesetzes. Das Positive selbst, die Wahrheit, die Freiheit, das Gesetz hat Kafka niemals dargestellt.[29]

Where Henel writes »das Gesetz,« read: »das Gewissen.« She has not carried the logic of her argument to its conclusion. The implied presence of that which is positive also implies an important question about the protagonist's relationship with the truth. Not only does K.'s guilt evoke a presentiment of the law; it also poses a question about the *origin* of this law. The court and K. are twins that together engender conscience, the authentic power of judgment in matters of guilt and innocence.

K. attempts intellectually to seize and interpret the court. He fails because he assumes the court is something wholly other than himself. But another unexamined assumption lies buried in imagining that the court is exclusively K.'s prismatic reflection. The court complements K.'s attempt to grasp the law with a hermeneutic gesture of its own. It seizes and interprets K. If Josef K. could only in some way participate in the hermeneutic that proceeds from the court, if he could allow the court to grasp him and offer it no resistance, he would be a man in harmony with himself and his conscience. There are two principle characters in the story. One is K. and the other is the court. Each player is actively autonomous to a certain degree, and each conditions the response of the other. The theme of conscience emerges for the reader as a result of this dialectical interaction between two figures that are paradoxically similar and different at the same time.[30]

---

[29] Ingeborg Henel, »Die Türhüterlegende und ihre Bedeutung für Kafkas *Prozeß*,« *DVjs*, 37 (1963), 68.

[30] It should not go unremarked that the reader is likewise engaged in a dialogue with the novel; the text is an active partner in the interaction and meaning emerges as a product of this conversation. Meaning is not a static something hidden behind a veil of words. It is a function of dynamic process.

A certain branch of Kafka criticism will presumably raise an objection to this interpretation. There is a prominent trend in readings of Kafka that accepts Josef K.'s observing consciousness as the origin of reality in the fictional world. I will call this view the »phenomenological fallacy,« if »phenomenological« is understood to mean an interpretive strategy that accords epistemic privilege to the observing subject. The objection would be that the court cannot be an active partner in dialectical confrontation because it is only a passive reflection of K.'s inner life, or even of Kafka's mental landscape. K.'s consciousness is prior to the court.

Ingeborg Henel's observation that the court is a »projection« of K.'s wretched soul has been understood by some as a psycholgistic metaphor.[31] Interpreters less circumspect than Henel have so radically set up K.'s mind as an absolute origin at the center of the fictional world that the court becomes the phantasm of a dreaming man. Friedrich Beißner has gone so far as to suggest that the court is the delusion of an isolated mind.[32] Such readings do violence to the integrity of the tale's narrative illusion. The motive behind such readings is perhaps a felt need to rationalize and thereby make harmless the dangerous irrationality that overwhelms the protagonist. This irrationality threatens not only K. but the reader who identifies with him as well. It would be a like error to suppose that Gregor Samsa is not really a verminous insect at all but only a man who is dreaming that he is a bug. It is a hermeneutical imperative that the integrity of the illusion remain intact. Gregor Samsa is really a cockroach or beetle of some sort, and Josef K. is really having a trial.

The psychologizing phenomenologists base their argument for the priority of K.'s consciousness on the much discussed phenomenon of

---

[31] See note 19.

[32] Friedrich Beißner advances the proposition that the court is the »innerseelisches Wahnbild eines in vollständiger Erschöpfung isolierten Geistes,« in *Der Erzähler Franz Kafka* (Stuttgart: Kohlhammer, 1952), 39. In *Der Schacht von Babel. Aus Kafkas Tagebüchern* (Stuttgart: Kohlhammer, 1963), p. 44, he writes: »Ich behaupte nochmals: alle Personen und alle Vorgänge, die mit dem Prozeß zu tun haben, sind nur in K.s Träumen und Halbträumen vorhanden.« The most thoroughgoing study of consciousness as the center of reality in Kafka's work is Jörgen Kobs, *Kafka. Untersuchungen zu Bewußtsein und Sprache seiner Gestalten*, hrsg. v. Ursula Brech (Bad Homburg: Athenäum, 1970), on *Der Prozeß* cf. esp. 391f. More in line with my »hermeneutical approach« is Cyrena N. Pondrom, »Kafka and Phenomenology: Josef K.'s Search for Information,« *Wisconsin Studies in Contemporary Literature*, 8 (1967), 78–95; rpt. in *Twentieth Century Interpretations of The Trial. A Collection of Critical Essays*, ed. James Rolleston (Englewood Cliffs, N.J.: Prentice-Hall, 1976), pp. 70–85.

»Einsinnigkeit« in Kafka's prose.[33] It is the narrative sleight-of-hand whereby the novelist largely restricts the reader's point of view to that of the protagonist, thereby forcing the reader to identify with K. The assumption is that K. is a mimetic double for a possible person in the real world, and that the court ought to be mimetic also. Since such courts have no objective existence in average reality, it is easy to jump to the conclusion that K. is demented or dreaming.[34] Intellectual historians rush to support this reading by fitting it into the context of Kafka's era, which witnessed the rise of phenomenology, empirical psychology, and the ›discovery‹ of the unconscious.

In spite of being covered by all this heavy artillery, the psychologizing phenomenologists are vulnerable because they have overlooked a decisive feature of *Der Prozeß*: its narrativity. The novel's self-conscious irony militates against a reading that places K.'s consciousness at the center of reality. The phenomenon of »Einsinnigkeit« is a trick, a narrative device that Kafka applies »mit Berechnung« in order to exploit his readers' empathetic sensibilities as the protagonist's suffering gathers them in. Kafka wants for us to see the court as K. sees it, a looming, inscrutable edifice apparently bent on our destruction. But he does not do so in order to establish consciousness as a generative force. Certainly K. suffers because of the limitations of his »Augenlicht,« but the reader who identifies too closely with him has fallen into Kafka's hermeneutical trap. Kafka plays with the reader by making him partake of K.'s miserable despair, never realizing that much more can be known about the court than the limited protagonist is aware of. The critics of K.'s consciousness have seen through this deception clearly enough, and have made what seems to them the next logical step, which is making K. the origin of his court. There is obviously a certain logic in this position, but narrativity qualifies consciousness in an important way. The bottom line of reality in *Der Prozeß* is not consciousness; it is narrative, words and images, signs and figures. K.'s personal subjectivity is no more an origin of the court than the reader's personal subjectivity is the origin of *Der Prozeß*. It is easy to accept the court as pure fiction, but it goes against the grain to think of K. as a literary arabesque, a printed puppet with no more »consciousness« than the court that is his double.

---

[33] See note 21.
[34] There is also another possibility, namely that the court *is* mimetic. J.P. Stern argues that this sort of trial does exist: »The Law of *The Trial*,« in *On Kafka. Semi-Centenary Perspectives*, ed. Franz Kuna (London: Paul Elek, 1976), 22–41.

Yet Kafka has gone to the trouble to reveal the fictionality of Josef K. and the world of his trial in various ways that I have tried to make clear. In so doing he has established narrativity as a deeper level of reality than consciousness and has disqualified K. as the mimetic double for a possible man in the so-called real world. K. is an eidolon, and the court is a figment of literary imagination. They are possible only in the charmed dimension of fictional narrative. When Gustav Janouch began to chatter enthusiastically about how lifelike he found the figures of *Der Verschollene*, Kafka is reported to have said: »Ich zeichnete keine Menschen. Ich erzählte eine Geschichte. Das sind Bilder, nur Bilder.«[35] A sidelong glance at Musil will shed some light on this matter of non-mimetic pictures. He describes the art of characterization in *Törleß*:

> Die Zeichnung der Charaktere ist stilisiert, alles auf die kürzeste Linie zu-sammengefaßt, keine volle Menschen dargestellt, sondern jeweils nur deren Schwerlinie.
> Das würde noch gut zum »psychologischen Roman« stimmen. Gleich aber geht es um einen Schritt weiter. Es findet sich keine reale Psychologie, we-nigstens ist sie ganz ohne Interesse, willkürlich, dilettantisch behandelt. . . . Die psychologischen Schwerlinien gehören mehr oder minder konstruierten Figuren an. Nie kam mir der Gedanke, ist dieser Mensch möglich? Im Gegenteil: ich frug, ist dieser Mensch konsequent? Und ist es, so ist es mir desto lieber, je unmöglicher er ist.[36]

Musil's comments ring true for *Der Prozeß* as well as for *Törleß*. The fictional world takes on an autonomy independent of the rules that govern the figures of life. We are free to regard K.'s machinations at a critical, perhaps even chilly, distance.

Such departures from accepted novelistic practice are only part of how Kafka subverts illusionism. As I have tried to show, he regarded the figurality of language the source of »fun and despair« in storytelling. He calls attention to this »Spaß und Verzweiflung« by making his tales relentlessly ambiguous. His despair is that a word-image – Josef K. for instance – is always only what it actually is and can never really be what it represents. But the figures of fiction are also fun because they can become gaming pieces in a contest between author and reader. He plainly states in his diary that the death scenes are a game for him. This

---

[35] Gustav Janouch, *Gespräche mit Kafka. Aufzeichnungen und Erinnerungen*, erw. Neuaufl. (Frankfurt a.M.: Fischer Taschenbuch Verlag, 1981), 45.
[36] Robert Musil, *Briefe 1901–1942*, hrsg. v. Adolf Frisé unter Mithilfe v. Murray G. Hall (Reinbek bei Hamburg: Rowohlt, 1981), 13. A letter of March 22, 1905 to Stefanie Tyrka. Cf. also Kessler's remarks on Kafka's non-mimetic procedures, esp. 119–126.

sport extends to playfully mocking and undoing real-seeming appearances. The gambit of nesting representations within representations in *Der Prozeß* is an example of the author having fun with the fictional, or figural, status of K.'s world. Yet this hide-and-seek playfulness does not trivialize the claims of fiction on truth; it relocates them. Kafka's game is an inquiry into the disposition of knowledge as literature.

The ironic »Geständnis« that K. and his world are »Lüge« does not abrogate the right of literature to its privileged place in the ways of human knowledge. It is, for example, self-evident that the lives and trials of other patently fictive figures – Don Quixote, Tom Jones, Tristram Shandy – are no less compelling for their fictionality. Kafka's Josef K. belongs in the ranks of these memorable fabulations. Setting narrativity into the foreground of *Der Prozeß* does not diminish the claim that the novel implicitly and justly makes to truth-telling. It does, however, qualify the traditional claim of mimesis that art is an imitation of reality, regardless of whether this reality is thought to be material or spiritual. Narrative art is necessarily mimetic art to a certain extent, but narrative does not exhaust its truth-potential in mimesis. The relationship of fiction to truth is not a matter of accurate representation; rather, it is to be sought in the »hermeneutical function« of narrative.

Conscience in *Der Prozeß* is not the object of mimetic or any other version of objectifying representation. It is much more the point at which narrative hermeneutical function becomes articulate. Indeed, conscience is itself a hermeneutical event. It is the act of setting to decision what is to be right and what is to be wrong, what is to be just and what is to be vicious, who is to be guilty and who is to be innocent. The hermeneutical function of the poetic word is precisely such an act of setting to decision.

The primary function of an imagined world of words is not to refer to a thing but to precipitate an event: the poetic word must elicit a response. *Der Prozeß* seeks to elicit a response from its readers inasmuch as it asks for a decision concerning the origin of authority in individual and collective conscience. The novel does not ask for an everyday judgment on some specific moral dilemma. Kafka withholds the crime of which K. is allegedly guilty for this reason. The novel does not demand a ruling on a specific case in accordance with the law of moral or juridical convention. It is instead asking for a decision concerning the origin of the law's authority. This origin is conscience, and it belongs to a dimension of human experience more fundamental than personal subjectivity or moral convention. Musil called this dimension »der andere Zustand,« a concept fully in place in the reality of K.'s trial.

133

Josef K.'s failure, then, is not the image of a cynical end to modern man. It is much more an appeal for intelligent and ethically tempered critical reflection. K.'s confrontation with his court contains an implicit query, which is to say that it sets to decision – *andeutungsweise* – the question of what claims a human being's conscience must play in the course of events. What at first seems to be obscurity and undecidability is in truth an appeal for a way of reading that is both responsive and responsible. Interpretation has an ethical dimension.

Der Prozeß is a celebration of conscience in the sense of a lamentation. Kafka's song of lament becomes the occasion for a reflective confrontation with one of human life's elemental events. It is the confrontation itself and not mimetic features of the narrative that are principally of interest. It is K.'s confrontation with the court and the reader's confrontation with the narrative from which meaning first arises. The novel is the site of the hermeneutical function in much the same way that an elegy is a song of sorrow: the song is not a likeness of the sorrow it laments yet the sadness is brought to language in the singing voice. Or again: a temple is not a likeness of the divinity it honors, yet for a believer this divinity suffuses the carved stone and wrought space of the entire construction. The temple celebrates its numen in the same sense that *Der Prozeß* celebrates conscience. There is in each case a call to active participation. The novel provokes its reader into assuming the responsibility for an interpretive response that Josef K., in his gnostic turpitude, has shirked. It is in this sense that the novel has a utopian aim: it is not a forecast for an apocalyptic end to a doglike humanity – a »bitch gone bad in the teeth« as Ezra Pound put it – instead it opens up onto the future as onto a realm of potentialities governed by the dynamics of response and responsibility. The novel is not an imitation of nature; it is an intimation of time to come. It is writing, and writing is, according to Kafka, a »Form des Gebetes« (H, 252).

CHAPTER V

IN THE CRYSTAL GARDEN:
The Replenishment of Art and the Ecology
of Man in Thomas Mann's *Doktor Faustus*

> . . . es sind
> noch Lieder zu singen jenseits
> der Menschen.
>
> Paul Celan[1]

To a reader casually familiar with the recent history of the novel, the modernism of Kafka, Broch, and Musil is self-evident. By way of contrast, Thomas Mann's novels seem more reserved, less modernistic than those of his contemporaries. It is in fact clear that Mann's fiction embraces and refines the literary practices of nineteenth-century realism. His imagined worlds have a true-to-life quality that situates their author squarely at the end of a lineage that includes the likes of Goethe, Tolstoy, Fontane, and Dickens, to name only a few. In keeping with their standards of realism, Mann depicts places and times in which memorable characters become enmeshed in events that are alive with the comedy and drama of human interest. His engaging plots move according to a principle of progressive linearity and are a realm within which individual psychology interacts with circumstance so as to press toward the final disaster or fulfillment. Mann's rich prose conjures forth an illusion of reality that seems by virtue of its imposing presence to be a defense of realist mimesis. Where, then, are the collapse of reality, the crisis of representation, and the inwardness that are supposed to typify modernist narrative? What makes Thomas Mann different from his contemporaries?

It is his response to the tradition that sets him apart from the other German and Austrian modernists. Mann's ambivalent posture might profitably be likened to that of the French expressionist painter Georges Rouault. On the face of it he and Rouault are diametric opposites. Rouault was as experimenter in abstract form, whereas Mann

---

[1] Paul Celan, *Ausgewählte Gedichte/Zwei Reden*, mit einem Nachwort v. Beda Allemann, suhrkamp taschenbuch, 604 (Frankfurt am Main: Suhrkamp, 1980), p. 105.

was a conservative practitioner of verisimilar mimesis. Yet at a deeper level their aesthetic impulse pivots on a common axis. Each of the two was simultaneously radical and conservative in his response to the tradition. Rouault put revolutionary form in the service of humanist and Christian values. The conservative intention of his revolt in form was to preserve and renew the legacy of tradition. Thomas Mann's most profound work, *Doktor Faustus*, claims for itself a like but precisely inverted intention. It puts traditional narrative form in the service of a project that asks thorny questions of the Western cultural heritage. The radical intention of his formal conservatism is to challenge the assumptions that underlie art in the tradition of the West.

These assumptions, which are at bottom those of the humanist tradition, have a direct bearing on the modernist tendencies of *Doktor Faustus*.[2] The action of the novel takes place in an era of crisis, a time in which war, nihilism, and moral bewilderment have made a shambles of orderly existence. Mann portrays this crisis as the failure of humanism because, in spite of its lofty ideals, it has served as an incubator to the political bestiality of the twentieth century. As the novel presents it, the faulty basis of humanism is its anthropocentric subjectivity, the strict division between man and nature. In the realm of aesthetics, humanistic egoism causes the artwork to become dislodged from its rightful place in the middle of life. In particular it estranges art from its religious function and isolates it in the academic solitude of high culture. Cut off from its deepest origins, artistic expression eventually exhausts the conventions that define and restrict it until it ultimately transforms itself into parody. This depletion of expressive schemata

---

[2] In conscious deviation from the two dominant ways of reading the novel I argue that the main theme of *Doktor Faustus* is the problem of humanism. The first style of interpreting this novel is based on a repressive notion of »social realism« that tries to make Thomas Mann the objective chronist of bourgeois decadence. The second major direction of interpretation reads the novel in terms of Thomas Mann's personal response to the specific historical situation. Certainly the criticism of bourgeois culture and Mann's confrontation with Nazi Germany are imposing and indispensable elements of *Doktor Faustus*, but they are also the epiphenomena of a more fundamental critique that is at work in the novel. I intend to show in this chapter how the concept of humanism itself emerges in *Doktor Faustus* as the unexpected root of the crisis of modernity. Like various other contemporary thinkers, Thomas Mann wondered how Western humanism, in spite of its high ideals, could produce – or at least fail to prevent – Nazism, Stalinism, and two World Wars. For an overview of the crisis in contemporary humanism see Paul Ricoeur, »Philosophy,« in *Main Trends of Research in the Social and Human Sciences*, ed. Jacques Havet, New Babylon, 21/2, Part II, Vol. II (The Hague, Paris, New York: Mouton/UNESCO, 1978), pp. 1449–1470.

demonstrates Thomas Mann's perception of the crisis of representation, and his critique of anthropocentric humanism pierces through to the core of the aesthetics of interiority.

This chapter will sketch out these problems in some detail and will attempt to show how Mann tries to resolve the impasse of modernist culture. At the heart of his fictionalized solution is the reconciliation of ethics and aesthetics. It is to this end that his Adrian Leverkühn founds a theory of composition that originates not from personal interiority but in the exteriority of nature as a whole. In so doing he replenishes the ability of art to achieve depths of humane expression inaccessible to the schemata of tradition. The source of this renewal is a conception of nature that understands her to encompass the entirety of the world, a holism that includes both the physical and the spiritual. According to Leverkühn, good and evil belong to nature, man belongs to nature, and art belongs to nature. A reconciliation between ethics and aesthetics is possible because the both of them are rooted in common ground. It is a function of art to articulate an ecology of man caught between the natural poles of good and evil.

I

As a preliminary to the discussion of *Doktor Faustus*, and in order to bring the novel into the context of modernism, it will be useful to specify provisionally the nature of the mimesis that is at work in the writings of Thomas Mann. Mimesis is the popularly acknowledged name for an ill-defined bond of representation between a literary sign and that for which it is a substitute. The stability of this bond has traditionally been the solid ground beneath the feet of both poet and critic. Yet we have seen that the novels of Kafka, Broch, and Musil refuse to take this stability for granted. Instead, they sound the theme of a crisis in representation. In these novels language appears as a tool that is inadequate when its role is thought to be recuperating the fullness of extra-literary reality. The way of mediation between fiction and the world for these novelists is irony. The language of illusion ironically offers the pretense of reality while simultaneously pointing up its true condition of narrativity. It admits that it is ›only‹ an ensemble of printed signs and uttered sounds that are never identical with the world they seem to represent.

Thomas Mann is the undisputed master of real-seeming illusion in German prose. His imaginary worlds satisfy the modern craving for verifiable historical and scientific facts; his sharply profiled characters seem as real, and often as not even more real, than the mundane people we are likely to know outside of novels; and the language in which he unfolds the vivid theater of his imagination is astonishing in its manifold virtuosity. It is a prose style to satisfy even the most exacting demands of any programmatic realist of the nineteenth century. Under these circumstances it ought to come as a surprise that most readers associate irony more readily with the novels of Thomas Mann than with those of Kafka, Broch, or even Musil. It is this paradoxical union of irony with realism that is the striking feature of Mann's narrative practice. The aesthetic distance generated by his sometimes sober, sometimes humorous, and occasionally wicked irony qualifies the piety of his realism in an important way.[3] The tension inherent in this unity is at the core of Mann's mimetic project.

At its least appealing, his so-called »ironical detachment« is something more like sarcasm. Posing as critique, it is sometimes designed to allow the willing reader to join the narrator – and presumably also the novelist himself – at some pretended Olympian vantage from which to smile down in smug self-satisfaction at foolish characters. The caustic wit of *Beim Propheten* or *Gladius Dei* are examples of his irony in this style. A brief passage from *Buddenbrooks* will help to specify the structure of his »detachment.« It concerns the seemingly objective narrator's description of Mamsell Jungmann, the Buddenbrook family's long-time governess. She was, he observes, a woman, »die nun schon fünfunddreißig Jahre zählte und sich rühmen durfte, im Dienste der ersten Kreise ergraut zu sein.‹[4] Obviously enough, the ›objective description‹ is an unqualified judgment passed on by an authority situated in Archimedean inaccessibility. The narrative voice frames its observations ironically so as to unmask the Mamsell's fatuous satisfaction in her servitude and to reproach her, or society, for allowing youth and personal dignity to be squandered in such a manner. The invisible narrator is similarly judgmental throughout the novel, yet poses as an objective reporter in the manner of Naturalism. It is tempting to regard this conflict of subjective vision with objective reportage as a a struc-

---

[3] On Thomas Mann's irony in general cf. esp. Erich Heller, *The Ironic German. A Study of Thomas Mann* (London: Secker and Warburg, 1958), cited as Heller; and Hans Mayer, *Thomas Mann* (Frankfurt am Main: Suhrkamp, 1980), pp. 171–183.

[4] Thomas Mann, *Buddenbrooks. Verfall einer Familie*, Gesammelte Werke, Frankfurter Ausgabe, hrsg. v. Peter de Mendelssohn, vol. III (Frankfurt am Main: S. Fischer, 1981), p. 326. Subsequent references to other volumes of the Frankfurter Ausgabe of the Gesammelte Werke will be cited in these notes as the *GWFA* followed by the appropriate volume number and preceded by the individual title.

tural flaw in the novel because, in the interest of narratological integrity, some account needs to be rendered for the point of view from which the story unfolds. Properly speaking, the narrator of a novel is a persona that belongs to the imaginary world within the book and is not identical with the writing novelist's individual psychology. Under certain circumstances it is probably licit for the reader to construct a limited amount of unity between author and narrator. Yet the unexamined assumption that the narrator and the author are twins can lead to absurd confusions. The critic who assumes the perverted narrator of Nabokov's *Lolita* to be a double for the author is not only confused but perhaps also guilty of libel. Novels such as *Buddenbrooks* run into trouble when they offer objective reporting from a narrative voice that is projected from within the nothingness of a disembodied anonymity. Its omniscience and invisibility militate against the reader's correct perception of its natural limitations and its origin in narrative convention. Mann, I believe, sensed the burden of this convention and set about lightening it when he invented figures to narrate *Doktor Faustus* and *Der Erwählte* from within the novel and when he cast *Felix Krull* in the form of its narrator's autobiography.

A middle step between the transcendental anonymity of the narrator in *Buddenbrooks* and the fully developed narrator-figures of Zeitblom and Krull is evident in *Der Zauberberg* and in the *Joseph* tetralogy. The narrator has not yet become an acting character within the story, but he does step obtrusively and humoristically into the narrative foreground. In these novels the narrator begins to take on more personality. He addresses the reader directly, muses over his characters and their lives, feigns ignorance, calls attention to his own limitations, and generally makes it known to his reader that the narrated world is one of illusion, of language-play, and self-critical literary parody.[5] In the essay »Meerfahrt mit *Don Quixote*« Thomas Mann takes due note of the kinship between his style of irony ,and that of Cervantes.[6] Like his Spanish

---

[5] Seidlin and Weigand have written perceptively on the self-conscious narrator figures in the novels of Thomas Mann's middle period. On *Der Zauberberg* see Hermann J. Weigand, *The Magic Mountain. A Study of Thomas Mann's Novel »Der Zauberberg*,« University of North Carolina Studies in Germanic Languages and Literatures, 49 (Chapel Hill: University of North Carolina Press, 1965; a rpt. of the 1933 ed.), esp. pp. 67f, 86. On the *Joseph* novels see Oscar Seidlin, »Thomas Mann's *Joseph the Provider* and Laurence Sterne's *Tristram Shandy*,« in his *Essays in German and Comparative Literature*, University of North Carolina Studies in Comparative Literature, 30 (Chapel Hill: University of North Carolina Press, 1961), pp. 182–202; German rpt. in *Thomas Mann*, hrsg. v. Helmut Koopmann, Wege der Forschung, 335 (Darmstadt: Wissenschaftliche Buchgesellschaft, 1975), pp. 140–164.

[6] In *Leiden und Größe der Meister*, *GWFA* VIII, 1018–68, esp. pp. 1035f.

predecessor, Mann uses parody and irony as a doubled-edged sword of critique and self-critique.

Not the least of Thomas Mann's mechanisms of self-consciousness is this use of irony from *Buddenbrooks* and *Felix Krull*. It is one of the means whereby the author makes it known that the reality of the text occurs at the level of its narrativity – i.e. of its words and conventions – and not at the level of referentiality. Such is also the irony that Mann attributes to Goethe's portrayal of Mephisto in *Faust*. Mephisto is actually a demon born in the depths of ancient superstition. Goethe had to dispose of certain traits in order to make him presentable to an intellectually sophisticated era. Horns, tail, claws, cloven hoof and the other standard appurtenances of the devil's colorful past in the popular imagination would have been comical anachronisms for Goethe's enlightened audience. So the poet recasts him as urbane and cosmopolitan, in keeping with the values of his time and place. Yet at one point in *Faust* even this Mephisto betrays his humble origins in primitive folklore when he balks and shys away from a crucifix, reverting fully to the slightly ridiculous manners of a medieval hobgoblin. This stylized aversion to the holy cross, suggests Mann, has the feel of well-worn literary claptrap when transferred onto the likes of this otherwise suave figure: »So spielt der Dichter mit seiner Figur, gibt ihr Augenblicke satirischer Selbst-Aufhebung und Einschränkung ihrer Wirklichkeit. Schließlich aber ist sie da – ein Teufel, dem mittelalterlichen Dämon-Zeremoniell unterworfen, der Beschwörung zugänglich.«[7]

Mann's point is that good-humored irony of the self-conscious variety is perfectly in keeping with the tone of a serious literary project. But the converse is also true. Serious ironies are in keeping with a humorous literary project. One thinks, for instance, of Felix Krull's chummy affinity for Professor Kuckuck's menagerie of stuffed animals. Like them, Felix is a sham and an impostor. He is not the Marquis that he is pretending to be and, even more to the point, he is himself the denizen of a menagerie. As a figure in a novel he is as lifeless as the lifelike figures in Kuckuck's frozen zoo. Krull is the product of self-conscious literary taxidermy.

Felix Krull's feeling of solidarity with the contrivances of Kuckuck's art is one facet of the novel's overriding theme, which is the relationship between illusion and reality. And this relationship folds back on the novel itself as a world of artifice and illusion. Imagination and pretense govern Krull's entire existence, and in this sense he is the literary word incarnate. In the same way that he is conscious of his

---

[7] »Über Goethes *Faust*,« in *Leiden und Größe der Meister*, *GWFA* VIII, p. 276.

cunning trickery and imposture, so also is the novel aware of itself as an artfully contrived ensemble of conventions, tropes, and verbal illusions. The rift between *Schein* and *Sein* seems utter. Precisely this problem is taken up and developed thematically by characters within the tale, especially Kuckuck and Krull, who defend illusion on the grounds that illusion and reality are both ultimately a function of being itself, a fundamental process of nature. Professor Kuckuck expounds to Felix on the inanimate crystals that are able to mimic living plants. Felix recounts:

> Im Schein- und Halbleben der flüssigen Kristalle spiele augenfällig das eine Reich ins andre hinüber. Immer, wenn die Natur uns gaukelnd im Unorganischen das Organische vortäusche, wie in den Schwefel-, den Eisblumen, wolle sie uns lehren, daß sie eines sei.[8]

Mimicry in nature and mimesis in art are a matched pair to which I will return at the end of this chapter. Here it is interesting to note that the notion of imitation and illusion in nature is also a self-reflective key to the status of literary illusion in *Doktor Faustus*.

In Chapter III Zeitblom recalls his childhood with Adrian Leverkühn and the influence that Adrian's father, Jonathan, exercised on them. Like Professor Kuckuck, the elder Leverkühn is a philosopher of nature, who enjoys »speculating the elements« with the two boys. This speculation concerns especially the games of imitation and illusion that nature plays with itself. It is he who shows them a picture book that contains a representation of the exotic butterfly *Hetaera esmerelda*. Because of its translucent pink and violet wings, it looks like a flower petal floating in the jungle breeze. In a similar vein, there is a reproduction of a moth that imitates in minute detail the appearance of a leaf. Jonathan points out to them that even the coloration, the »traumschönes Azurblau« that belongs to many insects of the tropics, is in truth an optical illusion. The color is not properly *in* the insects at all but is instead the play of light on the creatures' epidermal formations. Adrian's mother wonders out loud: »Es ist also Trug?«

> »Nennst du das Himmelsblau Trug?« erwiderte ihr Mann, indem er rückwärts zu ihr aufblickte. »Den Farbstoff kannst du mir auch nicht nennen, von dem es kommt.«[9]

---

[8] *Die Bekenntnisse des Hochstaplers Felix Krull. Memoiren erster Teil* (Frankfurt am Main: S. Fischer, 1979), pp. 276f.

[9] *Doktor Faustus/Die Entstehung des Doktor Faustus* (Frankfurt am Main: S. Fischer, 1967), p. 23. In the rest of this chapter both the novel and *Die Entstehung* will be cited from this edition parenthetically in the text.

The line of separation between illusion and reality, which ordinarily seems plain enough, suddenly becomes indistinct. The realization gradually emerges that nature itself engages in the sport of illusion-making that had seemed to be the exclusive province of poets and painters. Here – bent over a picture book we cannot see, among a group of fictional charaters gathered together in an imaginary world – is a discussion of the relationship between illusion and truth, fiction and reality.

The extraordinary twist that Mann gives to this familiar theme is to couch it not in terms of art, its accustomed context, but in terms of nature. Mimesis, the artifice of imitation, appears at once in a new light. There is a flash of illumination that reveals the fundament of art to be an entirely natural process and not the privileged activity of the autonomous human mind. Art originates at a level deeper than individual mind.

Skeptics will object that there is no insight here because this notion belonged to the programmatics of Romanticism. Lyric poets of the deepest, most original sensibilities – from Haller and Brockes to Goethe and Eichendorff – made a similar point long ago. These leaders have been followed by legions of slighter and inferior poets who have hammered away ad nauseam at the unity of man and nature. But these poets protest too much; the very necessity of asserting this unity is predicated on the scission between man and nature. In the wake of Cartesian dualism and in the grip of German Idealism, the Romantics perceived man, his putative consciousness and unique individuality to be at the center of, yet separate from nature. Mind imposes its categories on the world »out there,« on nature, and this nature is not permitted to be what it is but must instead become an objectification of mind, an expression of man and his order. When Descartes codified the epistemic privilege of mind by dint of its self-certainty, the human being became a »subject,« and everything else – nature – became its »object.«

Literally, *ob-ject* means ›that which is thrown into opposition‹ to the *sub-ject*, which is ›that which is thrown beneath‹ nature, i.e. its basis. The upshot of this paradigm is the loss, as it were, of nature. Subjective Romanticism responded to its sense of alienation from the objective world with a poetry that celebrates nature in its juxtaposition to man. The very appearance of valorized nature in painting and poetry is a *novum* of modernity, the sign of a nostalgia caused by the division of the world into subjects and objects. The artistic celebration of nature was an attempt to recover what had receded from self-certainty and immediate accessibility. But even the most persuasive attempts had to fail because the subject-object paradigm – which had precipitated the schism in the first place – also governed the way in which they tried to recapture nature. The modern concept of man as the interiority of personal subjectivity, perception, experience and creation became firmly entrenched as the center of reality, and the exterior world became the space into which this interiority poured forth. The world became anthropocentric and anthropomorphic.[10] It is the Age of Humanism, and it is Faust in his relentless will to knowledge, which is to say in his sometimes well-intentioned sometimes ruthless will to power, who is emblematic of the modern era.

In *Doktor Faustus*, perhaps surprisingly, the centrality of man and the romantic lordliness of human subjectivity are opened to question. The fulcrum of this question is the relationship between imitation as a process of nature and imitation as a contrivance of human artistry: mimesis. Jonathan Leverkühn's speculation about nature's unexpected talent for illusion-making is the springboard for this query about the interconnectedness of truth and illusion in literary art. He offers to Adrian and Serenus a series of examples that challenge their way of thinking about fiction and reality: a butterfly that mimics a leaf; a drop of chloroform that acts like a hungry beast; musically vibrated sand that translates sound into spatial patterns; ice crystals that imitate live fronds, grasses, and flower blossoms; and a crystal garden »grown« from the sandy bottom of a water-filled vessel.

The water crystals, which both Leverkühn and Kuckuck refer to as »Eisblumen,« are the occasion of a commentary on the reciprocity of imitation. Zeitblom recalls the scene at some length:

Bildeten, so lautete seine Frage, diese Phantasmagorien die Formen des Vegetativen *vor*, oder bildeten sie sie *nach*? Keines von beidem, erwiderte er wohl sich selbst; es waren Parallelbildungen. Die schöpferisch träumende Natur träumte hier und dort dasselbe, und durfte von Nachahmung die Rede sein, so gewiß nur von wechselseitiger. Sollte man die wirklichen Kinder der

---

[10] For a useful summary of the epistemological model that the eighteenth century inherited see Stephen Toulmin, *Human Understanding. The Collective Use and Evolution of Concepts* (Princeton: Princeton University Press, 1971), pp. 13–25. For a critique of the notion of the philosophical subject see Martin Heidegger, »Die Zeit des Weltbildes,« in his *Holzwege*, Gesamtausgabe, Abt. I, Bd. 5 (Frankfurt am Main: Vittorio Klostermann, 1977), pp. 75–113; Michel Foucault, *The Order of Things. An Archaeology of the Human Sciences* (New York: Vintage Books, 1973); and Karl Popper, »Epistemology Without a Knowing Subject,« in his *Objective Knowledge. An Evolutionary Approach* (London: Oxford, 1972), pp. 106–152. It is no doubt very significant that as unlikely a trio as Popper, Heidegger and Foucault can at least in principle agree upon this point.

Flur als die Vorbilder hinstellen, weil sie organische Tiefenwirklichkeit besaßen, die Eisblumen aber bloße Erscheinungen waren? Aber ihre Erscheinung war das Ergebnis keiner geringeren Kompliziertheit stofflichen Zusam-
menspiels als diejenige der Pflanzen. Verstand ich unseren Gastfreund recht,
so war, was ihn beschäftigte, die Einheit der belebten und der sogenannten
unbelebten Natur, es war der Gedanke, daß wir uns an dieser versündigen,
wenn wir die Grenze zwischen beiden Gebieten allzu scharf ziehen, da sie
doch in Wirklichkeit durchlässig ist und es eigentlich keine elementare Fähigkeit gibt, die durchaus den Lebewesen vorbehalten wäre, und die nicht der
Biologe auch am unbelebten Modell studieren könnte. (29)

This tantalizing ambiguity between imitation and intimation is not re-
solvable, because each of the two – recapitulation and precapitulation –
arises from a deeper unity. The principle of creativity that generated
and governs organic nature also generates and governs anorganic nature. Animate and inanimate phenomena, as old Leverkühn rightly
perceives, are rooted in common ground. The boundary between them
is uncertain, determined more by habits of classification than by incontrovertible fact.

Zeitblom finds the ice flowers unsettling enough, but old Leverkühn's crystal garden is even more chilling. This garden is a crystalline
landscape cultivated in a jar. When Jonathan asks the boys what they
think of the jar's contents, they reply that the little structures seem to
be plants. Jonathan points out that they only look like plants and adds
significantly that these imitations are not less remarkable for appearing
to be of a second-order reality, mere copies. The butterfly that copies a
leaf cannot fill the niche in the ecosystem that the leaf fills, but it does
fill its own proper niche. The reality of an ›imitation‹ is of an order
equal to but not identical with the supposed ›original.‹

But when the butterflies' game of imitation extends to anorganic
nature it takes on sinister connotations. The chemical crystals in old
Leverkühn's garden seem demonic and unholy to Zeitblom, and even
Jonathan Leverkühn is ill at ease with them. In contrast to his father
and his friend, Adrian reacts to this play of similitudes with an odd
mirth. The beautiful garden both attracts and repels old Leverkühn,
who finally reaches the tearful conclusion: »Und dabei sind sie tot«
(32). Zeitblom, the novel's die-hard traditionalist, retreats from the garden in sanctimonious indignation, retiring into the security of his faith
in humanistic values: »Gespenstereien wie diese sind ausschließlich die
Sache der Natur. . . . Im würdigen Reich der Humaniora ist man sicher
vor solchem Spuk« (32). But Zeitblom is not as secure from this sort of
sorcery as he thinks he is. What Zeitblom cannot recognize is that he
himself is in a crystal garden. Old Leverkühn's demonstrations fold
back on the novel self-referentially to reveal the lifelike simulacra who

speak and act in it for what they really are: »Spuk« and »Gespenstereien« that belong squarely in the noble realm of the Humaniora. The novelist, camouflaged here momentarily as old Leverkühn, has grown a real-seeming garden of words and tropes inside a vessel from which they cannot escape. Should the reader of a novel shed a tear – like Jonathan Leverkühn – because the figures in the vessel behind the glass are not real people, because they are »dead?« Adrian, for one, does not share the »humanism« of his father and his friend. As tears well up in old Leverkühn's eyes and as Serenus recoils in disgust, Adrian has to choke back his amusement, presumably at their anthropomorphic sentimentalism. When viewed from within Zeitblom's frame of reference, this laughter has a pathological note in it, and since he is our narrator we are compelled to accept his view, at least provisionally. Adrian rejects their anthropocentricity, and the tension between his post-nihilist anthropology and Zeitblom's conservative humanism informs much of the rest of the novel.

Zeitblom and Leverkühn share a love for art, yet it is also this common territory upon which they are divided from one another, as between the *humaniora* and the *elementa*. For Zeitblom, art is the fruit of culture; it is that which separates man from the beasts and from soulless, inanimate nature. Like his father before him and like Dr. Faustus of the 1587 chapbook, Adrian is a speculator of the elements. He pursues the implications of his father's nature mysticism to their uppermost and nethermost reaches. Old Leverkühn's comments – or rather his questions – concerning the games of imitation between butterflies and leaves lend a sharp relief to the difference between Adrian and Serenus. »»Wie hat das Tier das gemacht? . . . Wie macht es die Natur durch das Tier? Denn dessen eigener Beobachtung kann man den Trick unmöglich zuschreiben. . . . Ich frage das euch, damit nicht gar ihr mich danach fragt.‹« (24). This open question is set also to the reader of the novel. How is it that a butterfly can imitate a leaf? How is it that lifeless crystals imitate living plants? How is it that a few words and letters printed on a page are able to contain deathless images, penetrating thoughts, and entire worlds of laughing, crying, living people?

The central point, which is implied in old Leverkühn's puzzlement at nature's impostors and is kept alive in his unanswered questions to the boys, is the relationship between art and life, culture and nature. The butterfly does not »know« how to imitate a leaf, as the old speculator surmised, but nature does »know« how to bring about this ingenious bit of mimetic artistry. According to this line of logic, the artistry of a human being is only secondarily the product of individual genius in the form of personal subjectivity. It is primarily the voice of a deeper unitary field that speaks through man and nature alike, through the speaking poet, through the mimicking insect.

Anthropocentric humanism fails to situate the phenomenon of consciousness properly. It is first and foremost the expression of a holonomic principle that underlies it and all other creative phenomena. The conventional duality of mind and nature is misleading, for each of the two is grounded in the nourishing soil of a deeper authority, the authority of imagination. In my unconventional use of the word ›imagination‹ there remains little of its meaning in ordinary usage. It is not the discrete faculty of individual or even collective subjectivity in the sense of psychology or of the brain's circuitry. Imagination is to be understood here as a fundamental principle of the selective, stochastic process of transformation that governs the future-oriented creativity of image-making in man and nature. The individual, no matter whether it is a butterfly pretending to be a leaf or a storyteller creating the illusion of people and deeds, is the instrument and not the instigator of this process. In both nature and culture imitation functions doubly as the recapitulation of what has been and the prefiguration of what is to be.

For the present it is important only to note that from the outset of *Doktor Faustus*, or at least from Chapter III, the novel presents a question. This question poses itself in an ironical motion of self-reference, and it concerns the interrelatedness of the mechanisms of imitation in nature and culture. It is a query of the most authentic sort because it does not come with a ready-made answer, but is formulated as an invitation to active thinking. The voice of the novel, speaking now through Jonathan Leverkühn, responds to the question in a way that shifts the burden of thought onto the shoulders of the reader: »Ich frage das euch, damit nicht gar ihr mich danach fragt.«

II

Doktor Faustus contains in discernable form a remarkable amount of German history and biography, and the traditions of Western philosophy, music and literature shape its contents to an equally remarkable degree. The elegance and compression of the deftly interwoven threads of fact and fabulation are interesting in their own right, and scholars have examined its warp and woof in considerable detail.[11] Source hunt-

---

[11] Gunilla Bergsten, *Thomas Manns »Doktor Faustus«: Untersuchungen zu den Quellen and zur Struktur des Romans*, Studia Litterarum Upsaliensia, 3 (Stockholm: Svenska, 1963); Liselotte Voss, *Die Entstehung von Thomas Manns Roman »Doktor Faustus.« Dargestellt anhand von unveröffentlichten Vorarbeiten*, Studien zur deutschen Literatur, 39 (Tübingen: Niemeyer,

ers, allusion scalpers, and theory skinners find themselves on a hunting preserve of special abundance. And the sportive Thomas Mann, a gamekeeper who enjoys a good chase, was friendly enough to write a guide to good hunting on his preserve.

Die Entstehung des »Doktor Faustus.« Roman eines Romans records among other things the author's various readings during the period he was at work on the novel. His account reads as if it were a simple autobiographical record but it is actually shrewd in its artful inclusions and exclusions. For instance, he notes in passing that »Stevensons Meisterstück *Dr. Jekyll and Mr. Hyde*« belonged to the readings that made an impression on him during the period when the as yet inchoate novel began to occupy his mind (692). Stevenson's tale is of course the classic example of *dédoublement* in the history of the novel. It is the story of two men who are actually inverse reflections of the same man. A similar mode of antithetical pairing is the cornerstone of *Doktor Faustus.* Zeitblom and Leverkühn are inverse doubles of each other, covertly parodistic enfigurations of opposing Jekyll-and-Hyde poles: the good and kindly Dr. Zeitblom vs. the mad and raging genius Mr. Leverkühn. But the doubling only begins here. Zeitblom is also a conspicuous double for the traditional narrator and latter-day Erasmus to Leverkühn's Luther; and Leverkühn also echoes the lives of Faust, Nietzsche, Hugo Wolf, and Judas; the artist manqué Schildknapp, whose eyes are an eerie repetition of Adrian's, is a negative reflection of the true artist in Leverkühn; the limping Dozent Schleppfuß, the stuttering Herr Kretzschmar, and Adrian's Leipzig tourguide are mirrors to his Mephisto – and their infirmities prefigure the paralysis that will eventually overtake him; the flowers of the crystal garden imitate in diabolical mummery their animate counterparts; Frau von Tolna doubles Esmerelda, who also doubles as a butterfly and a musical motif; the landscape, circumstances, and even the people of Adrian's adult home at Pfeiffering resemble in uncanny detail those of his childhood home at the Buchelhof near Kaisersaschern. The novel's system of interior reflections and exterior allusions is unusually complex, but there is one in particular that should not go unnoticed.

At the beginning of the last chapter I suggested that the protagonist-pair in *Doktor Faustus* are contemporary variants of Don Quixote and Sancho Panza. The composer Leverkühn is a demonic Quixote, out of

1975); T. J. Reed, *Thomas Mann. The Uses of Tradition* (London: Oxford, 1974), pp. 360–402; J.P. Stern, *History and Allegory in Thomas Mann's »Doktor Faustus«*, An Inaugural Lecture Delivered at University College, London 1 March 1973 (London: H. K. Lewis, 1975), cited as Stern.

step with his time, bent on an improbable quest, and dedicated to his true Dulcinea. She is Esmerelda, and she appears in various guises, now a diseased whore, now an elusive butterfly, or again as a haunting motif borne through the whole of Leverkühn's composition like a flower petal on the wind. In her Faustian persona she is the fabulous concubine Helena, the most beautiful hetare of them all. As Faustus, Leverkühn must have his Famulus Wagner, and as Quixote he needs a squire. The figures of the professorial drudge and the sententious peasant are blended wonderfully in Serenus Zeitblom. His slightly preposterous name is a clue to the mixture of playfulness and seriousness with which he ought to be regarded. Literally it means something like ›blossom of the serene age.‹ The age at issue is that of humanism, and its flower is the mandarin intellectual who is dedicated to the values and ideals that have dominated the Western way of thinking since the Renaissance. This fastidiously erudite man of culture has supplanted the crusty peasant of the *Quixote* and the stuffy pedant of *Faust*, but the role remains the same. Sancho in *Don Quixote*, Wagner in *Faust*, and Zeitblom in Mann's novel are the carriers of average reality in their respective times and places. In each of the three masterworks, the main protagonists challenge the prevailing standards of reality. Each takes upon himself a quixotic mission that destines him for acts of madness and criminality that are made bearable by irony and humor.

Even though Don Quixote and Sancho Panza are worlds apart as individuals, they appear in the novel and in our memories as an inseparable pair. One without the other is unthinkable because the real action of the novel arises from the contrasting but complementary points of view that they express. They are Jekyll-and-Hyde inverted images of each other: the staunchly average man and his ›mad‹ alter ego. The sturdy conservative's sure grip on reality counterbalances the visionary's subversive madness. Zeitblom and Leverkühn are opposed yet inseparable doubles caught in the same dynamic counterpoise. Between these two positions is an interstice that offers itself as a stage upon which the act of interpretation can play itself out.

The first position is that of Serenus Zeitblom, who begins his long reminiscence with an ironic assertion. In the novel's first sentence, he thrusts himself into the foreground of his narrative to assert that he has no desire to thrust himself into the foreground of the narrative. He makes himself conspicuous from the very beginning and dominates the narrated world until the end.[12] With very few exceptions his point of

---

[12] On Zeitblom's structural role see Margit Henning, *Die Ich-Form und ihre Funktion in Thomas Manns »Doktor Faustus« und in der deutschen Literatur der Gegenwart*, Studien zur deutschen Literatur, 2 (Tübingen: Niemeyer, 1966).

view determines that of the reader. His overstated eloquence, the secrets that the author keeps from him, and his repeated insistence that he is not writing a novel are some of the ways in which his domination is ironized and undermined.

By way of explaining Zeitblom's presence and role in the novel, Thomas Mann writes in *Die Entstehung* that he cannot recall when he first thought of introducing him into the story. But he does point out that his sense of parody as well as the need for irony and humor were decisive factors: »Gewiß hatte die Erinnerung an die parodistische Autobiographie Felix Krulls dabei mitgewirkt, und überdies war die Maßnahme bitter notwendig, um eine gewisse Durchheiterung des düsteren Stoffes zu erzielen und mir selbst, wie dem Leser, seine Erschrecknisse erträglich zu machen« (700). Parodic autobiography has become the parody of a biography; and the serio-comic figure of the narrator-biographer introduces an element of irony and understated humor that help to create some aesthetic distance between the grim events depicted and the emotional plane that the author and reader inhabit.

By introducing an observer into the field of observation Mann has opened his writing to a dimension that at best had only been implied in *Buddenbrooks* or *Der Zauberberg*. In his *Schlafwandler*, Hermann Broch had similarly interposed an obtrusive narrator between the reader and the story, and had given this practice a careful theoretical justification in his essay »James Joyce und die Gegenwart« (1936).[13] There is no reason to believe that Broch's theory influenced Thomas Mann. Nevertheless, what matters here is that the presence of the storyteller in the story has been stock-in-trade for the self-conscious novelist since Cervantes and Sterne. It is the earmark of the greater tradition to which both Broch and Mann belong. Old Zeitblom seems aware of his place in this tradition – ironically of course – when in the course of his narration he likens himself to Laurence Sterne (97).

Zeitblom's presence in the work renders the narrator, which in Mann's earlier work had only been an invisible voice, into a known quantity. No longer is the narrative point of view an Archimedean point located at some vantage outside of the narrated world. It has become a character with its own history, its own intellectual commitments, beliefs, prejudices, and limitations. This figure makes distinct the line of division that always exists between the empirical author of a fiction and the voice that speaks from within the fiction itself during its

---

[13] Hermann Broch, »James Joyce und die Gegenwart,« in his *Schriften zur Literatur 1, Kritik*, Kommentierte Werkausgabe, hrsg. v. Paul Michael Lützeler, vol. IX/1 (Frankfurt am Main: Suhrkamp, 1976), pp. 63–95.

real life in its own history, as opposed to the interpretation its author might give it. Thomas Mann is not Zeitblom, even though he may bear various traits that match our perception of the author. Zeitblom is more of a working hypothesis, a judgmental point of view from which the action of the story unfolds, as well as a full-fledged actor in the cast of characters. The introduction of the observer into the sphere of observation is a gesture of renunciation on the part of the author. Rather than exploit the traditional privilege of the realist author-narrator, i.e. the right to impose authoritative views and judgments, this author has merged with the novel as whole to become a function of its pronouncements. Mann has absented himself as a external point of reference and left in his place a hermeneutical configuration that is open to the act of imaginative, affective, and critically intelligent reading.[14]

In the hermeneutical configuration of *Doktor Faustus*, Zeitblom holds a place from which reality and its provisional borderlines are marked out. His voice is that of tradition, and it is he who eloquently reaffirms and reinforces the generally acknowledged versions of the Good, the True and the Beautiful. His point of view is that of the bourgeois humanist and enlightened liberal. Dr. phil. Serenus Zeitblom presents himself as a man of finely honed intellect and critical discrimination; he has cultivated his aesthetic sensibilities yet has not indulged them to excess nor allowed them to become overripe; by profession he is an educator of the young, and his fields are Latin, Greek, and History; he advocates an ideal of mankind that is based upon the concept of individualism and the liberal values associated with it: freedom, truth, progress, right, and reason. For Zeitblom, the sum of these values is the occidental achievement in art and letters and their reflection in human affairs in the form of political, social, and religious institutions. It is significant that Zeitblom composes the German libretto for Leverkühn's version of *Love's Labour's Lost*, for the humanist's labor of love has truly been lost. In two lacerating World Wars the meliorist tradition, its eternal verities, and its human values come crashing down around Zeitblom's horrified ears:

> Das Gefühl, daß eine Epoche sich endigte, die nicht nur das neunzehnte Jahrhundert umfaßte, sondern zurückreichte bis zum Ausgang des Mittelalters, bis zur Sprengung scholastischer Bindungen, zur Emanzipation des Individuums, der Geburt der Freiheit, eine Epoche, die ich recht eigentlich als die meiner weiteren geistigen Heimat zu betrachten hatte, kurzum, die Epo-

---

[14] Hans Mayer notes a similar point in *Felix Krull*. H. M., »Felix Krull und Oskar Matzerath. Aspekte des Romans,« in his *Das Geschehen und das Schweigen. Aspekte der Literatur*, edition suhrkamp, 342 (Frankfurt am Main: Suhrkamp, 1969), pp. 35–67, esp. 56f.

che des bürgerlichen Humanismus; – das Gefühl, sage ich, daß ihre Stunde geschlagen hatte, eine Mutation des Lebens sich vollziehen, die Welt in ein neues, noch namenloses Sternzeichen treten wollte, – dieses zu höchstem Aufhorchen anhaltende Gefühl war zwar nicht erst das Erzeugnis des Kriegsendes, es war schon das seines Ausbruchs, vierzehn Jahre nach der Jahrhundertwende, gewesen und hatte der Erschütterung, der Schicksalsergriffenheit zum Grunde gelegen, die meinesgleichen damals erfahren hatte. (468f)

Have the humanists, the teachers of mankind not only in Germany but in all of the West, simply failed to live up to their obligations, or could it be that Humanism contained within itself the seeds of its own eventual destruction? In Chapter XXXIV Zeitblom argues that the intellectuals of his day, with Georges Sorel leading the pack of renegades, have betrayed the ideals of humanism and turned jubilantly to barbarism, violence, and mere chaos. The Kridwiß Circle of Munich intellectuals spouts a Sorelian philosophy »der Gewalt, der Autorität und der Glaubensdiktatur« that illustrates Zeitblom's critique (485). These avant-garde analysts of culture, in a spasm of reaction to the evident failure of humanism, have only turned the values of tradition upside down. Their fashionably mannered pessimism revels merrily in its own smug and sterile nihilism, pointing the way to fascism. It is perhaps their unabashed delight in gloom and destruction that unsettles Zeitblom most of all. Like him, they are students of the *humaniora*, but their interest in knowledge has shriveled up into an unregenerate »academism« that is a correlate of the aestheticism that flourished at the same time. Their advocation of power and violence is not the reflection of a desire to recover an old order or even to begin a new one. They are interested in the regime of learning for its own sake because it enhances feelings of aloof superiority. Their diagnostic pronouncements on the diseased culture of Europe are an exercise in nihilistic self-absorption, a narcissistic pose, a hyper-intellectual expression of impotence and despair.

Still, it is not the effete literati alone who are filled with the sense of an ending. Zeitblom himself feels and even embodies the exhaustion of humanism. He is by natural disposition and profession an educator. By the same token, humanism has been the mentor of the West in general, and perhaps of Germany in particular. Zeitblom's personal failure as an *Erzieher* dovetails lamentably with the inability of the doctrines and institutions of humnanist culture to prevent the rise of totalitarian bestiality in the modern era: Zeitblom has no doubt whatsoever that his own sons would turn him over to the Nazi authorities if they were to discover his true political sentiments. Zeitblom's failure to pass on his values to his children marks the failure of the tradition in general. He feels morally obliged to withdraw from the teaching profession as he

151

witnesses the rise of National Socialism in his civilized, cultivated homeland, and even after the final defeat of the oppressors, Zeitblom senses that his ideals are out of step and out of place:

> Werde ich wieder einer humanistischen Prima den Kulturgedanken ans Herz legen, in welchem Ehrfurcht vor den Gottheiten der Tiefe mit dem sittlichen Kult olympischer Vernunft und Klarheit zu *einer* Frömmigkeit verschmilzt? Aber ach, ich fürchte, in dieser wilden Dekade ist ein Geschlecht herangewachsen, das meine Sprache sowenig versteht wie ich die seine, ich fürchte, die Jugend meines Landes ist mir zu fremd geworden, als daß ich ihr Lehrer sein könnte .... (669)

It is true that the decadent humanists of the Kridwiß variety betrayed the very ideals that had given rise to their way of life. But it is also true that a humanist of authentic conviction and moral intelligence such as Zeitblom turned out to be powerless to prevent or oppose the malignant growth of political aggression and terror. This state of affairs suggests that the real problem lies deeper than a betrayal of timeless ideals, that there is in humanism itself a hidden flaw. If this is the case, then there must be some position beyond the customary alternatives, *either* humanism *or* brutal, insensate barbarism.

Leverkühn moves in a direction that leads beyond the helpless humanism of Zeitblom and beyond the perverse nihilism of the Kridwiß Circle. What makes him different from them is his eccentric sense of humankind's place in the order of the world. Zeitblom's image of man is classically humanistic. It attaches prime importance to the uniqueness of man and to the absoluteness of human values (63). Historically, the birth of Homo humanus at the dawn of modernity coincides with the ›discovery‹ of Culture and Nature, which in turn gives rise, respectively, to the Humanities and to the Scientific Revolution. In his essence man has suddenly become more than a natural being in the world among other natural beings. Now he is the creator, preserver, and product of culture, the subject of values, the master and perceiver of soulless nature. The natural world becomes the object of precise investigation because as mere material it can be weighed, measured, counted and otherwise quantitatively analyzed. Its subjective analyzer, the scientist-investigator with the immaterial essence of mind, stands above and beyond the merely natural in a position of sovereign objectivity.

Zeitblom repeatedly avows his distaste for the natural world and defends the innate superiority of the »lettered-humane,« the »Sprachlich-Humane.« »»Es ist dem Menschen natürlich,‹ sagte Goethe, ›sich als das Ziel der Schöpfung zu betrachten, und alle übrigen Dinge nur in bezug auf sich, und insofern sie ihm dienen und nützen.‹«[15] The poet's

---

[15] Johann Peter Eckermann, *Gespräche mit Goethe in den letzten Jahren seines*

comment to his secretary is symptomatic for modernity's prevailing notion of man's place in the world. Zeitblom's humanism is full of the Goethean spirit of a benevolent Faustian domination. It underlies even the counterhumanism of the poseurs in the Kridwiß Circle. Salon poet Daniel zur Höhe's marauding hero »Christus imperator maximus« is an all-too-accurate caricature of the Faustian will to power run amok. Indeed, these drawing-room thinkers openly advocate violence and barbarism as an alternative to the vitiated present. But their bogus philosophy is only the shadow cast by traditional humanism. Its fundamental point of reference remains man and his dominion over the earth, a dominion that extends to nationalistic aggression and man's domination of man. This concept of humankind as the subject of power – no matter whether it comes in the form of traditional individualism or quasi-radical collectivism – is common to humanist and counterhumanist alike.

Leverkühn's response to the natural world is a clue to his subtle movement towards a post-nihilistic view of man. Early in the novel Adrian evinces an affinity for the *elementa* that sets him apart from his childhood companion. In his contrasting commitment to the *humaniora*, Zeitblom peremptorily dismisses Jonathan Leverkühn's crystal garden as mere »Spuk« and »Gespenstereien.« In Chapter XXVII this thematic opposition resurfaces when Zeitblom is a skeptical audience to Leverkühn's reflections on the *elementa*. Their point of departure is Klopstock's ode »Frühlingsfeyer,« which Adrian has set to music. It is of particular interest to him because of the mysticism of its »Tropfen am Eimer« strophe, in which art, nature, and religious humility are thought to converge. Zeitblom recollects that in those days his friend was preoccupied with questions of nature and the cosmos, a topic concerning which their opinions were very much at a cross-grain.

Adrian's sympathy for the abyss takes a literal form in his playful enthusiasm for the creatures of the ocean's nethermost depths and for the celestial vastness of galactic expanses. Zeitblom recalls that Leverkühn enjoyed teasing him with his philosophical »speculations:« »denn er kannte wohl meine bis zur Abneigung gehende Interesselosigkeit an den Faxen und Geheimnissen des Natürlichen, an ›Natur‹ überhaupt, und an meine Anhänglichkeit an die Sphäre des Sprachlich-Humanen« (358). The humanist objects that nature's deep-sea grotesqueries as well as the exponential »Zahlenspuk« of astrophysical time and space are not religiously productive nor otherwise relevant to the essence of man.

Lebens, hrsg. v. H. H. Houben (Wiesbaden: Brockhaus, 1959), p. 348. The entry is dated 20 February, 1831.

Such dalliance with the immeasurable and the nonhuman, thinks Zeitblom, can give no nourishment to authentic piety:

Frömmigkeit, Ehrfurcht, seelischer Anstand, Religiosität sind nur über den Menschen und durch den Menschen, in der Beschränkung auf das Irdisch-Menschliche möglich. Ihre Frucht sollte, kann und wird ein religiös tingierter Humanismus sein, bestimmt von dem Gefühl für das transzendente Geheimnis des Menschen, von dem stolzen Bewußtsein, daß er kein bloß biologisches Wesen ist, sondern mit einem entscheidenden Teil seines Wesens einer geistigen Welt angehört; daß ihm das Absolute gegeben ist, die Gedanken der Wahrheit, der Freiheit, der Gerechtigkeit, daß ihm der Verpflichtung auferlegt ist zur Annäherung an das Vollkommene. In diesem Pathos, dieser Verpflichtung, dieser Ehrfurcht des Menschen vor sich selbst ist Gott; in hundert Milliarden Milchstraßen kann ich ihn nicht finden. (363)

Zeitblom takes seriously and literally the dictum that man is the measure of all things. Whatever lies beyond the precincts of Homo humanus recedes into irrelevance, and since man »ist kein bloß biologisches Wesen,« it must be that his natural part is somehow exterior to his truer essence. The spiritual part – a subjective egoism – is reified in Culture, the apogee of human achievement in contradistinction to the »Faxen« of mindless nature.

If Zeitblom sounds the clarion of *human* nature, then it is fair to say that Leverkühn is an advocate of human *nature*. He replies to his humanistic alter ego:

»So bist du gegen die Werke,« antwortete er, »und gegen die physische Natur, der der Mensch entstammt und mit ihm sein Geistiges, das sich am Ende auch noch an anderen Orten des Kosmos findet. Die physische Schöpfung, dieses dir ärgerliche Ungeheuer von Weltveranstaltung, ist unstreitig die Voraussetzung für das Moralische, ohne die es keinen Boden hätte, und vielleicht muß man das Gute die Blüte des Bösen nennen – une fleur du mal. Dein Homo Dei ist doch schließlich – oder nicht schließlich, ich bitte um Entschuldigung, aber vor allem einmal – ein Stück scheußlicher Natur mit einem nicht gerade freigebig zugemessenen Quantum potentieller Vergeistigung. Übrigens ist es amüsant zu sehen, wie sehr dein Humanismus, und wohl aller Humanismus, zum Mittelalterlich-Geozentrischen neigt, – mit Notwendigkeit offenbar. Populärerweise hält man den Humanismus für wissenschaftsfreundlich; aber er kann es nicht sein, denn man kann nicht die Gegenstände der Wissenschaft für Teufelswerk erachten, ohne auch in ihr selbst dergleichen zu sehen. Das ist Mittelalter. Das Mittelalter war geozentrisch und anthropozentrisch. Die Kirche in der es überlebte, hat sich gegen die astronomischen Erkenntnisse im humanistischen Geist zur Wehr gesetzt, hat sie verteufelt und verboten zu Ehren des Menschen, hat auf Unwissenheit bestanden aus Humanität. Du siehst, dein Humanismus ist reines Mittelalter.« (363f)

Leverkühn is vaunting the priority of nature as the ultimate source of all things physical *and* spiritual. His objection to Zeitblom's humanism pivots on two hinges: the ethical and the anthropological. In suggesting that the ethical is rooted in nature, Adrian varies a theme learned from his mephistophelean theology professor in Halle. The demonologically informed Privatdozent Eberhard Schleppfuß – the sign of the cloven hoof survives here as an onomastic residue – taught that good and evil are the twin siblings of natural creation, that each depends on its opposed complement for reality and meaning. The good becomes a Baudelairean »fleur du mal« because it is anchored in demonic nature, inextricably intertwined with its counterpart. This flower image is a variation on the »Eisblumen« theme, a renewed evocation of the anorganic *fleurs du mal* in Jonathan Leverkühn's crystal garden. The implication is that the hand of art and contrivance somehow plays a role in the ecology of good and evil. A vague interrelationship between art, nature, and ethics is showing its blurry outline.

Adrian's attitude toward the reciprocity of the sacred and the demonic will help to sharpen the edges of this outline. At his sister's wedding, unsentimental Adrian contends to Zeitblom that the bourgeois sacrament of matrimony is a way of artificially containing within socially productive boundaries the violent passion of lust. This domestication of demonic eros could be regarded as *une fleur du mal*. The artifice of ecclesiastical ritual has the power to transform animal lust into the holy bond of connubial piety: the demonic passes over into the sacred, which means also that there always exists the immanent danger that evil can explode from its confines.

The proper place of art, according to Leverkühn, is in the service of the ecology of good and evil, straining against chaos, effecting the transformation of the demonic into the sacred. Zeitblom seems to hold a similar view: »oft habe ich. . .meinen Primanern vom Katheder herab erklärt, daß Kultur recht eigentlich die fromme und ordnende, ich möchte sagen, begütigende Einbeziehung des Nächtig-Ungeheueren in den Kultus der Götter ist« (17). But the agreement is only apparent. Zeitblom's pompous condescension – »vom Katheder herab« – gives him away. Art as »Kultur« is an art that has become a humanistic end in itself, that has denied its roots in nature and so has robbed itself of the vitality it needs to contain »das Nächtig-Ungeheuere.« The exhaustion of modern art reflects the failure and end of certain humanistic presuppositions. For instance, art that sentimentalizes nature, that refashions it into the image of bourgeois liberal ideals, that fails to mediate it in its ethically ambivalent truth is destined for crisis: »Das Werk! Es ist Trug. Es ist etwas, wovon der Bürger möchte, es gäbe das noch. Es ist gegen die Wahrheit und gegen den Ernst« (241). Adrian protests that art must reveal truth, and that when it becomes a function of high-minded self-deception in an era of dire need, such an art becomes an ethical liability.

--und nun fragt es sich, ob bei dem heutigen Stande unseres Bewußtseins, unserer Erkenntnis, unseres Wahrheitssinnes dieses Spiel noch erlaubt, noch geistig möglich, noch ernst zu nehmen ist, ob das Werk als solches, das selbstgenügsam und harmonisch in sich geschlossene Gebilde, noch in irgendeiner legitimen Relation steht zu der völligen Unsicherheit, Problematik und Harmonielosigkeit unserer gesellschaftlichen Zustände, ob nicht aller Schein, auch der schönste, heute zur *Lüge* geworden ist. (241)

This degeneration from the aesthetic plenitude of *Schein* to the moral poverty of *Lüge* stands in direct relation to art's formal self-indulgence, its tendency to allow originality to ossify and endlessly rehearse its past successes according to the patterns of its conventions. Only irony and parody remain as intellectually honest formal possibilities.

The similarity of Mann's Adrian to Musil's Ulrich on this count is worth noting. Each is aware that the rules governing average art and average reality, respectively, are old truths that have petrified into autotelic schemata: self-perpetuating conventions pretending to be eternal verities. Ulrich would no doubt applaud Adrian's critique of modern religiosity. The »numinous chaos« of authentic religious experience has succumbed to the ever increasing secularization of the bourgeois church and its scientific, humanistic theology (cf. esp. Chapter XIV). Religion and art that do admit of the demonic lose touch with the sacred as well. Enfeebled, exhausted conventions of art and culture can no longer contain the terror of the latent evil that will eventually shatter their worn-out framework and overpower the sleeping humanists. The icy »Mann ohne Eigenschaften« in *Doktor Faustus* refuses to compromise his sense of the sacred in much the same way that his Viennese counterpart refuses to betray his utopian pursuit of the »Other Condition« and its numinous chaos. The measure of Ulrich's ethical sincerity is his willingness to flout firmly seated convention by entering into an incestuous experiment in mystical union with his sister. The allegorical measure of Adrian's proud seriousness is his readiness to take on Esmerelda's fatal disease in the interest of regained creativity and, ultimately, renewed health.

Before we examine Adrian's ›ethical aesthetic‹ in greater detail, the second, anthropological prong of Adrian's critique of Zeitblom's humanism remains to be considered. For Zeitblom, only man and the things that have a determinate relation to humanness come into the fullness of being. Leverkühn likens this subjective egoism to the geocentric Middle Ages, implying that modernity's anthropocentric humanism is as benighted as precopernican astronomy. The Cartesian *ego cogito* and the transcendental ego of Kantian philosophy are the academic codification of the man-centered universe. Adrian's cool sympathy for the crystal garden, his unsentimental affinity for the creatures of the darkest oceanic night and for the incalculable depths of stellar infinitude mark his rejection of man-the-measure. Zeitblom's dualism sets man into a position of superior opposition to nature; Leverkühn's holism situates man in the midst of nature among its other essents. The denatured man of humanism forfeits his connectedness with the rest of the world. The unbroken continuum of man and nature is visible in the potent work of art. For Adrian, the secularization of art, its loss of cultic resonance, leaves the serious artwork with the burden of an alienated solemnity, a would-be profundity that discharges its pathos into a void. It is for this reason he must turn to parody. Yet his irony is not entirely identical with the cynical fatalism of the Kridwiß Circle. He insists that this burden of dislocated pathos, of art as »Culture« does not have to be the fate of art in the future. Zeitblom reports his friend's position with skepticism: »Was [das Schicksal der Kunst] denn sein sollte, wußte er nicht zu sagen. Aber daß die Kultur-Idee eine geschichtlich transitorische Erscheinung sei; daß sie sich auch wieder in anderem verlieren könne; daß ihr nicht notwendig die Zukunft gehöre, diesen Gedanken hatte er entschieden aus Kretzschmars Vortrag ausgesondert« (82). It is a thought that stays with him. This »Kultur-Idee,« the secularization of art, and the anthropocentric universe are various aspects of the same humanism that is in the process of collapsing noisily around Zeitblom and Leverkühn.

But the humanist is reluctant to give up his time-honored ideals and objects on ethical grounds to the artist's vague intimations: »›Aber die Alternative,‹ warf ich ihm vor, ›zur Kultur ist die Barbarei‹« (82). Adrian in his turn refuses to accept Zeitblom's either-or formulation: »Die Barbarei ist das Gegenteil der Kultur doch nur innerhalb der Gedankenordnung, die sie uns an der Hand gibt« (82). The hazy goal of Leverkühn's quixotic struggle is an ethically viable art that supersedes the constricting binary opposition Culture/Barbarism. Years later he gives a clearer picture of his vision:

> Die ganze Lebensstimmung der Kunst, glauben Sie mir, wird sich ändern, und zwar ins Heiter-Bescheidenere, – es ist unvermeidlich, und es ist ein Glück. Viel melancholische Ambition wird von ihr abfallen und eine neue Unschuld, ja Harmlosigkeit ihr Teil sein. Die Zukunft wird in ihr, sie selbst wird wieder in sich die Dienerin sehen an einer Gemeinschaft, die weit mehr als »Bildung« umfassen und Kultur nicht haben, vielleicht aber sein wird. Wir stellen es uns nur mit Mühe vor, und doch wird es das geben und wird das Natürliche sein: eine Kunst ohne Leiden, seelisch gesund, unfeierlich, untraurig-zutraulich, eine Kunst mit der Menschheit auf du und du . . . . (429)

This transport of utopian faith stands out in its uniqueness. Zeitblom thinks it out of character with Leverkühn's more usual chilly pride, but in this passage the composer has revealed the side of himself that Zeitblom cannot see. This artist has an unexpected messianic-quixotic sense of calling, the yearning for a soul traced out allegorically in his fascination with Andersen's little mermaid. He has been born into a tradition whose arteries have hardened. Historical circumstance compels him to seek a means to resuscitate the vitality of the work of art. It is a project that requires a fundamental rethinking of man's place in the world.

The relocation of human being into the natural world is a decisive factor for Adrian's aesthetic. The nexus between his desophistocated, ›fundamental‹ art and elemental nature is a special understanding of mathematics. Its emblem is the »magisches Quadrat« of Dürer's »Melancolia« (125), but it is prefigured as early as Chapter III. Among the curiosities in Jonathan Leverkühn's collection of naturalia were exotic mussels inscribed by nature with a strange »writing.« The marks on the shell of one particular mussel incite Jonathan and the boys to try to decipher its message by comparing them with ancient near-eastern forms of writing. Obviously these attempts can lead to nothing, but the assumption that leads to these attempts is crucial because it stays with Adrian. It is the assumption that *nature speaks* and that its ciphers can be made intelligible. This »Zeichenschrift« motif later re-emerges as Adrian's interest in math. Its formative period is during his student days in Halle under the tutelage of the philosophy professor Nonnenmacher. His lectures on Pythagorean nature-mysticism and its idea that number is the primal essence of nature – an essence that also embraces the domain of the ethical – lay the cornerstone of Leverkühn's later theory of musical composition (cf. 126f, 213). It was Pythagoras who first established the connection between musical harmonies and the ratio of string lengths, which led him and his disciples to develop a cosmology based on a religiously conceived notion of arithmetic and geometry.[16] The idea of mathematical relations governing the cosmos

---

[16] In this specific instance, Mann's source was likely John Redfield's *Music: A Science and an Art* (New York: Knopf, 1926), pp. 67–72, 107, 184. Mann refers to this work in the *Entstehung*. But in general he derived much of his musicological information from Adorno's *Philosophie der neuen Musik*. Adorno's opinions occur sometimes from Zeitblom's perspective and sometimes from Leverkühn's. Adorno himself decides against Schönberg's twelve-tone technique of composition because it sacrifices spontaneity to the repressive authority of the system's autotelic rationale: »Die totale Rationalität der Musik ist ihre totale Organisation. Durch Organisation möchte die befreite Musik das verlorene Ganze, die verlorene Macht und Verbindlichkeit Beet-

has an obvious bearing on Leverkühn's music. The sacred decad of Pythagorean mysticism is a short step from the twelve-tone chromatic series that undergirds Leverkühn's technique of composition.

Galileo's optimism that the »Book of Nature« is written in mathematical ciphers, or Leibniz's theory that there is a mathematically preestablished harmony of the cosmos are thoughts that impend tacitly in the background of *Doktor Faustus*. Yet on the whole, this isomorphic identity of number and nature is a thin place in the novel's otherwise convincing illusion. The dream of an all-encompassing grammar of symbolic logic had already been laid to rest a few years before when Kurt Gödel published his now-famous »Incompleteness Theorem.« His paper of 1931 proved that even the most powerful mathematical systems can never be made complete. Like any other ›language,‹ mathematical signification is limited by its own interior logic that ultimately and necessarily ends in self-contradiction.[17] A philosopher of science, Karl Popper, has argued persuasively that the isomorphic positivity that has traditionally been attributed to rigorous mathematical descriptions of nature is a delusion of sorts. A mathematical observation, suggests Popper, is always only a hypothesis that can exclude the false but that can never identify the true with absolute positivity. The scientist is like a navigator in the fog who must steer his craft through narrow shoals. He makes his calculations and follows them, never knowing with absolute certainty where he is. He knows only that he has not run aground. The calculations have served their purpose and are to be regarded as »true,« or at least as useful, until they can be falsified under other circumstances. Relativity theory and quantum mechanics have in

---

hovens wieder herstellen. Das gelingt ihr bloß um den Preis ihrer Freiheit, und damit mißlingt es. Beethoven hat den Sinn von Tonalität aus subjektiver Freiheit reproduziert. Die neue Ordnung der Zwölftontechnik löscht virtuell das Subjekt aus.« (Cf. Zeitblom's critique, pp. 126, 253f.) Perhaps Adorno's critique of Schönberg is valid, but in the imaginary world of *Doktor Faustus*, Adrian Leverkühn – the composer, the author, *das Subjekt* – also dissolves into the system, symbolically into madness and death. However, Thomas Mann's version of the subject's dissolution finally takes on a positive valuation because it signals the »Rekonstruktion des Ausdrucks« when comingled with the elemental need to articulate sorrow over the loss of little Nepomuk. This is the difference between Adorno's Schönberg-critique and Mann's presentation of Leverkühn's achievement: Schönberg's system removes art from life, whereas Leverkühn's number-magic – because it is unmediated Nature – returns art to the middle of life. See: Theodor W. Adorno, *Philosophie der neuen Musik*, Suhrkamp Taschenbuch Wissenschaft, 239 (Frankfurt am Main: Suhrkamp, 1978), pp. 69–70.

[17] Ernest Nagel and James R. Newman, *Gödel's Proof* (New York: New York University Press, 1958).

this sense falsified, or shown the limits of, Newtonian mechanics. Any map of reality can always only approach isomorphy.[18]

Still, all of this niggling does no damage to *Doktor Faustus*. For the same reason we are able to believe that carpets can fly in *Arabian Nights*, we can also accept mathematics in *Doktor Faustus* as an un-mediated transcription of nature. The real point is that Leverkühn believes he has rediscovered the possibility of artistic expression not as subjective expression in the sense of Goethe, Beethoven, and humanism, but as an expression of man in nature and nature in man, what he would regard as an »objective« frame of reference. But in point of fact the terms *objective* and *subjective* become superfluous when the barrier between man and nature has been broken down. Leverkühn's art is not, as Zeitblom fears, inhuman because man is part of nature. The natural world, as Leverkühn has pointed out to him, is a condition of the possibility of ethics. It follows that his aesthetic program is not an »aestheticism« but a step toward the recovery of fundamentals. It recognizes good and evil as a part of the world to which man belongs and that art has a responsibility to them. Leverkühn's culminating work, the *Weheklag Dr. Fausti*, is the aesthetically and ethically determined expression of grief within coordinates set forth by nature herself.

Zeitblom refers to Leverkühn's quest to break through irony into the fullness of authentic expression as the »Rekonstruktion des Ausdrucks« (643). Yet before any such renewal can occur there must first be a clearing of ground. This destructive impulse is a critique of the tradition that takes the form of ironical imitation. Thus Leverkühn's early works are parody. They are ironically self-conscious exercises in the received forms of musical expression. The composer finds himself unable to take seriously the threadbare conventions that too many hands have passed down to him. High culture indulges the formulae of »fine art« in a ritual of excessively cultivated self-congratulation. When art becomes the refined pastime of the professional academy and esoteric cognoscenti, and when its forms become autotelic conventions, values in themselves, expression loses its ability to seize the demonic and transmute it into the sacred.

Mann satirizes the impotence of high culture in the grisly scene of Rudi Schwerdtfeger's murder. The hollow clichés of education and good breeding are torn apart when the pampered daughter of *Besitz und Bildung*, Ines Rodde, pumps five pistol shots into her ex-lover after an evening at the concert. As the horribly mutilated Rudi lies wounded on

---

[18] Karl Popper, *Logik der Forschung*, 5. verb. Aufl., Die Einheit der Geisteswissenschaften, 4 (Tübingen: J. C. B. Mohr, 1973).

the floor of a Munich street car, gurgling red bubbles, Zeitblom and his humanistic colleague Dr. Kranich stand by in erudite uselessness:

>Was für eine entsetzliche, besinnungslose, unvernünftige Tat!« sagte [Dr. Kranich], bleichen Angesichts, in seiner klaren, akademisch wohlartikulierten und dabei asmathischen Sprechweise, indem er das Wort »entsetzlich,« wie man es öfters, auch von Schauspielern, hört, »entsetzlich« aussprach. Er fügte hinzu, nie habe er mehr bedauert, nicht Mediziner, sondern nur Numismatiker zu sein, und wirklich erschien mir in diesem Augenblick die Münzenkunde als die müßigste der Wissenschaften, noch unnützer als die Philologie, was keineswegs aufrechtzuhalten ist. (596f)

The macabre humor of this caricature lies in the unmasking of the humanists' self-deceiving detachment from elemental passion and death. Dr. Kranich's final appearance in the novel is during another scene in which demonic evil erupts from its flimsy containment. At the outbreak of Leverkühn's madness, the wheezy scholar testily announces his regret that no representative of the »irrenärztliche Wissenschaft« is on hand: »ich, als Numismatiker, fühle mich unzuständig« is his parting comment. As Leverkühn's madness becomes increasingly obvious during this scene, his cultivated listeners begin to depart in varying degrees of disgust and distress. Only the uncultivated Frau Schweige still shows compassion and wisdom where the humanists have failed.

The art of high culture is in a similar state of disaffection from the fundamental situation of human being. Because Adrian has sensed this estrangement he seeks uneasy refuge in irony and parody. With a prolix lucidity that is peculiar to him, Zeitblom expresses precisely the nature of his friend's response to his artistic heritage: »In Wahrheit war hier das Parodische die stolze Auskunft vor der Sterilität, mit welcher Skepsis und geistige Schamhaftigkeit, der Sinn für die tödliche Ausdehnung des Bereichs des Banalen eine große Begabung bedrohten.« In a tone of apologetic diffidence and with a touch of irony that is not his own, Zeitblom adds, »Ich hoffe das richtig zu sagen« (202f). The novelist has formulated the biographer's phrasing in a way that calls attention to this key passage. It is the point at which theme and structure converge.

In order to clarify this intersection it will be helpful to invoke once again Marthe Robert's idea of functional identity: »When imitation imposes a way of writing on the novelist and a way of living on the hero, it creates a functional identity between the two similar yet disparate figures that tells us more than any external circumstance about the true extent of their relation.«[19] I have tried in my third chapter to

---

[19] Marthe Robert, *The Old and the New. From Don Quixote to Franz Kafka*, trans. Carol Cosman (Berkeley: University of California Press, 1977), p. 13.

show how Musil's literary problematics are mirrored in Ulrich's problem of finding a suitably original way of life. In *Doktor Faustus* this initial *dédoublement* doubles itself again when the author's literary problems fall to both of his protagonists. Leverkühn feels doomed to rehearse endlessly the weary forms and feints of an already exhausted musical tradition. Self-conscious imitation as a form of criticism is the only acceptable solution for him. Thomas Mann's problem as a novelist is identical. In the era of Kafka, Mann's rhetorical elegance and weighty periods make him a literary dinosaur. This sense of anachronism materializes in the novel as Serenus Zeitblom, whose formidable learning and near-comic eloquence belong to another era. It is one of many ways in which the novel's condition of narrativity is made prominently visible.

The novel's repertoire of self-conscious devices is large. Mann is both a master of verisimilitude and a devious hand at subverting the illusions that he has constructed with such care. Adrian's critique of convention is the novel's critique of itself as a conventional construct. Realist assumptions about form and representation can no longer be taken for granted, and as soon as this insight takes hold of the novel's reader an extensive array of friendly swindles goes on parade: outlandish names and caricatured personalities, intentionally overwrought style, manifold allusions and »citations,« allegories, puzzle games (who is Frau von Tolna?), and a large number of interpolated narratives that recapitulate and magnify certain aspects of the narrative upon which they have been superimposed. These devices serve to question the relationship between the *narrated world*, which is set together from the verbal odds and ends that convention will allow, and the *lived world*, which is always in excess of the stories told about it.

Not the least of Mann's mirrors to the text is its companion novel, *Die Entstehung*. Its autobiographical protagonist resembles Leverkühn when he comments on a real-life lecture delivered by Bruno Franks: »Er benutzt den humanistischen Erzähl-Stil Zeitbloms vollkommen ernst, als seinen eigenen. Ich kenne im stilistischen nur noch die Parodie. Darin nahe bei Joyce...« (716, cf. 741). When Joyce patterns his narrative parodistically on Homer's *Odyssey*, Thomas Mann rather more abstractly sets his story into an aesthetically theoretical frame of reference that the figures construct for themselves. The imaginary characters, especially Leverkühn, Zeitblom, and the devil, constantly talk about the conditions, assumptions, intentions, forms, failings, and alienation of modern art. Thomas Mann and James Joyce, each in his own way, both make the conditions of their novels' reception largely internal to the novels themselves and completely internal to the novel as a contrivance of tradition and individual imagination. This process of interior self-replication in Mann's work has prompted Erich Heller's perceptive observation that the ironic German's style makes his critic's task doubly difficult, for it is hard to think a thought about the novel that it has not already thought about itself.[20]

The novel is thinking about itself when the devil offers Adrian a critique of the prevailing assumptions about the representation of reality in art:»Gewisse Dinge sind nicht mehr möglich. Der Schein der Gefühle als kompositorisches Kunstwerk, der selbstgenügsame Schein der Musik selbst ist unmöglich geworden und nicht zu halten, – als welcher seit alters darin besteht, daß vorgegebene und formelhaft niedergeschlagene Elemente so eingesetzt werden, als ob sie die unverbrüchliche Notwendigkeit dieses einen Falles wären« (321). Composition occurs within the framework of prescriptive formulas, which means that the rendering of emotion is equally formulaic. The representation of unique reality turns out to be nothing more than a set of conventions masquerading as the unmediated record of something that is not actually susceptible of schematic reconstitution.

The unique is by definition exterior to convention. A rupture between lived life and prescriptive form has opened up in the modern period. The uniqueness of modern experience no longer corresponds to its supposed image in the art of high culture.

The devil views the same crisis of representation from its other angle:»der Sonderfall gibt sich die Miene, als wäre er mit der vorgegebenen, vertrauten Formel identisch. Seit vierhundert Jahren hat alle große Musik ihr Genügen darin gefunden, diese Einheit als bruchlos geleistete vorzutäuschen, – sie hat sich darin gefallen, die konventionelle Allgemeingesetzlichkeit, der sie untersteht, mit ihren eigensten Anliegen zu verwechseln. Freund, es geht nicht mehr. Die Kritik des Ornaments, der Konvention und der abstrakten Allgemeinheit ist ein und dasselbe. . . . Die Subsumtion des Ausdrucks unters versöhnlich Allgemeine ist das innerste Prinzip des musikalischen Scheins. Es ist aus damit. Der Anspruch, das Allgemeine als im Besonderen harmonisch enthalten zu denken, dementiert sich selbst« (321f). Art deludes itself when it pretends that the unique instance can assimilate itself to prefabricated aesthetic categories. Yet since the Renaissance this ungrounded presupposition has served as a basis for mimetic practices.

---

[20] Heller, p. 277. Gunter Reiß has written a lengthy study of the ways of self-allegory in Thomas Mann's work as a whole: »Allegorisierung« und moderne Erzählkunst. Eine Studie zum Werk Thomas Manns (München: Wilhelm Fink, 1970).

The end of humanism in the contemporary era is of a piece with the crisis of representation that comes with the unmasking of convention. Formal paradigms of expression have revealed themselves to be arbitrary constructs that are never continuous with the object of representation; and the unique object of representation in its solitude is powerless to create general laws of representation within which to formulate itself as an aesthetic articulation. No matter whether the direction of motion is from the unique to the paradigmatic or from the paradigmatic to the unique, the possibility of an undisrupted continuum has been disqualified.

The devil's terminology is a tacit critique of Goethe's favored strategy of representational rhetoric. *Das Allgemeine* and *das Besondere* are famous watchwords of his conceptual vocabulary. In the *Maximen and Reflexionen* he writes:»Das ist die wahre Symbolik, wo das Besondere das Allgemeine repräsentiert, nicht als Traum und Schatten, sondern als lebendig-augenblickliche Offenbarung des Unerforschlichen.«[21] This »true symbolism« is a mode of expression that the devil forbids Adrian and that the critically self-conscious novel denies to itself: »Es ist aus damit. Der Anspruch, das Allgemeine als im Besonderen harmonisch enthalten zu denken, dementiert sich selbst. Es ist geschehen um die vorweg und verpflichtend geltenden Konventionen, die die Freiheit des Spiels gewährleisteten« (322). The genius of unmediated vision, that of a Goethe or a Beethoven, turns out to be the mediated vision of subliminal convention. The latecomer, unable to accept the traditional assumptions about »wahre Symbolik« must turn to the nihilism of parody.

Another passage from Goethe will help to clarify the ideal of representation that *Doktor Faustus* rejects. In an 1820 essay on one of Philostratus's paintings, Goethe defines the symbol as follows:

> Es ist die Sache, ohne die Sache zu sein, und doch die Sache; ein im geistigen Spiegel zusammengezogenes Bild, und doch mit dem Gegenstand identisch. Wie weit steht dagegen nicht Allegorie zurück; sie ist vielleicht geistreich witzig, aber doch meist rhetorisch und konventionell und immer besser, je mehr sie sich demjenigen nähert, was wir Symbol nennen.[22]

These Goethean standards consign Thomas Mann – a self-confessed allegorist, parodist, and ironist – to a purgatory for the »geistreich-

---

[21] Johann Wolfgang von Goethe, *Die Wahlverwandtschaften, Die Novellen, Die Maximen und Reflexionen*, Gedenkausgabe, hrsg. v. Ernst Beutler, vol. IX (Zürich: Artemis, 1949), p. 532.

[22] Johann Wolfgang von Goethe, *Schriften zur Kunst*, Gedenkausgabe, 2. Aufl., hrsg. v. Ernst Beutler, vol. XIII (Zürich: Artemis, 1965), p. 868.

witzig.« Unable to share Goethe's faith that the symbol is less »rhetorical and conventional« than allegory, Mann practices an art that thrives on rhetoric and convention as a mode of criticism and self-criticism.

By Thomas Mann's day the sense of emancipation that Goethe had almost single-handedly brought to German literature had already run its course. The habits of mind and the conventions of expression that he set into motion had gradually slowed down and finally hardened into prescriptive schemata for writing and reading. The notion of a 'natural genius' who transmutes his inner life – Erlebnis – into objective form had begun to have the resonance of a cracked plate.[23] The categories of subjective experience and its objectification had reached a high point in one sense – the names of Dilthey, Husserl, Mach, Proust, Broch, or Virginia Woolf come readily to mind – yet the leveling effect of convention worked simultaneously to undermine the possiblity of a poetics of true interiority.

Joyce is the outstanding example of both tendencies at work against each other: the stream-of-consciousness ›realism‹ of Bloom's sheer interiority is pitted against an imaginary world that is the baldest contrivance of irony and parody that a modern novelist has produced. The ›essayistic‹ approaches of Robert Musil and Thomas Mann show an especially high degree of awareness concerning the role that convention plays, respectively, in human experience and literary creation. They are skeptical of any claims to an »unmittelbares Anschauen« because they realize that exterior reality is mediated by subliminal expectations and assumptions on the part of the individual who is having the Erlebnis. Moreover, »inner« experience is in no way autonomous or discrete because, as Musil's persuasive critique in Der Mann ohne Eigenschaften has shown, these unrecognized conventions constitute the features of that experience. Inner experience is a function of conventions that precede, and are thus exterior to, the individual. In a precisely parallel process, literary expression proceeds not from within the subject but imposes itself on experience from the »exteriority« of convention and tradition.

The privileging of personal subjectivity as an absolute origin is the hallmark of humanism's anthropocentric aesthetics. Both Leverkühn and Mann reject this position. Leverkühn turns to his mathematical nature-mysticism as a solution. Mann is less radical. He is acutely aware

---

[23] For a concise critique of the origins and limits of the aesthetic Erlebnis-concept see Hans-Georg Gadamer, Wahrheit und Methode. Grundzüge einer philosophischen Hermeneutik, 4. Aufl. (Tübingen: J. C. B. Mohr, 1975), pp. 39–77.

of the burden of tradition and convention on him, and his techniques of composition bear witness to this awareness. His parodic style as well as his so-called »Montage-Technik« – what his detractors call plagiarism – militate against the interiority of subjective Romanticism. His writing is not an objectification of his inner being. Thomas Mann is much more the willing instrument of a tradition that is prior and exterior to his personal individuality. He has at his disposal not an »unmittelbares Anschauen« but a great diversity of preformed materials waiting to be reshaped in the alembic of his magisterial *ars combinatoria* (cf. 776). Without a viable concept of the symbol to guarantee the continuity of the lived world with the literary word, Mann finds it necessary to rehabilitate the practice of allegorical writing.

Allegory is the mode of representation in which identity yields to difference. The correlation of the allegorical sign to its signandum is an arbitrary determination, or »unmotivated« in Benveniste's precise sense.[24] The allegory is a substitute for the absent and is therefore itself »other« than that which is represented. Parody and irony are extreme forms of allegory inasmuch as they are signs that intentionally reveal themselves as such and consequently deny their ultimate identity with the object of representation. Indeed, it turns out that the object of representation of Leverkühn's musical compositions and Mann's literary ones is not even »the world« but is actually the conventional forms that have customarily served as the vehicle for represented reality. Leverkühn's parodic explorations of the musical tradition are allegories of symbols that do not know they are really only allegories. Yet he is not satisfied with games that are »geistreich witzig« and feels himself compelled to discover a means to replenish art as a positive form of expression.

At this juncture there is a divergence of ways between the writer of the novel and the protagonist who shares his problem of composition. Leverkühn manages to break through into renewed creativity beyond

---

[24] At the level of the linguistic sign, de Saussure regards the connection between a signifier and a signified as *arbitrary*. Benveniste objects that the signifier-signified link is in fact logically necessary in the same sense that one side of a coin presupposes the other. It is the relation between the linguistic sign and the objective *signandum* that is arbitrary. In the light of this argumentation Benveniste proposes that the nature of the sign's interior order is not arbitrary but »unmotivated.« If Benveniste's argument holds good at the level of the linguistic sign, then it will also be applicable at a higher level of discourse, i.e. that of the literary sign. Emile Benveniste, »The Nature of the Linguistic Sign,« in his *Problems in General Linguistics*, transl. Mary Elizabeth Meele, Miami Linguistics Series, 8 (Coral Gables, Florida: University of Miami Press, 1971), pp. 43–48.

parody and irony, but Mann remains a parodist and ironist to the end of the novel and to the end of his own career. His final achievement is his finest parody, *Felix Krull*. In *Doktor Faustus* it remains to be seen whether the ›negative‹ aspect of ironic presentation merely qualifies the ›positive‹ achievement inside the story, or whether it nullifies it entirely. The first order of business will be to follow the elaborate tracery of allegorical design in Leverkühn's striving. In particular, the roles of Esmerelda and Echo are in need of translation into their respective aesthetic and ethical meanings. The second step will be to discuss the effects of ironical intention on these meanings.

III

The allegorical marker of artistic creativity in *Doktor Faustus* is eros. It is the link between amoral nature, its intrinsic power of creation, and its human manifestations as passion and love. The decisive formulation of the erotic as a problem in the novel appears as a tale that the demonologist Schleppfuß offered in one of his lectures. This anecdote is one of the many parables by which the novel reproduces itself *en abyme*. It is the story of a fifteenth-century cooper named Klöpfgeißel and his sweetheart, Bärbel (143–47). Because the young man had no money he was unable to marry Bärbel. But mere economic considerations did not keep them from consummating their union in secret. However, it happened once that Klöpfgeißel was in a nearby town and allowed himself to be bullied by co-workers from the coopery into a visit to a brothel. To his great consternation, when finally in the arms of an accommodating woman he found himself unable to rise to the occasion. Yet an ensuing visit to Bärbel found him once again in best form. On still another occasion of potential infidelity, he was once again dismayed to discover an unaccountable lack of cooperation on his part. With the aid of a priest experienced in such matters, Klöpfgeißel is able to reach the obvious conclusion: Bärbel had bewitched him. The authorities summarily extract a confession from her and burn her at the stake in order to save her eternal soul from perdition. Pious Klöpfgeißel watches the grisly execution, secure in the knowledge that her hideous screams are those of the demon flying out of her. Afterwards the hexed barrel-maker recovers full control of his natural creative potential.

The novel's autocommentary in this parable is not subtle. Leverkühn, in order to recover the artistic creativity that has been lost to the artist of his era, will stop at nothing to achieve his ends. His sacrificial offering, his Bärbel, is little Nepomuk Schneidewein. The prostitute

167

Esmerelda is his diabolical temptress. These simple correspondences must be examined with care.

Leverkühn's attraction to Esmerelda is overt allegory. She is the personification of art; a fallen Helena, a new Dulcinea. Once the most beautiful of all, now she has passed through too many hands, been used and abused, cruelly reduced to a diseased whore. Leverkühn's love for her – it is not a base craving but a deeply sensual love – is a quixotic gesture in the term's fullest ambiguity, for it is never really clear whether Don Quixote sees more or less than we do. He knows that Dulcinea is a coarse peasant girl, yet he holds stubbornly to his vision of her. Adrian knows that Esmerelda is a whore, yet he sees her in a different light. A demonic Schleppfuß-double leads him to her in a Leipzig brothel, where he discovers his fallen angel wrapped in her transparent butterfly wings, surrounded by glass, glinting crystal, and mirrors. These reflecting surfaces are the emblems of art. Adrian has found his way into the crystal garden.

Confused, aroused, suspended between fascination and revulsion at the voluptuous surroundings, Adrian's erotic energy discharges into a piano that is standing open in the room. He moves as if by instinct to the instrument and hammers out his Esmerelda-motif for the first time – *h e a e es* – as almond-eyed Esmerelda herself strokes his arm and cheek. Disoriented and excited, Adrian dashes away from her and plunges back out into the street. This brief flirtation with eros and creativity whets his carnal appetite. It draws him inexorably on to consummate his pact with the chthonic forces of creativity that inhere in nature and have been awakened in him. Adrian returns to Esmerelda a year later only to discover she has disappeared from Leipzig and retired to an eastern province of Austria-Hungary. Under the pretense of traveling to Graz for a performance of *Salomé*, he pursues her to Pozsony, the capital of Slovakia.

He finds her there, syphilitic but convalescent, and makes to her a declaration of his passionate love. She responds to him in kind with a loving and sincere warning about her sickness. Adrian goes on to make love to her in full knowledge of what dangers are in store. His pact with the devil some years later is a mere formality that raises to consciousness the many implications of the decision he has made.

Zeitblom says that Adrian never sees her again, but he does not know as much as he thinks he does. Unknown to the narrator, Adrian's butterfly-angel undergoes a metamorphosis to re-emerge as the mysterious Hungarian noblewoman Frau von Tolna. In an adroit bit of riddle-solving, Victor A. Oswald has showed that the »unsichtbare Figur« hovering near Adrian – her epithet reminds us of her invisible wings –

is in truth the prostitute from Pozsony.[25] »Pozsony« is the Hungarian name for the Slovakian *Bratislava*, German *Preßburg*, which is only one of the clues that the cagey novelist slips past his dozing narrator. The association with Hungary is important because Frau von Tolna is the widow of a Hungarian nobleman famous for his lusty excesses. He was a man of the uninhibited sort who would be liable to fall in love with a Dostoyevskian Sonja and marry her. The weightiest clue to Frau von Tolna's secret identity is her gift to Adrian, a ring of »Edel-Beryll:« in English an emerald, in Spanish – *esmerelda*. Adrian always wears it on his left hand when he is composing. It is a potent emblem of his demonic-sacred union with Esmerelda.

Adrian has joined himself to this exotic figure in whom love and sickness, warmth and creativity, carnality, spirituality, and death are all intermingled. When he made love to her she was a poor, sick whore, abused, exhausted, and infected by an anonymous succession of men who only *took* from her. Adrian has *given* to her a measure of authentic love, and in so doing has taken on the disease that she carries. Subsequently she recovers and rises to wealth and reclusive prominence. Now that Adrian has taken her disease on himself, it is she who sustains him – as his patroness literally, and as the wellspring of his creativity allegorically. But this communion of individual talent with its origins replenishes art only at the highest of costs. The disease festers in the composer's brain as a twofold sign: first, it is the mark of an enormous imaginative fecundity that penetrates well beyond the borders of average reality; second, it is the sign of an ethical flaw, pathological and evil.

The Nietzschean theme of disease and genius as an inseparable doublet is frequent in Thomas Mann's work. For this reason it will be best to let the novelist gloss his version of this idea himself. While working on *Doktor Faustus* Mann also wrote an essay on Dostoyevsky, in which he discusses the matter in some detail:

> Die Wahrheit ist, daß ohne das Krankhafte das Leben seiner Lebtage nicht ausgekommen ist, und es gibt schwerlich einen dümmeren Satz als den, daß »aus Krankem nur Krankes kommen kann.« Das Leben ist nicht zimperlich, und man mag wohl sagen, daß schöpferische, Genie spendende Krankheit, Krankheit, die hoch zu Roß die Hindernisse nimmt, in kühnem Rausch von Fels zu Felsen sprengt, ihm tausendmal lieber ist als die zu Fuße latschende Gesundheit. Das Leben ist nicht heikel, *und irgendwelchen moralischen Unterschied zwischen Gesundheit und Krankheit zu machen, liegt ihm sehr fern.* . . . Gewisse Errungenschaften der Seele und der Erkenntnis sind nicht mög-

---

[25] Victor A. Oswald, »The Enigma of Frau von Tolna,« *Germanic Review*, 23 (1948), pp. 249–53.

lich ohne die Krankheit, den Wahnsinn, das geistige Verbrechen, und die großen Kranken sind Gekreuzigte und Opfer, der Menschheit und ihrer Erhöhung, der Erweiterung ihres Fühlens und Wissens, kurz ihrer höheren Gesundheit dargebracht. Daher die religiöse Aura, die das Leben dieser Menschen umgibt und auch ihr Selbstbewußtsein so tief beeinflußt.[26]

This rousing apologia for the pathological element in genius goes overboard where I have italicized the claim that a »moral« distinction between health and disease is irrelevant. The essay implies a distinction between the regulations of moral convention and the more genuine good and evil that are rooted in nature itself. The genius recognizes this distinction and challenges repressive moral convention in the interest of ultimate good health. This act of ignoring morality becomes, finally, a moral deed.

The situation in *Doktor Faustus* is a good deal more complex and more honest. Leverkühn chooses evil not out of an interest in ultimate good health, but out of pride, a lust for power and self-aggrandizement (324–33). This is the disease that is characteristic of his culture. He renounces human responsibility in order to devote himself fully to the pursuit of a new art, hence the only term of the devil's assistance: »Du darfst nicht lieben.« Love is suffused with the ethical determination that is intrinsic in nature and beyond the mock-up ethical categories of cultural and religious convention. It is only after the experience of love and the evil of its irretrievable loss that Leverkün's art reaches fulfillment.

The devil's »nicht« is not a simple prohibition. Adrian breaks the terms of his agreement, or so it seems, by loving his nephew. Yet it is not Adrian but Nepomuk who is punished. This »nicht« does not mean that Adrian will fail if he loves; it means that the *loss* of love is the condition of his success. Art rushes in to fill this vacant space, but only at the cost of guilt and suffering.

If the Esmerelda-theme is an allegory of aesthetics, then the Nepomuk scenes allegorize the concomitant ethical situation. The composer's sickness as a sign for evil and moral culpability is too abstract to be very convincing. Mann supplements it with a concrete extrapolation of

---

[26] »Dostojewski – mit Maßen,« in *Leiden und Große der Meister, GWFA* VIII, pp. 973–74. Cf. J. P. Stern's remarks to the ethical question of National Socialism in Stern, pp. 6ff. Mann's phrase, »vom Kranken kann nur Krankes kommen,« is a quote from Gerhard Hauptmann. See Thomas Mann's letter of 27 August 1944 to Fritz Kaufmann, in *Dichter über ihre Dichtungen: Thomas Mann*, Dichter über ihre Dichtungen 14/III, hrsg. v. Hans Wysling unter Mitarbeit von Marianne Fischer, part III (Passau: Heimeran, S. Fischer, 1981), p. 27.

its effects. Adrian's love for Esmerelda is real enough, but it belongs to a sphere of spiritualized carnality that is outside of ordinary human relations. The figure of Adrian's little nephew, five-year-old Nepomuk Schneidewein, returns the question of love to a manageable dimension. Already Adrian's affection for another human being has resulted in that person's death. Rudi Schwerdtfeger came too close to Leverkühn and paid with his life. The aura of evil that emanates from the icy composer becomes even more sinister when Nepomuk comes to visit his uncle at the Schweigestill home. By loving him Adrian destroys him.

This »wundersame Knabe« is a variation on the »schöne Seele« theme, a figure that recalls such literary innocents as Shakespeare's Ariel or Goethe's Mignon, and bears traces of Gretchen and Euphorion as well. His is a goodness that dooms him in the fallen world of actual reality. Nepomuk calls himself *Echo*, as if in description of his relationship to his uncle. On the allegorical level he is an echo of the part of Leverkühn that must be sacrificed, namely innocence. Echo is first of all a blood relation to the composer, but figuratively he is Adrian's child by Esmerelda, Faust's child by Helena. Little Echo's oddly antiquated way of speaking mimics his uncle's eccentric taste for medieval archaisms. The child's headaches duplicate those of Adrian, and his disease – cerebro-spinal meningitis – attacks the central nervous system in the same way that syphilis does. Echo's agonizing death is a two-fold sign: allegorically it is the image of Leverkühn's self-sacrifice, and literally it is the cause of his guilt. Echo is preternaturally innocent and good, not at all fit for life in an era ridden with black guilt. He must go the way of Mignon, Gretchen, and Euphorion. Echo is also a reflection of the part of himself that Adrian has sold to the devil, i.e. his own naivité and innocence, his right to love. But on the literal level Nepomuk – now a literal human being and not the protagonist's »echo« – is a child whom a ruthless egoist cruelly destroys. The primary emphasis in the novel is on the literal level so as to press home unequivocally Leverkühn's personal responsibility for the death of an innocent.

Within the coordinates of meaning that the novel has set up for itself, the virulent malignancy of evil cannot appear alone. Its inevitable complement is always there beside it. The good belongs to evil like the mountain to a valley. The novel has set the stage for evil's transmogrification into the sacred. Leverkühn's response to the child's death is simultaneously ethical and aesthetic. Raging with grief and pain, he unleashes his darkest fury on Zeitblom and makes his strange pronouncement: »Es soll nicht sein.« Leverkühn means that he despairs of the good and the noble, that Beethoven's song of jubilation, *The Ninth*

Symphony, must be *taken back*. At first sight this »taking back« seems to be a peculiar idea, but the history of art is full of examples for it. No doubt Miguel de Cervantes experienced *Amadis of Gaul* in much the same way that Leverkühn experiences Beethoven. Reality did not bear out the noble claims made in the epics of knightly deeds. With his *Don Quixote* Cervantes takes back courtly romance and in so doing founds a new tradition. Henry Fielding takes back Richardson's grand sentiments; Voltaire takes back Leibniz; Heine takes back the Romantics; Leverkühn takes back Beethoven. And *Doktor Faustus* takes back Goethe's *Faust*. With Cervantes the chivalric Middle Ages came to an end that was the beginning of the novel. With Leverkühn the age of Faust, of anthropocentric humanism, comes to an end, and a new work of art stands on the threshold of a nascent tradition.

»The Lamentation of Dr. Faustus« is Leverkühn's breakthrough into an idiom in keeping with the needs of his era. In it Leverkühn supersedes the affective and formal schemata of tradition, and, most importantly, he transcends the notion of art as an expression of personal subjectivity. The quasi-natural number magic of his composition technique has removed man from the center and relocated human experience in the midst of nature.[27] There are no vocal solos in the *Weheklag*; the human voice and the voice of instruments interpenetrate and exchange places: »Das Echo, das Zurückgeben des Menschenlautes als Naturlaut und seine Enthüllung *als* Naturlaut, ist wesentlich Klage, das wehmutsvolle ›Ach, ja!‹ der Natur über den Menschen . . .« (644). This reintegration of man into nature is not a renunciation of ethics. A lamentation is by its very nature an ethical utterance. In this particular case it is the articulation of contrition and an acknowledgment of guilt. Its twelve-syllable vocal theme could serve as an epitaph for its composer: »Denn ich sterbe als ein guter und ein böser Christ« (646). The utter despair of his lamentation is the voice of its sincerity. It inverts the joyful *Ninth Symphony* not in cynical mockery but in soul-wrenching disappointment. Yet precisely where such disappointment is possible is where hope thrives, and the possibility of hope is always implicit in the counterfactuality of art, in the knowledge that all could be otherwise. Leverkühn loved young Nepomuk, but in so doing he ›looked back,‹ like Orpheus turning to see if Eurydice was following him up into the light. Because they love they lose their love, and the evil of this

---

[27] It is interesting to note that Kandinsky's intention in his theory of non-objective art is strikingly similar. Instead of number magic, Kandinsky relies on the »mystical« power of pure form and color. See Wassily Kandinsky, *Über das Geistige in der Kunst*, 5. Aufl. mit einer Einführung v. Max Bill (Bern-Bümpliz: Benteli, 1956), pp. 80–85.

loss generates the song of sorrow that fills the empty place, a reminder of the sacred. Leverkühn has exorcised his demon and contained the unmitigated terror of suffering and death within bounds that make them manageable for a natural being. He has not reached »das Heiter-Bescheidenere« but he has supplied future generations with the formal tools they will need to fulfill his vision.

IV

At least two objections to my positive account of the novel's implied aesthetic of ethical anti-subjectivity will come readily to mind. The first is the problem of irony, which threatens at least to suspend any affirmative assertion if not reduce it entirely to paradox and aporia. Doesn't the ironic superstructure of the novel subvert the positivity of Leverkühn's achievement, since this achievement exists only within the rhetorically enchanted infrastructure of the narrative's imaginary world? Secondly, even if Leverkühn's »Rekonstruktion des Ausdrucks« manages to elude the deconstructive irony that surrounds it, this reconstruction looks more like a nostalgic remystification of expression than an authentically new avenue of aesthetic possibilities. Doesn't Leverkühn fall right back into the self-deluded rhetoric of symbolism that both he and the novel have rejected? The narrative anticipates and confronts both of these objections, and once again its response leads back to the special conception of nature at work in the novel.

Taken together, these objections reveal themselves as the old rivalry between symbol and allegory as epistemological figures of discourse. Symbol claims to represent its object by somehow becoming that object in a process of poetic transubstantiation; and irony, as a form of allegory, claims that the gap between *signum* and *res* is unbridgeable. Modern Leverkühn is unable to believe in symbol at all, and he doubts that allegory as irony will ever lead, as the Romantics had hoped, to positive expression. This skepticism leads him to scoff at the devil's promises. Leverkühn denies the possibility of a »Durchbruch« because he believes only another sham reality would result: »Ich werde osmotische Gewächse ziehen.« The allusion is to the cold, »dead« flowers of his father's crystal garden. To this the devil replies:

> Ist doch gehupft wie gesprungen! Eisblumen oder solche aus Stärke, Zucker und Zellulose, – beides ist Natur, und fragt sich noch, wofür Natur am meisten zu beloben. (323)

Jonathan Leverkühn had made the same point years before: »Die schöpferisch träumende Natur träumte hier und dort dasselbe, und durfte von Nachahmung die Rede sein, so gewiß von wechselseitiger« (29). In this same sense all works of art are »osmotische Gewächse,« deceptions that are never identical with the ›object of representation.‹ Yet resemblances are where you see them, no matter whether they are classified as symbols, allegories, or as any other figure of discourse. Crystal gardens and works of art exist by their own autonomous right, and when resemblance to another domain occurs, it is best to speak not of an original and a copy but of mutually illuminating realms joined at their origin.

Resemblances are naturally occurring phenomena in all of the world, and man's mind belongs to the world – not vice versa. Leverkühn's Copernican Revolution is the restoration of artistic creativity, a product of mind, to its natural ›objectivity‹ as it were. He establishes an objective framework that derives directly from the essence of nature. Within this framework it becomes possible to articulate the truth unencumbered by exhausted clichés. Paradoxically, authentic humanness returns to aesthetic form only when expression – or better: *articulation* – is no longer the objectification of exclusively human subjectivity. Leverkühn's *Weheklag* returns the elemental truth of grief and despair to creative artifice by returning to the ground-principle of art and ethics. His song of sorrow is beyond symbol and allegory, beyond subject and object because each of these categories is predicated on a man-centered cosmos. When Leverkühn de-subjectifies his art, it does not become truly objective. With the disappearance of the subject, there can be no object, only world in its phenomenal diversity. Similarly, the conflicting claims of symbol and allegory are relevant only within the subject/object epistemology of language-as-signification and literature-as-representation. The fusion of the subject and the object into the holism of world makes the semiotic model of truth superfluous. Resemblances are a basic fact of the world in which both *signum* and *res* are equally originary. It is pointless to ask whether a butterfly that looks like a dead leaf is really a symbol or only an allegory of that which it resembles.

Finally, a word must be said about the ethical claims of *Doktor Faustus*. Its concept of man in nature sounds suspiciously like Rousseauist sentimentality, but nothing could be further from the truth. As man dissolves back into nature he is not a »noble savage« but a finite being in an ongoing world, tragically susceptible of good and evil. In full knowledge of his freedom to choose, Leverkühn opts willingly for evil because of his pride and ambition. It is this experience of evil that makes it possible or even necessary for him to fulfill his artistic calling. This fulfillment is the direct result of his guilt in Echo's horrible death.‹ There are in this ethical scenario the rumblings of ancient myth. Near the beginning of Western literature the wrathful pride of Achilles brings about the death of a beloved friend. Only after the needless death of Patroclus, for which the grief-stricken Achilles knows himself to be fully responsible, does the hero return to the Achaeans to fulfill his proper role. The hybris of Leverkühn causes a similar tragedy. Only after his descent into the blackest shame, guilt, and despair, only after he has descended into the depths of wretchedness is he able to rise to a new, deepened and unrhetorical articulation of elemental humanness.

CHAPTER VI

EPILOGUE: The Quixotic Word

> ... The quixotic word ... is
> invocation and critique, con-
> juration and radical probing,
> both one and the other with
> their risks and perils.
>
> Marthe Robert[1]

This study began with an allusion to the myth of Orpheus, which served to illustrate a crucial aspect of the modernist aesthetic. The literature of modernism is conditioned by a gnawing sense of loss – Nietzsche's ›death of God‹ gave to the modern sense of dearth its most lasting formulation – an emptiness that even the finest poetry cannot assuage. Like Orpheus' songs of mourning for a dead wife, the modernist work of art is typically a gesture of lamentation that knows itself to be ›mere fiction‹ and so realizes also that it cannot resurrect a happier past or make present once again that which is absent.

In the history of the German novel, literary criticism has codified this insight for itself as a »Romankrise:« »Wirklichkeitsverlust,« »Sprachskepsis,« »die Wendung nach Innen,« and »Selbstreflexion.« The loss of certainty concerning external reality, the decentering of internal reality, and skepticism toward the epistemic reliability of language in general and toward literary language in particular all conspired together to cause the poetic word to fold back upon itself. Cut off from the outside, it meditates on its relation to the world beyond itself. For the modernist, there was no self-evident link between the poetic word and lived reality.

It is plain that in the novels of Broch, Musil, Kafka, and even in Thomas Mann, the resemblance between the fictional world and the real one is intentionally discontinuous. Each writer in one way or another reflects on the fictionality of his narrative and in so doing reveals

---

[1] Marthe Robert, *The Old and the New. From Don Quixote to Franz Kafka*, trans. Carol Cosman (Berkeley: University of California Press, 1977), p. 21.

176

the crucial distance between the world as it is and the stories told about it. While seeming to represent reality in the received sense of Aristotelian mimesis, the Cervantic irony of modernist fiction simultaneously asserts its own separation from the world.

This conclusion is hardly a surprise in the present atmosphere of literary criticism. At least since New Criticism and especially since the widespread acceptance of structuralist premises and the subsequent rise of deconstruction, a new orthodoxy of critical opinion has developed around the idea that the literary artwork is an autotelic thing. That the works of German modernists will support this thesis is no doubt a foregone conclusion among a large number of critics. The advocates of poststructuralism have seized on this concept with notorious delight. Their more traditional colleagues perceive the idea that ›literature refers to nothing outside of itself‹ as a notion that is hostile both to literature and to the critical enterprise. The nihilistic gaiety of poststructuralism in its popular form has served at least to raise the question of how, if at all, the literary word catches hold of the world.

Precisely this question, which is at bottom an ethical one, was of the utmost importance to the German modernists. We have seen that Broch, Musil, Kafka, and Thomas Mann – each in his own way and each for his own reasons – rejected the assumption that the novel was a representation of reality. Is, then, the modernist novel an empty flourish, a nihilistic giggle in the rubble of modern culture? Popular variants of poststructuralism and the ›postmodern‹ novel have a reputation for implying this conclusion. But the modernist novel offers an alternative resolution to this dilemma.

This final chapter will review first of all the individual attempts of Broch, Musil, Kafka, and Mann to respond to this question, and then it will pursue the answer that their work collectively implies. I mean to suggest here that literature does not draw its primary strength from the imitation of outward appearances, and also that this supposed ›failure‹ of representation does not relegate the poetic word to an empty gesture. Literature is much more the scene of a dynamism – the two-pronged event of its creation and continuous recreation during its historical life among successive generations of readers – the primary function of which is not to refer to a thing but to elicit a response. Literature is the activity in which the nonobjective values that govern our thinking, feeling, and doing articulate themselves. Along with the more obviously non-representational modes of aesthetic activity – music and architecture – literature is one of the privileged spaces in which we encounter ourselves: our beliefs and values, our history, and perhaps most importantly, the dimly apprehended outlines of our own incipient future.

177

The poetic word is a utopian gesture that is, in the word's most profound ambiguity, Quixotic.

* * *

Let me begin this final portion of my study by returning to modernism's one most salient feature: the break with nineteenth-century realist assumptions. In Chapter II I attempted to show that the »inward turn« of narrative was actually only an extension of these assumptions. Their true antagonist was the crisis of representation. The representation of inner reality is as much a ›verisimilar‹ mimesis as that of external reality. It only seems anti-mimetic because the terms of comparison have not yet been settled – the rapid assimilation of Freudian psychoanalytic vocabulary notwithstanding. If any such terms were ever to become widely accepted conventions, they would be as mimetic as the terms of traditional realism. What must be emphasized is that the modernist crisis of representation militates against *any* sort of representation, no matter whether the referent is supposed to be inner or outer reality. And, as we have seen, »reality« itself – as that which is to be represented – was a far from stable object of representation.

Hermann Broch believed that his era had lost its grip on the real for historical reasons. The language of fiction in the new age had lost its mythopoeic potency in inverse proportion to the rise of science. The skeptical objectivity of the scientific mind forfeited the possibility of unity with the overarching »Platonic« realm of nonobjective values. Mythic narrative, which had been the traditional voice of these values, was demoted by science to the status of benighted superstition. The turn of history to the era of science meant the disintegration of the all-encompassing system of values that had united European culture in the past. The scientific imperative that truth is the accurate representation of objectively existing facts reduced myth to an indefensible form of untruth. Storytelling could no longer lay claim to being a purveyor of truth because it could not represent that which has no objective existence.

Broch's historicist value-philosophy has been much criticized, but his notion that the aesthetic impulse is linked somehow to the existence of non-objective, temporally conditioned entities is fundamentally rightheaded. Take for example his presentation of the Baddensen family in the *Pasenow*-novel of *Die Schlafwandler*. In order to arrest the passage of time and thereby assuage the numbing fear of death they become compulsive collectors of objects. These objects idealize moments of the past to such an extent that this aestheticized past threatens to transform the present into a lifeless museum (see above, pp. 49–50). Broch pre-

178

sents this hypostasis as an alienation from time, death, and love – e.g. the virgin Elisabeth Baddensen sitting alone in her father's obsessively tidy private garden – and as an abuse of the aesthetic impulse. Elisabeth's counterpart is the tragic Ruzena, a woman whose erotic and essentially ›aesthetic‹ or creative nature condemns her to wretchedness in a world that refuses to acknowledge the power and presence of Eros and Thanatos. Broch is implying that the age needs an art that can admit of the passage of time. However, this insight remains underdeveloped in his work.

Musil carries the notion further than Broch does. Musil believed that in institutions such as law, politics, art, morals, and education – in short, all phases of the public and private sphere that are under the governance of our shared mental life – there occurs a gravely debilitating hypostasis. Whenever the temporal flow of the mind's affective experience is halted at one point – as when a once valid law or a custom outlives its usefulness – a static representation has falsified the dynamic nature of its object. Ulrich takes a vacation from represented reality in order to discover the truer world beyond representations. He is seeking »die Welt ohne feste Form,« which is the world of his own and his culture's hidden ›soul.‹

Musil's special problem is that the novel in which these ideas occur is itself an example of the hypostatizing institutions under critique. In his attempt to resolve this impasse, Musil constructs a theory of metaphoric expression that aims to ›intimate‹ but not to ›represent‹ reality. The psychologist Musil reasons that because our innermost being is in a state of constant flux and because its state is necessarily unique at any given time, only an expression that is itself unique can give voice to the true nature of this event. Insofar as language is a system of conventional signs, it is incapable of capturing and expressing that which is unique. The loophole in this system is metaphor. It throws together two conventional signs to create a third, unique sign that by virtue of its tentative status can articulate the truth of the sought-after inner event. So long as the crucial tension between the two terms of the metaphor is upheld, the expression will remain fresh and effective. If the tension collapses, the metaphor will die, reduced to a conventional denotative sign. As long as it lives it continues to demand intensively imaginative participation on the part of the reader, who must work to construe it in accordance with its context and his own experience. It is this strategy of articulation that makes stories such as *Die Vollendung der Liebe* and *Die Versuchung der stillen Veronika* so extraordinarily alien and difficult.

Musil's notion of representing reality is plainly distinct from the received conventions of nineteenth-century fiction. He rejects the very idea of representation because it cannot help him in his pursuit of unique inner events. A look at *Die Verwirrungen des Zöglings Törleß* will help to clarify this matter. The novel's young protagonist is a »boy without qualities,« an adolescent version of Ulrich. Each of the two reaches toward an understanding of the world beyond representations. Ulrich refers to this realm as a state of being, »der andere Zustand,« and Törleß refers to it as »das Unendliche.« When Törleß learns of the non-representational character of a certain mathematical concept – $\sqrt{-1}$ – he suspects that he has found a clue to this world that he intuits (6: 73f). The boy turns to his math professor for an explanation of how imaginary numbers can be true yet have no referents in the real world. The professor explains that such expressions are »Denknotwendigkeiten,« heuristic fictions that do not imitate reality yet nevertheless reach outward towards the truth (6: 77).

For Musil, literary fictions have a similar status. The poetic trope – *Gleichnis* is the term that Musil prefers – is likewise a non-representational notation that reaches outward toward the truth. It is the »Denknotwendigkeit« of what Ulrich calls »das ahnende Denken« (4: 1307). It is his »mystical« way of thinking that honors the integrity of true reality by refusing to tether it to a denotative representation. The poetic trope addresses the indeterminate world of feeling better than referential language can because, like feeling, the well wrought trope is both unique and indeterminate. It does not denote or represent an inner event. Instead, it simultaneously evokes and suspends a tentative sense of the affective moment. Because the *Gleichnis* lacks conceptual fixity it allows full sway to the reader's participating imagination. In reading, writes Musil, »wir lösen das Erwünschte los und lassen das Unerwünschte zurück« (8: 1238). Because a poetic articulation lacks fixity and because it does not purport to »represent« its non-objective object, it is able to keep pace with the ephemeral ›life of the soul‹ and remain always fresh.

The trouble with Musil's considerations of metaphor in *Der Mann ohne Eigenschaften* is that he seldom rises above his theorizing metalevel. He talks more *about* using evocative metaphors than he actually uses them. Musil's praise of Rainer Maria Rilke reveals his own poetic aims along with his shortcomings as a writer:

> Würde man eine Reihe aufstellen, an deren einem Ende das Lehrgedicht, die Allegorie, das politische Gedicht zu stehen kämen, also Formen eines schon fertigen Wissens, so stünde am entgegengesetzten Ende Rilkes Gedicht als reiner Vorgang und Gestaltung geistiger Mächte, die in ihm zum erstenmal Namen und Stimme bekommen. (8: 1241).

Because Musil's novels – and those of Hermann Broch as well – are highly theoretical allegories of concepts and ideas, they qualify as »Formen eines schon fertigen Wissens:« Broch writes allegories of his philosophy of history and values; and Musil tells the story of a theorist who unsuccessfully tries to live out a life based on theory. Musil seldom passes from theorizing about poetic language to the full use of it. With Kafka it is otherwise.

Kafka's tales have a powerful and spontaneous originality that is emphatically untheoretical in inception and appeal. His images and parables do not exhaust themselves in the conceptual rigidity of hyperintellectual allegory. Kafka's work approximates Musil's ideal of writing as »reiner Vorgang und Gestaltung geistiger Mächte, die . . . zum erstenmal Namen und Stimme bekommen.« A foray through the vast secondary literature around Kafka shows that his work has aroused and continues to arouse an overwhelming response, some of which is deeply imaginative and much of which is pedestrian. Regardless of individual quality, the sheer numbers of Kafka studies are a testimony to the presence of a felt truth that Kafka's skill brings to language. But it remains a truth that has thus far largely escaped the conceptual nets of literary criticism.

Like Musil, Kafka was keenly aware of the limits of denotative language. And like Musil, Kafka wanted in his fiction to give a name and voice to inner experience. But as we have seen in Chapter IV, he did not believe that language, even metaphor, could represent the inner world in an affirmative way. »Die innere Welt läßt sich nur leben, nicht beschreiben« (H, 72). Franz Kafka rejects the idea of representation more fully than either Broch or Musil and sets in its place another narrative strategy that is ›non-affirmative‹ in character. This rather obscure-sounding concept of negative articulation is not as gratuitous as it may seem.

I argued in Chapter IV that Josef K.'s court, when spoken of in the affirmative language of representation, is something like a symbol or allegory of his conscience. ›Conscience‹ belongs to the inner world; we therefore witness in Josef K.'s confrontation with his court a kind of writing that lives up to Musil's call for one that is »reiner Vorgang und Gestaltung geistiger Mächte.« But in likening K.'s court to a conscience I have fallen back into the logic of representation that Kafka sought to escape. Literary criticism is conceptual and has to reduce its object of analysis to a conventional term. »Conscience« is an acceptable, if reductionist, compromise between the integrity of Kafka's novel and the needs of interpretation.

The problem here is that conscience is a philosophical and theological concept that has a history of its own. To insist too strongly that the court is an allegory of conscience runs the risk of imposing this concept and its burdensome history onto the unique experience that the story of Josef K. brings to life. This is precisely the danger that Musil warns against and that Kafka's non-conceptual imagery forbids. Properly speaking, the historical concept »conscience« and Kafka's *Prozeß* both address a non-objective tertium that exists outside the jurisdiction of language. The great virtue of Kafka's way of storytelling is its refusal to fasten a label to this tertium. Instead, it encircles it, pressing at its boundaries and thereby forcing it to show at least its dark contours.

A short dialogue from Kafka's »Betrachtungen« will help to clarify the logic of contrapositive articulation that is at work in much of his fiction:

> »Daß es uns an Glauben fehle, kann man nicht sagen. Allein die einfache Tatsache unseres Lebens ist in ihrem Glaubenswert gar nicht auszuschöpfen.« »Hier wäre ein Glaubenswert? Man kann doch nicht nichtleben.« »Eben in diesem ›kann doch nicht‹ steckt die wahnsinnige Kraft des Glaubens; in dieser Verneinung bekommt sie Gestalt.« (H, 40, No. 109)

The simple fact of Josef K.'s trial is just such a »kann doch nicht.« He ›awakens‹ to this fact one fine morning, yet insists throughout his experience that it cannot be so. His denial of the trial calls it forth in its ever-increasing complexity. Within this very nay-saying is lodged the court's irrepressible power over K.; in this negation it takes on form. K.'s guilt and his conscience inform the being of the court, and his repudiation of it only tightens its grasp on him. His denial of his deepest self ultimately leads to a bizarre execution-suicide.

Kafka's bleak novel is, then, an inverted affirmation of the claims of the ethical. It is a cautionary tale. Such an insight helps to clarify Kafka's general attitude toward the ends of writing as an art form. »Diese ganze Literatur,« writes Kafka, »ist Ansturm gegen die Grenze . . . . Allerdings ein wie unbegreifliches Genie wird hier verlangt, das neu seine Wurzeln in die alten Jahrhunderte treibt oder die alten Jahrhunderte neu erschafft und mit all dem sich nicht ausgibt, sondern jetzt erst sich auszugeben beginnt« (T, 345). It is not customary to think of Kafka as a utopian writer, but there are nonetheless good reasons for doing so. This passage reveals Kafka's perception of literature itself as a »border raid.« These borders are the limits of the world *as it is*, the borders of a reality that is too confining. By its very existence, regardless of its content, literature serves the utopian function of articulating our subliminal knowledge that the as yet unformed future can be better than the present. By means of literature we insinuate our needs, desires, and expectations into the future. Like Orwell's *1984* or Nabokov's *Invitation to a Beheading*, the seeming dystopias of Kafkan making are actually an unequivocal rejection of the worlds they depict with pretended coolness and impartiality. The unrelieved despair of *Der Prozeß* or *Das Schloß* is nothing other than a gesture of protest against anonymous forces of oppression.

In Kafka's work, this intention finds its clearest voice in the figure of Amalia, a major character from the village beneath the castle. In her, Kafka reveals his soberly utopian turn of mind: her refusal to submit to Sortini's vile demands is an act of open defiance against the castle. Her village otherwise knows only unquestioning obedience to the customs of the castle and the desires of its officials. In the lowly Amalia's resounding »*No!*« is lodged that irrational power of the Kafkan »kann doch nicht.« In the claustrophobic world of the village, where conformity is a principle carried to exponential extremes, only Amalia has the courage and insight to imagine that things could be other than they are. In obeying the call of her moral imagination, Amalia enacts the deed of the poetic word. And this deed is the defiance of the world as it is, the refusal to accept a reality that is too confining. Amalia's *no* is an »Ansturm gegen die Grenze.«

In a similar vein, Kafka once described the project of literature as a form of prayer: »Schreiben als Form des Gebetes« (H, 252). Certainly Kafka did not have in mind the bogus religiosity of a Stefan George or any similar devotee of the poet-as-priest fervor that crops up from time to time in literary history. Kafka's work is quite opposed to such vagaries, which makes his comment all the more interesting. From the perspective of philosophical anthropology, the function of art and of prayer in culture is similar: each is an elemental articulation of desire itself. The language of prayer, poem, and tale is the discursive space in which occurs a ceremony of creative imagination. This ceremony is the verbal enactment of the values and ideals that will govern the choices to be made in the future. Poetry and fiction are in secular culture the correlative of prayer in the theocentric culture. Each is an open space in which the desires and fears of individuals and of the culture as a whole are brought to language. Frequently, as in Kafka, the articulation is non-affirmative in character. Orpheus' lamentations, his refusal to accept the death of Eurydice, also illustrates this *via negativa*. Adrian Leverkühn's masterwork »Die Weheklag Dr. Fausti,« – an outraged refusal to accept an innocent's death – is likewise a contrapositive affirmation.

Leverkühn's great threnody is, as it were, a prayer on behalf of his much loved nephew, Nepomuk. Lamentation arises from the experience of a lack, out of something that is missing, and is thus a kind of invocation and conjuration of the spirit of that which is not at hand. It cannot restore the lost, but it can indeed affirm and reinforce the potency of the deeply felt values that motivate the lamentation. Leverkühn's definition of prayer suggests as much:

> Ich glaube zu verstehen, was Aristoteles mit der Entelechie meinte. Sie ist der Engel des Einzelwesens, der Genius seines Lebens, auf dessen wissende Führung es gern vertraut. Was man Gebet nennt ist eigentlich die mahnende oder beschwörende Anmeldung dieses Vertrauens. Gebet aber heißt es mit Recht, weil es im Grunde Gott ist, den wir damit anrufen. (127f)

Leverkühn's »Weheklag« for Nepomuk is precisely such a self-revelation of this immanent faculty of individual and communal mind. The composer transforms his personal outrage and self-condemnation into an unremitting howl of anguish that is, at the same time, an avowal of guilt and a »prayer« for atonement. It was little Nepomuk himself, who is also an »Echo« of Leverkühn's own soul, who provided his uncle with a sense of the possibility of redemption. Zeitblom and Leverkühn overhear the strange child recite his archaic bedtime prayer:

> Merkt, swer für den andern bitt',
> Sich selber löset er damit.
> Echo bitt' für die ganze Welt,
> Daß Got auch ihn in Armen hält. Amen. (626)

As Leverkühn observes, »Er bittet für die ganze Schöpfung, ausdrücklich um selbst eingeschlossen zu sein« (626). Leverkühn's own final word is his »Weheklag.« It is a dystopian avowal of grief at his guilt in the death of Nepomuk, and is similarly a ›prayer‹ »für die ganze Schöpfung.« The composer speculates on his own redemption by offering up an expression of profound regret that simultaneously speaks for an entire era. »Dr. Fausti Weheklag« is an orphic lamentation (647) for the fallen child, and it is also a song of mourning for the innocent dead of an entire generation:

> Nun kann nur dieses uns frommen, und dieses nur wird uns aus der Seele gesungen sein: die Klage des Höllensohns, die furchtbarste Menschen- und Gottesklage, die, ausgehend vom Subjekt, aber stets weiter sich ausbreitend und gleichsam den Kosmos ergreifend, auf Erden je angestimmt worden ist. (643)

Like Orpheus and Faustus before him, Leverkühn is a conjuror of the dead (647). But the dead cannot return to life; all that can remain in their absence is the song of lamentation. Zeitblom's exaggerated pathos in the passage cited above must not be allowed to obscure the authenticity of Leverkühn's achievement. The richness of his musical expression transcends his personal tragedy to become the voice of lamentation for his wretched era. By embracing the whole of his generation, Leverkühn's lament follows the logic of Nepomuk's prayer: »swer für den andern bitt' / Sich selber löset er damit,« and enfolds its own author. The mad composer's confession in Chapter XLVII is the verbal counterpart of his musical »Weheklag.«

His lamentation is a prayer by his own definition. It is the self-assertion of a monitory, conjuring daemon that guides the individual in his thinking and striving. The »Weheklag Dr. Fausti« is the self-assertion of this inner voice not only for the composer personally. It is much more the voice of his entire era speaking through him, offering up a prayer for itself. He, the artist, speaks the confession of an era's guilt-ridden self-knowledge.

Leverkühn's point is well taken. If prayer is the articulation of the individual's in-born *genius*—i.e. the objective (even if not referential) form of hopes, desires, fears, and values that move his thoughts and deeds – then it makes sense to think of major works of art as the secular ›prayer‹ of an entire culture. In the art it produces, a given community reveals itself to itself, and in so doing casts its shadow into the future.

The point here is that the functional status of art in the modern era resembles that of prayer in a culture dominated by the presence of the gods. Central to both is not so much the ›representation of reality‹ but more the sense of expectancy and the implied possibility of renewal. Like prayer, poetic fiction is a ceremonial space in which desires and values are expressed, and which opens up onto the future. The same novelist who wrote of »Schreiben als Form des Gebetes« also wrote: »Ist es möglich, daß ich die Zukunft zuerst in ihren kalten Umrissen mit dem Verstand und dem Wunsch erkenne und erst, von ihnen gezogen und gestoßen, allmählich in die Wirklichkeit dieser gleichen Zukunft komme?« (T, 319). It is rather too literal a reading to understand Kafka to be a prophet of National Socialism; a man pressed forward by intellect and drawn forth by desire does not invent a hell for himself to live in. But he may well postulate a hell as a precondition of the liberation to which he aspires. Kafka's dystopias are not refutations of the yearned-for liberation so much as they are the ironic precondition of its possibility:

Es ist keine Widerlegung der Vorahnung einer endgültigen Befreiung, wenn am nächsten Tag die Gefangenschaft noch unverändert bleibt oder gar sich verschärft oder, selbst wenn ausdrücklich erklärt wird, daß sie niemals aufhören soll. Alles das kann vielmehr notwendige Voraussetzung der endgültigen Befreiung sein. (T, 337)

Amalia embodies this sentiment, and Kafka's fiction more than that of any ordinary utopian insists on the necessity of hope and sober opposition to false authority. By presenting us with the mundane horror of hopeless conformism and by pretending to deny the most self-evident of human values, Kafka forces us to wake up to the presence of these values, very much like Josef K. »awakens« to them on the morning of his thirtieth birthday. Those who read Kafka as the prophet of doom and aporia overlook passages such as this:

> Es ist sehr gut denkbar, daß die Herrlichkeit des Lebens um jeden und immer in ihrer ganzen Fülle bereitliegt, aber verhängt, in der Tiefe, unsichtbar, sehr weit. Aber sie liegt dort, nicht feindselig, nicht widerwillig, nicht taub. Ruft man sie mit dem richtigen Wort, beim richtigen Namen, dann kommt sie. Das ist das Wesen der Zauberei, die nicht schafft, sondern ruft. (T, 339)

This sorcerer's call is, of course, the Quixotic word of poetry and fiction.

There is no talk here of represented reality. Instead, the task of fiction, of *la verbe donquichotesque*, is – in the elegant formulation of Marthe Robert – »invocation and critique, conjuration and radical probing, both one and the other with their risks and perils.« Such fiction invokes in us a sense of reality, perhaps, but much more compelling is the sense of futurity that is native to the utopian *counter*reality of the poetic word. Robert Musil, too, was keenly aware of the poetic word as critique and invocation. According to him, imaginative literature is »ein auf ›Herstellung‹ gerichteter Vorgang, ein ›Vorbildzauber‹, und keine Wiederholung des Lebens oder Ansichten darüber, die man ohne sie besser ausdrückt ...« (8: 1224f). The hermeneutical function of mimesis is not to offer representations of reality but instead to enliven and to challenge the receptive mind that, in turn, will construe in accordance with it needs and desires. The ongoing interaction of human beings with the stories they tell about themselves is the stuff that the spiritual world is made of. These words are the fundament of deeds: the course of Western culture is unthinkable without the narrated realities of the Bible, and the Greeks, and the classics of modernity. While there are certainly words that do not call forth deeds, there can be no deeds of moment that do not ultimately float on a sea of words. And words in the condition of their greatest vitality comprise the finest literary achievements of tradition. They are the words that speak from the past with a voice of authority that is self-evident in its spontaneous appeal to the modern imagination.

Bibliography

Adorno, Theodor W. »Form und Gehalt des zeitgenösschischen Romans.« *Akzente*, 1 (1954), 410–16.
- *Die Philosophie der neuen Musik*. Suhrkamp Taschenbuch Wissenschaft, 239. Frankfurt am Main: Suhrkamp, 1978.
Albertsen, Elisabeth. *Zur Dialektik von Ratio und Mystik im Werk Robert Musils*. München: Nymphenburg, 1968.
Allemann, Beda. »Wahrheit und Dichtung.« In *Weltgespräch 7. 2.* Folge. Hrsg. v. Arbeitsgemeinschaft Weltgespräch Wien-Freiburg. Wien, Freiburg: Herder, 1969, pp. 32–45.
Alter, Robert. *Partial Magic. The Novel as a Self-Conscious Genre*. Berkeley, Los Angeles, London: University of California Press, 1975.
- »Mimesis and the Motive for Fiction.« In *Images and Ideas in American Culture. Essays in Memory of Philip Rahv*. Ed. Arthur Edelstein. Hanover, New Hampshire: Brandeis University Press, 1979.
Arntzen, Helmut. *Satirischer Stil. Zur Satire in Robert Musils »Mann ohne Eigenschaften.«* 2. erg. Aufl. Abhandlungen zur Kunst-, Musik-, und Literaturwissenschaft, 9. Bonn: Bouvier, 1970.
Auerbach, Erich. *Mimesis. Dargestellte Wirklichkeit in der abendländischen Literatur*. 2. verb. und erw. Aufl. Bern: Francke, 1959.
Bahr, Hermann. »Die Moderne.« In *Hermann Bahr. Zur Überwindung des Naturalismus. Theoretische Schriften, 1887–1904*. Hrsg. v. Gotthart Wunberg. Sprache und Literatur, 46. Stuttgart: Kohlhammer, 1968, pp. 35–38.
Balet, Leo and E. Gerhard. *Die Verbürgerlichung der deutschen Kunst. Literatur und Musik im 18. Jahrhundert*. Hrsg. v. Gert Mattenklott. Ullstein Buch, 2995. Frankfurt am Main: Ullstein, 1973.
Barth, John. »The Literature of Exhaustion.« *The Atlantic*, Aug. 1967, pp. 29–34.
- »The Literature of Replenishment.« *The Atlantic*, Jan. 1980, pp. 65–71.
Barthes, Roland. *S/Z*. Trans. Richard Miller. New York: Hill and Wang, 1974.
Bataille, Georges. *L'Erotisme*. Paris: Les Editions de Minuit, 1957.
Baudelaire, Charles. *Oeuvres Complètes*. Ed. Y.-G. Le Dantec, rev. Claude Pichois. Paris: Gallimard, 1961.
Bauer, Gerhard. »Die ›Auflösung des anthropozentrischen Verhaltens‹ im modernen Roman.« *DVjs*, 42 (1968), 677–701.
Bauer, Sibylle, and Ingrid Drevermann. *Studien zu Robert Musil*. Literatur und Leben, NF 8. Köln, Graz: Böhlau, 1966.
Beckett, Samuel. »Dante... Bruno.. Vico.. Joyce.« In *Our Exagmination Round his Factification for Incamination of Work in Progress*. London: Faber and Faber, 1929, pp. 3–22.
Beckett, Samuel, and Georges Duthuit. *Proust/Three Dialogues*. London: John Calder, 1965.

Beebe, Maurice. »Ulysses and the Age of Modernism.« In *Fifty Years »Ulysses.«* Ed. with an Intro. by Thomas F. Staley. Bloomington, London: Indiana University Press, 1974, 172–88.
- »What Modernism Was.« *Journal of Modern Literature*, 3 (1974), 1065–84.
- »Reflective and Reflexive Trends in Modern Fiction.« In *Twentieth Century Poetry, Fiction, Theory*. Eds. Harry R. Garvin and John D. Kirkland. Lewisburg: Bucknell University Press, 1977, pp. 13–26.
Beicken, Peter. »*Berechnung* und *Kunstaufwand* in Kafkas Erzahlrhetorik.« In *Franz Kafka, eine Aufsatzsammlung nach einem Symposium in Philadelphia*. Hrsg. v. Marie Luise Caputo-Mayr. Schriftenreihe Agora, 29. Berlin, Darmstadt: Agora, 1978, pp. 216–34.
- *Franz Kafka. Eine kritische Einführung in die Forschung*. Frankfurt am Main: Athenäum Fischer Taschenbuch, 1974.
- »Kafka's Narrative Rhetoric.« *Journal of Modern Literature*. 6 (1977), 398–409.
Beißner, Friedrich. *Der Erzähler Franz Kafka*. Stuttgart: Kohlhammer, 1952.
- *Kafka der Dichter*. Stuttgart: Kohlhammer, 1958.
- *Der Schacht von Babel. Aus Kafkas Tagebüchern*. Stuttgart: Kohlhammer, 1963.
- *Kafkas Darstellungen des »traumhaften inneren Lebens«*. Bebenhausen: L. Rotsch, 1973.
Benjamin, Walter. *Ursprung des deutschen Trauerspiels*. Hrsg. v. Rolf Tiedemann. Suhrkamp Taschenbuch Wissenschaft, 225. Frankfurt am Main: 1982.
Benn, Gottfried. *Gesammelte Werke in zwei Bänden*. Hrsg. v. Dieter Wellershoff. Wiesbaden: Limes, 1968.
Benveniste, Emile. *Problems in General Linguistics*. Trans. Mary Elizabeth Meele. Miami Linguistics Series, 8. Coral Gables, Florida: University of Miami Press, 1971.
Berger, Peter. »The Problem of Multiple Realities: Alfred Schutz and Robert Musil.« In *Phenomenology and Social Reality. Essays in Memory of Alfred Schutz*. Ed. Maurice Natanson. The Hague: Martinus Nijhoff, 1970, pp. 213–33.
Bergsten, Gunilla. *Thomas Manns »Doktor Faustus«: Untersuchungen zu den Quellen und zur Struktur des Romans*. Studia Litterarum Upsaliensa, 3. Stockholm: Svenksa, 1963.
Bertschinger, Andreas. *Hermann Brochs »Pasenow« - ein künstlicher Fontane-Roman? Zur Epochenstruktur Wilhelminismus und Zwischenkriegszeit*. Zürcher Beiträge zur deutschen Literatur und Geistesgeschichte, 55. Zürich: Artemis, 1982.
Binder, Hartmut. *Kafka-Kommentar zu den Romanen, Rezensionen, Aphorismen und zum Brief an den Vater*. München: Winkler, 1976.
- hrsg. *Kafka-Handuch in zwei Bänden*. Stuttgart: Alfred Kröner, 1979.
Böckle, Franz, et al. *Christlicher Glaube in moderner Gessellschaft*. Enzyklopädische Bibliothek in 30 Teilbänden, 2. Freiburg, Basel, Wien: Herder, 1981.
Boorstin, Daniel. *The Image, or What Happened to the American Dream*. New York: Atheneum, 1962.
Bradbury, Malcolm and James Mcfarlane, eds. *Modernism 1890–1930*. Sussex: Harvester; New Jersey: Humanities, 1978.
Brinkmann, Richard. *Wirklichkeit und Illusion. Studien über Gehalt und Grenzen des Begriffs Realismus für die erzählende Dichtung des neunzehnten Jahrhunderts*. 3. Aufl. Tübingen: Niemeyer, 1977.

- »Romanform und Werttheorie bei Hermann Broch.« *DVjs*, 31 (1957), 169–97.

Broch, Hermann. *Kommentierte Werkausgabe*. Hrsg. v. Paul Michael Lützeler. 13 Bde. Frankfurt am Main: Suhrkamp, 1978ff.

Brod, Max. *Franz Kafka. Eine Biographie*. 3. erw. Aufl. Berlin, Frankfurt am Main: S. Fischer, 1954.

Bultmann, Rudolf. *Glauben und Verstehen*. 4 Bde. Tübingen: J. C. B. Mohr, 1960ff.

Bürger, Peter. *Theorie der Avantgarde*. Mit einem Nachwort zur 2. Aufl. Edition Suhrkamp, 727. Frankfurt am Main: Suhrkamp, 1981.

Calinescu, Matei. *Faces of Modernity: Avant-Garde, Decadence, Kitsch*. Bloomington: University of Indiana Press, 1977.

Celan, Paul. *Ausgewählte Gedichte/Zwei Reden*. Mit einem Nachwort von Beda Allemann. Suhrkamp Taschenbuch, 604. Frankfurt am Main: Suhrkamp, 1980.

Church, Margaret. *Time and Reality. Studies in Contemporary Fiction*. Chapel Hill, North Carolina: University of North Carolina Press, 1963.

Cohn, Dorrit. *Transparent Minds. Narrative Modes for Presenting Consciousness in Fiction*. Princeton, New Jersey: Princeton University Press, 1978.

Corino, Karl. »Der erlöste Tantalus. Robert Musils Verhältnis zur Sprache.« *Annali: Studi Tedeschi*, 23 (Naples, 1980), 339–56.

Corngold, Stanley. *The Commentator's Despair. The Interpretation of Kafka's »Metamorphosis.«* Port Washington, N.Y.: Kennikat, 1973.

David, Claude. »Form und Gehalt in Robert Musils *Mann ohne Eigenschaften*.« *Euphorion*, 64 (1970), 221–30.

de Man, Paul. »Allegorie und Symbol in der europäischen Frühromantik.« In *Typologia Litterarum. Festschrift für Max Wehrli*. Hrsg. v. Stefan Sonderegger, Alois M. Maas, und Harald Burger. Zürich: Atlantis, 1969.

- »The Rhetoric of Temporality.« In *Interpretation. Theory and Practice*. Ed. Charles Singleton. Baltimore: Johns Hopkins University Press, 1969, pp. 173–209.

Derrida, Jacques. *Speech and Phenomena and other Essays on Husserl's Theory of Signs*. Evanston: Northwestern University Press, 1973.

Dinklage, Karl, hrsg. *Robert Musil: Leben, Werk, Wirkung*. Reinbek bei Hamburg: Rowohlt, 1960.

Dinklage, Karl, hrsg. zusammen mit Elisabeth Albertsen und Karl Corino. *Robert Musil. Studien zu seinem Werk*. Reinbek bei Hamburg: Rowohlt, 1970.

Eckermann, Johann Peter. *Gespräche mit Goethe in den letzten Jahren seines Lebens*. Hrsg. v. H.H. Houben. Wiesbaden: Brockhaus, 1959.

Eliot, T.S. *The Use of Poetry and the Use of Criticism: Studies in the Relation of Poetry to Criticism in England*. London: Faber and Faber, 1933.

Elm, Theo. »Problematisierte Hermeneutik. Zur ›Uneigentlichkeit‹ in Kafkas kleiner Prosa.« *DVjs*, 50 (1976), 477–510.

Emmel, Hildegard. *Geschichte des deutschen Romans*. 3 Bde. Sammlung Dalp, 103. Bern, München: 1972.

Emrich, Wilhelm. *Franz Kafka*. Bonn: Athenäum, 1958.

- *Protest und Verheißung. Studien zur klassischen und modernen Dichtung*. Frankfurt am Main: Athenäum, 1960.

Eykman, Christoph. *Geschichtspessimismus in der deutschen Literatur des 20. Jahrhunderts*. Bern: Francke, 1970.

Faulkner, Peter. *Modernism*. The Critical Idiom, 35. London, New York: Methuen, 1980.

Fletcher, Angus. *Allegory. The Theory of a Symbolic Mode.* Ithaca: Cornell University Press, 1964.

Foucault, Michel. *The Archaeology of Knowledge.* Harper Torchbook, 1901. New York: Harper and Row, 1976.

– »La Pensée du dehors.« *Critique,* 22 (1966), 523–46.

– *The Order of Things. An Archaeology of the Human Sciences.* New York: Vintage Books, 1973.

Frey, John R. »Author-Intrusion in Narrative: German Theory and some Modern Examples.« *Germanic Review,* 23 (1948), 274–89.

Fritz, Horst. »Die Dämonisierung des Erotischen in der Literatur des Fin de Siècle.« In *Fin de Siècle. Zur Literatur und Kunst der Jahrhundertwende.* Hrsg. Roger Bauer et al. Studien zur Philosophie und Literatur des 19. Jahrhunderts, 35. Frankfurt am Main: Vittorio Klostermann, 1977, pp. 442–64.

Fuder, Dieter. *Analogiedenken und anthropologische Differenz. Zu Form und Funktion der poetischen Logik in Robert Musils Roman »Der Mann ohne Eigenschaften.* Musil-Studien, 10. München: Fink, 1979.

Geißler, Rolf, hrsg. *Möglichkeiten des modernen Romans.* 3. Aufl. Frankfurt am Main: Diesterweg, 1962.

Gide, André. *Les Faux-Monnayeurs.* Paris: Gallimard, 1925.

Goethe, Johann Wolfgang von. *Gedenkausgabe der Werke, Briefe und Gespräche in 24 Bänden.* Hrsg. v. Ernst Beutler. Zürich: Artemis, 1948ff.

Grimm, Reinhold, hrsg. *Deutsche Romantheorien.* Frankfurt am Main: Athenäum, 1968.

Havet, Jàcques, ed. *Main Trends of Research in the Social and Human Sciences.* New Babylon, Studies in the Social Sciences, 21. Part II, vol. II. The Hague, Paris, New York: Mouton/UNESCO, 1978.

Hauser, Arnold. *Der Manierismus. Die Krise der Renaissance und der Ursprung der modernen Kunst.* München: Beck, 1964.

Heald, David. »All the World's a Stage – A Central Motif in Musil's *Der Mann ohne Eigenschaften.*« *German Life and Letters,* 27 (1973/74), 51–59.

– »Musil's Conception of ›Schauspielerei‹ as Novelist and Critic.« *Maske und Kothurn,* 23 (1977), 244–55.

Heidegger, Martin. »Die Zeit des Weldbildes.« In his *Holzwege.* Gesamtausgabe, Abt. I. Bd. 5. Frankfurt am Main: Vittorio Klostermann, 1977, pp. 75–113.

Heller, Erich. *The Disinherited Mind.* Cambridge: Bowes and Bowes, 1952.

– *The Ironic German. A Study of Thomas Mann.* London: Secker and Warburg, 1958.

Henel, Ingeborg. »Die Türhüterlegende und ihre Bedeutung für Kafkas *Prozeß.*« *DVjs.* 37 (1963), 50–70.

– »Die Deutbarkeit von Kafkas Werken.« *Zeitschrift für deutsche Philologie.* 86 (1967), 250–66.

Henning, Margrit. *Die Ich-Form und ihre Funktion in Thomas Manns »Doktor Faustus« und in der deutschen Literatur der Gegenwart.* Studien zur deutschen Literatur, 2. Tübingen: Niemeyer, 1966.

Hillebrand, Bruno. *Theorie des Romans.* 2 Bde. München: Winkler, 1972.

Hochstätter, Dietrich. *Sprache des Möglichen. Stilistischer Perspektivismus in Robert Musils »Mann ohne Eigenschaften.*« Gegenwart der Dichtung, 6. Frankfurt am Main: Athenäum, 1972.

Hofmannsthal, Hugo von. *Gesammelte Werke in 10 Einzelbänden.* Hrsg. v. Bernd Schoeller in Beratung mit Rudolf Hirsch. Frankfurt am Main: Fischer Taschenbuch Verlag, 1979.

Honig, Edwin. *Dark Conceit. The Making of Allegory.* London: Faber and Faber, 1959.

Howe, Irving. *The Decline of the New.* New York: Harcourt, Brace & World, 1963.

Jakobson, Roman. »Closing Statement: Linguistics and Poetics.« In *Style in Language.* Ed. Thomas A. Sebeok. Cambridge, Mass.: MIT Press, 1960, pp. 350-77.

James, Henry. *The Art of Fiction and Other Essays.* Ed. with an Intro. by Morris Roberts. New York: Oxford University Press, 1948.

Janouch, Gustav. *Gespräche mit Kafka. Aufzeichnungen und Erinnerungen.* Erw. Neuaufl. Frankfurt am Main: Fischer Taschenbuch Verlag, 1981.

Johnston, William. *The Austrian Mind. An Intellectual and Social History 1848-1938.* Berkeley, Los Angeles, London: University of California Press, 1972.

Jüngel, Eberhard. »Metaphorische Wahrheit.« *Evangelische Theologie,* Sonderheft (1974), 71-122.

Kafka, Franz. *Briefe an Felice.* Hrsg. von Erich Heller und Jürgen Born. Frankfurt am Main: Fischer Taschenbuch Verlag, 1976.

– *Der Prozeß.* Hrsg. v. Max Brod. Frankfurt am Main: Fischer Taschenbuch Verlag, 1980.

– *Tagebücher 1919-1923.* Hrsg. v. Max Brod. Frankfurt am Main: Fischer Taschenbuch Verlag, 1980.

– *Hochzeitsvorbereitungen auf dem Lande und andere Prosa aus dem Nachlaß.* Hrsg. v. Max Brod. Frankfurt am Main: Fischer Taschenbuch Verlag, 1980.

– *Sämtliche Erzählungen.* Hrsg. v. Paul Raabe. Hamburg: S. Fischer, 1970.

Kahler, Erich. »Untergang der epischen Kunstform.« *Neue Rundschau,* 64 (1953), 1-44.

– »The Transformation of Modern Fiction«. *Comparative Literature,* 7 (1955), 121-128.

– »Die Verinnerung des Erzählens.« *Neue Rundschau,* 68 (1957), 501-46 and 70 (1959), 1-54.

– *The Inward Turn of Narrative.* Trans. Richard and Clara Winston. The Bollingen Series, 83. Princeton, N.J.: Princeton University Press, 1973.

Kandinsky, Wassily . *Über das Geistige in der Kunst.* 5. Aufl. Mit einer Einführung von Max Bill. Bern-Bümpliz: Benteli, 1956.

Kant, Immanuel. *Kants Gesammelte Schriften.* Hrsg. v. der Preußischen Akademie der Wissenchaften. Berlin: Georg Riemer, 1900ff.. .

Kayser, Wolfgang. »Die Anfänge des Romans im 18. Jahrhundert und seine heutige Krise.« *DVjs,* 28 (1954), 417-46.

Kermode, Frank. *The Sense of an Ending. Studies in the Theory of Fiction.* New York: Oxford University Press, 1967.

– *Modern Essays.* London: Fontana Books, 1971.

Kessler, Susanne. *Kafka – Poetik der sinnlichen Welt. Strukturen sprachkritischen Erzählens.* Germanistische Abhandlungen, 53. Stuttgart: Metzler, 1983.

Kittler, Friedrich A. and Horst Turk. *Urszenen. Literaturwissenschaft als Diskursanalyse und Diskurskritik.* Frankfurt am Main: Suhrkamp, 1977.

Kluckhohn, Paul. »Die Wende vom 19. zum 20. Jahrhundert in der deutschen Dichtung.« *DVjs,* 29 (1955), 1-19.

Kobs, Jörgen. *Kafka. Untersuchungen zu Bewußtsein und Sprache seiner Gestalten.* Hrsg. v. Ursula Brech. Bad Homburg: Athenäum, 1970.

Krapoth, Hermann. *Dichtung und Philosophie. Eine Studie zum Werk Hermann Brochs.* Literatur und Wirklichkeit, 8. Bonn: Bouvier, 1971.

Kreutzer, Leo. *Erkenntnistheorie und Prophetie. Hermann Brochs Romantrilogie »Die Schlafwandler.«* Studien zur deutschen Literatur, 3. Tübingen: Niemeyer, 1966.
Kristeva, Julia. »The System and the Speaking Subject.« *Times Literary Supplement,* 12 Oct. 1973, pp. 1249-50.
Kudszus, Winfried. »Erzählperspektive und Erzählgeschehen in Kafkas *Prozeß«.* *DVjs,* 44 (1970), 306-17.
Kühne, Jörg. *Das Gleichnis. Studien zur inneren Form von Robert Musils Roman »Der Mann ohne Eigenschaften.«* Studien zur deutschen Literatur, 13. Tübingen: Niemeyer, 1968.
Lacan, Jacques. *The Language of the Self.* With an Essay by Anthony Wilden. Baltimore: Johns Hopkins University Press, 1968.
Lévi-Strauss, Claude. *The Savage Mind.* Chicago: University of Chicago Press, 1966.
Levin, Harry. *The Gates of Horn. A Study of Five French Realists.* New York: Oxford University Press, 1963.
- *Refractions. Essays in Comparative Literature.* New York: Oxford University Press, 1966.
Loos, Beate. *Mythos, Zeit und Tod. Zum Verhältnis von Kunsttheorie und dichterischer Praxis in Hermann Brochs Bergroman.* Gegenwart der Dichtung, 1. Frankfurt am Main: Athenäum, 1971.
Lukács, Georg. *Wider den mißverstandenen Realismus.* Hamburg: Claasen, 1958.
Mandelkow, Karl Robert. *Hermann Brochs Romantrilogie »Die Schlafwandler.« Gestaltung und Reflexion im modernen deutschen Roman.* Probleme der Dichtung, 6. Heidelberg: Carl Winter, 1962.
Mann, Thomas. *Doktor Faustus/Die Entstehung des Doktor Faustus.* Frankfurt am Main: S. Fischer, 1967.
- *Die Bekenntnisse des Hochstaplers Felix Krull. Memoiren erster Teil.* Frankfurt am Main: S. Fischer, 1979.
- *Gesammelte Werke in Einzelbänden.* Frankfurter Ausgabe. Hrsg. und Nachbemerk. v. Peter de Mendelssohn. Frankfurt am Main: S. Fischer, 1980 ff.
Mayer, Hans. *Das Geschehen und das Schweigen. Aspekte der Modernität.* Edition Suhrkamp, 342. Frankfurt am Main: Suhrkamp, 1969.
- *Thomas Mann.* Frankfurt am Main: Suhrkamp, 1980.
Michaels, Walter Benn. »The Interpreter's Self: Peirce on the Cartesian ›Subject.‹« *Georgia Review,* 31 (1977), 383-402.
Mieth, Dietmar. *Epik und Ethik. Eine theologisch-ethische Interpretation der Joseph-Romane Thomas Manns.* Studien zur deutschen Literatur, 47. Tübingen: Niemeyer, 1976.
Musil, Robert. *Gesammelte Werke in Einzelausgaben.* Hrsg. v. Adolf Frisé. 2 Bde. Hamburg: Rowohlt, 1952.
- *Tagebücher.* Hrsg. v. Adolf Frisé. Reinbek bei Hamburg: Rowohlt, 1976.
- *Gesammelte Werke in neun Bänden.* Hrsg. v. von Adolf Frisé. Reinbek bei Hamburg: Rowohlt, 1978.
- *Briefe 1901-1942.* Hrsg. v. Adolf Frisé unter Mithilfe von Murray G. Hall. Reinbek bei Hamburg: Rowohlt, 1981.
Nagel, Ernest and James R. Newman. *Gödel's Proof.* New York: New York University Press, 1958.
Neumann, Gerhard. »Umkehrung und Ablenkung: Franz Kafkas ›Gleitendes Paradox.‹« *DVjs.* 42 (1968), 702-44.

Nietzsche, Friedrich. *Werke in drei Bänden.* Hrsg. v. Karl Schlechta. München: Hanser, 1956.
Novalis. *Werke/Briefe/Dokumente.* Hrsg. v. Ewald Wasmuth. 2 Bde. Heidelberg: Lambert Schneider, 1957.
Nusser, Peter. *Musils Romantheorie.* Paris, the Hague: Mouton, 1967.
Oswald, Victor A. »The Enigma of Frau von Tolna.« *Germanic Review,* 23 (1948), 249–53.
Pascal, Roy. »Narrative Fictions and Reality. A Discussion of Frank Kermode's *The Sense of an Ending.*« *Novel,* 11 (1977/78), 40–50.
Payne, Philip. »Robert Musil's Reality – A Study in Some Aspects of Reality in *Der Mann ohne Eigenschaften.*« *Forum for Modern Language Studies,* 12 (1976), 314–28.
Peper, Jürgen. *Bewußtseinslagen des Erzählens und erzählten Wirklichkeiten. Dargestellt an amerikanischen Romanen des 19. und 20. Jahrhunderts insebesondere am Werk William Faulkers.* Studien zur amerikanischen Literatur und Geschichte, 3. Leiden: E.J. Brill, 1966.
Poggioli, Renato. *The Theory of the Avant-Garde.* Trans. Gerald Fitzgerald. Cambridge, Mass. and London: The Belknap Press of Harvard, 1968.
Politzer, Heinz. *Franz Kafka, der Künstler.* W.P.: S. Fischer, 1965.
Pondrom, Cyrena N. »Kafka and Phenomenology: Josef K.'s Search for Information.« *Wisconsin Studies in Contemporary Literature,* 8 (1967), 70–85.
Popper, Karl. »Epistemology without a Knowing Subject.« In his *Objective Knowledge. An Evolutionary Approach.* London: Oxford University Press, 1972, pp. 106–152.
– *Logik der Forschung.* 5. verb. Aufl. Die Einheit der Geisteswissenschaften, 4. Tübingen: J.C.B. Mohr, 1973.
Reed, T.J. *Thomas Mann. The Uses of Tradition.* London: Oxford University Press, 1974.
Reinhardt, Hartmut. *Erweiterter Naturalismus. Untersuchungen zum Konstruktionsverfahren in Hermann Brochs Romantrilogie »Die Schlafwandler.*« Kölner germanistische Studien, 7. Köln: Böhlau, 1972.
Reiß, Gunter. *»Allegorisierung« und moderne Erzählkunst. Eine Studie zum Werk Thomas Manns.* München: Wilhelm Fink, 1970.
Reiss, Hans. *The Writer's Task from Nietzsche to Brecht.* London: MacMillan, 1978.
Richards, Donald Ray. *The German Bestseller. A Complete Bibliography and Analysis 1915–1940.* German Studies in America, 2. Bern: Peter Lang, 1968.
Ricoeur, Paul. »The Function of Fiction in Shaping Reality.« *Man and World,* 12 (1979), 123–41.
Rilke, Rainer Maria. *Sämtliche Werke.* Hrsg. v. Rilke Archiv. Bd. 6. Frankfurt am Main: Insel, 1966.
Robert, Marthe. *The Old and the New. From Don Quixote to Franz Kafka.* Trans. Carol Cosman. Berkeley, Los Angeles, London: University of California Press, 1977.
Rolleston, James. *Kafka's Narrative Theater.* University Park and London: Pennsylvania University Press, 1974.
Rorty, Richard. »Philosophy as a Kind of Writing: An Essay on Derrida.« *New Literary History,* 10 (1978), 141–60.
Ryan, Judith. »The Vanishing Subject: Empirical Psychology in the Modern Novel.« *PMLA,* 95 (1980), 857–69.

Sandberg, Beatrice. »Der Roman zwischen 1910 und 1930.« In *Handbuch des deutschen Romans*. Hrsg. v. Helmut Koopmann. Düsseldorf: Bagel, 1983, pp. 489-509.

Sarraute, Nathalie. *The Age of Suspicion. Essays on the Novel.* Trans. Maria Jolas. New York: George Braziller, 1963.

Schmidt, Jochen. *Ohne Eigenschaften. Eine Erläuterung zu Musils Grundbegriff.* Untersuchungen zur deutschen Literatur, 13. Tübingen: Niemeyer, 1975.

Schnitzler, Arthur. *Gesammelte Werke in zwei Bänden.* Frankfurt am Main: S. Fischer, 1962.

Schöne, Albrecht. »Zum Gebrauch des Konjunktivs bei Robert Musil.« *Euphorion*, 55 (1961), 196-220.

Schramm, Ulf. *Fiktion und Reflexion. Überlegungen zu Musil und Beckett.* Frankfurt am Main: Suhrkamp, 1967.

Seidlin, Oscar. *Essays in German and Comparative Literature.* University of North Carolina Studies in Comparative Literature, 30. Chapel Hill: University of North Carolina Press, 1961.

Sokel, Walter. *Franz Kafka – Tragik und Ironie. Zur Struktur seiner Kunst.* München, Wien: A. Langen, G. Müller, 1964.

- »Kafka's Poetics of the Inner Self.« *Modern Austrian Literature.* 11 (1978), 37-58.

- »Language and Truth in the Two Worlds of Franz Kafka.« *German Quarterly*, 52 (1979), 364-84.

Spender, Stephen. *The Struggle of the Modern.* London: Hamish Hamilton, 1963.

Spiegel, Marianne. *Der Roman und sein Publikum im 18. Jahrhundert 1700-1767.* Abhandlungen zur Kunst-, Musik-, and Literaturwissenschaft, 41. Bonn: Bouvier, 1967.

Steinecke, Hartmut. *Hermann Broch und der polyhistorische Roman.* Bonner Arbeiten zur deutschen Literatur, 17. Bonn: Bouvier, 1968.

Steiner, George. *After Babel. Aspects of Language and Translation.* New York, London: Oxford University Press, 1975.

Stephan, Doris. »Vom Ungenügen des Dichters: Anmerkungen zur Todeserkenntnis Hermann Brochs.« *Forum*, 8 (1961), 181-83.

Stern, J(oseph) P(eter). »The Law of *The Trial*.« In *On Kafka. SemiCentenary Perspectives*. Ed. Franz Kuna. London: Paul Elek, 1976, pp. 22-41.

- *History and Allegory in Thomas Mann's »Doktor Faustus«.* An Inaugural Lecture Delivered at University College, London 1 March 1973. London: H.K. Lewis, 1975.

- *A Study of Nietzsche.* Cambridge: Cambridge University Press, 1979.

- »Die Wiener Wirklichkeit im Roman *Der Mann ohne Eigenschaften*.« *Literatur und Kritik*, 15 (1980), 525-31.

Strelka, Joseph. »Der Roman zwischen 1930 und 1945.« In *Handbuch des deutschen Romans*. Hrsg. v. Helmut Koopmann. Düsseldorf: Bagel, 1983, pp. 510-529.

Sussman, Henry. »The Court as Text: Inversion, Supplanting, and Derangement in Kafka's *Der Prozeß*.« *PMLA*, 92 (1977), 41-55.

Thieberger, Richard, hrsg. *Hermann Broch und seine Zeit.* Akten des Internationalen Broch-Symposiums Nice, 1979. Jahrbuch für Internationalen Germanistik, Reihe A, Bd. 6. Bern, Frankfurt am Main, Las Vegas: Peter Lang, 1980.

Todorov, Tvetan. *Littérature et Signification.* Paris: Larousse, 1967.

Toulmin, Stephen. *Human Understanding. The Collective Use and Evolution of Concepts.* Princeton, New Jersey: Princeton University Press, 1971.

Trommler, Frank. *Roman und Wirklichkeit. Eine Ortsbestimmung am Beispiel von Musil, Broch, Roth, Doderer, und Gütersloh.* Sprache und Literatur, 30. Stuttgart, Berlin: Kohlhammer, 1966.

Vaihinger, Hans. *Die Philosophie des Als Ob: System der theoretischen, praktischen und religiösen Funktionen auf Grund eines idealistischen Positivismus.* Berlin: Reuther & Reichard, 1911.

Voss, Liselotte. *Die Entstehung von Thomas Manns Roman »Doktor Faustus«. Dargestellt anhand von unveröffentlichten Vorarbeiten.* Studien zur deutschen Literatur, 39. Tübingen: Niemeyer, 1975.

Wahrenburg, Fritz. *Funktionswandel des Romans und ästhetische Norm.* Studien zur allgemeinen und vergleichenden Literaturwissenschaft, 11. Stuttgart: Metzler, 1972.

Walser, Martin. *Beschreibeung einer Form. Versuch über Franz Kafka.* München: Hanser, 1961.

Warnke, Frank J. *Versions of the Baroque. European Literature of the Seventeenth Century.* New Haven, London: Yale University Press, 1972.

Watt, Ian. *The Rise of the Novel. Studies in Defoe, Richardson, and Fielding.* London: Chatto and Windus, 1957.

Willenberg, Heiner. *Die Darstellung des Bewußtseins in der Literatur. Vergleichende Studien zu Philosophie, Psychologie und deutscher Literatur von Schnitzler bis Broch.* Diss. Frankfurt. N.p.: Studienreihe Humanitas, Akademische Verlagsgesellschaft, 1974.

Weigand, Hermann J. *The Magic Mountain. A Study of Thomas Mann's Novel »Der Zauberberg.«* University of North Carolina Studies in Germanic Languages and Literatures, 49. Chapel Hill: University of North Carolina Press, 1965; a rpt. of the 1933 ed.

Wittgenstein, Ludwig. *Briefe.* Hrsg. v. B.F. McGuinness und G.H. von Wright. Frankfurt am Main: Suhrkamp, 1980.

Wittgenstein, Ludwig. *Tractatus Logico-Philosophicus.* Edition Suhrkamp, 12. Frankfurt am Main: Suhrkamp, 1968.

Woolf, Virginia. »Modern Fiction.« In her *Collected Essays.* Vol. II. London: Hogarth, 1966, pp. 103–110.

Wysling, Hans, Hrsg. unter Mitarbeit von Marianne Fischer. *Dichter über ihre Dichtungen: Thomas Mann.* 3 Bde. Dichter über ihre Dichtungen, 14. Passau: Heimeran/S. Fischer, 1981.

Ziolkowski, Theodore. »Zur Entstehung und Struktur von Hermann Brochs Schlafwandlern.« *DVjs,* 38 (1964), 40–69.

– »Hermann Broch and Relativity in Fiction.« *Wisconsin Studies in Contemporary Literature,* 8 (1967), 206–16.

– *Dimensions of the Modern Novel. German Texts and European Contexts.* Princeton, New Jersey: Princeton University Press, 1969.

Zukav, Gary. *The Dancing Wu Li Masters. An Overview of the New Physics.* Toronto, New York: Bantam, 1979.